# TWENTIETH CENTURY VIEWS

The aim of this series is to present the best
in contemporary critical opinion on major
authors, providing a twentieth century perspective on their changing status in an era
of profound revaluation.

**Maynard Mack,** *Series Editor*
**Yale University**

# DOSTOEVSKY

# DOSTOEVSKY

## A COLLECTION OF CRITICAL ESSAYS

Edited by
*René Wellek*

A SPECTRUM BOOK

Prentice-Hall, Inc., *Englewood Cliffs, N. J.*

LIBRARY OF CONGRESS CATALOG CARD NO.: 62-16963

*Printed in the United States of America*

21878-C

# Table of Contents

# DOSTOEVSKY

# Introduction

# A Sketch of the History of Dostoevsky Criticism

## by René Wellek

The effect of a writer on his readers can be analyzed into aspects which are, though interlocking, nevertheless distinguishable: the reputation he acquires (which may assume the proportions of a legend or myth with little relation to reality), the criticism that attempts to define his characteristic traits and debates their significance and value, the actual influence he exerts on other writers, and—finally—the patient scholarship that tries to illuminate objectively his work and his life.

Dostoevsky's reputation—and one main trend of criticism—was established more than a hundred years ago when Vissarion Belinsky (1811-48), still revered as the greatest Russian critic, welcomed his first novel, *Poor People* (1846), with excited praise: "Honor and glory to the young poet whose Muse loves people in garrets and basements and tells the inhabitants of gilded palaces: 'look, they are also men, they are also your brethren.' " But Dostoevsky's second novel, *The Double* (published only two weeks after his first) sorely disappointed Belinsky. It was fantastic, he complained, and the fantastic "can have its place only in lunatic asylums, not in literature. It is the business of doctors and not of poets." These sentences set the tone of much Russian criticism even to the present day: Dostoevsky is either the compassionate friend of the insulted and injured or the dreamer of weird dreams, the dissector of sick souls.

Dostoevsky's early reputation faded with his ten-year banishment to Siberia (1849-59). It recovered only slowly because he had developed a political point of view similar to that of the Slavophiles and seemed to have deserted the radicals with whom he was supposed to sympathize. In the 1860's, Dostoevsky was still treated by the "radical" critics with sympathy and respect, though he now attacked their narrowly utilitarian and political view of literature. Nikolay Dobrolyubov (1836-61) reviewed *The Insulted and the Injured* (1861) very much in the spirit of Belinsky. He welcomed the novel's social pathos and compassion for the downtrodden, but could not bring himself to consider the book a work of art. Dmitri Pisarev (1840-68), the most violent of the "radical" critics, realized

1

that *Crime and Punishment* (1866) was an attack on the revolutionaries. While praising the author's humanity and artistic power, he tried to fend off the implications of Dostoevsky's antinihilistic message by blandly arguing that Raskolnikov's theories had nothing in common with those of the revolutionary youth and that "the root of Raskolnikov's illness was not in the brain but in the pocket."

But after Dostoevsky's return from Germany in 1871, with the publication of *The Possessed* (1871), with his journalistic activity, and finally with *The Brothers Karamazov* (1880), no doubt could be left that he had become the spokesman of conservative religious and political forces. After his speech on Pushkin (June 8, 1880) Dostoevsky, according to his own account, was hailed as a saint and prophet. (" 'Prophet! Prophet!' shouted the crowd.") Soon after Dostoevsky's death, his young friend, Vladimir Solovyov (1853-1900), delivered three speeches (1883) in which he interpreted Dostoevsky as a "prophet of God," a "mystical seer." In 1890 V. V. Rozanov (1856-1919)—the critic who had married Dostoevsky's friend, Appolinaria Suslova—examined *The Grand Inquisitor* for the first time almost as a religious text and interpreted its bearing on a philosophy of history. The radical intelligentsia, however, necessarily turned against him. The famous "populist" Nikolay Mikhailovsky (1842-1904) found the formula: Dostoevsky is "A Cruel Talent" (the title of his article, 1882), a sadist who enjoys suffering, a defender of the order of things which creates torturers and tortured. Dostoevsky, he declared, is most successful in describing the "sensations of a wolf devouring a sheep and of a sheep being devoured by a wolf." His picture of Russia and the Russian revolutionaries is totally false: he missed "the most interesting and most typical features of our time." Thus two widely divergent interpretations of Dostoevsky had developed in Russia before 1900.

Abroad, Dostoevsky's reputation spread only slowly. He was discussed in Germany relatively early (*e.g.,* by Victor Hehn in 1864) but the decisive breakthrough was made by a French aristocrat and diplomat, Count Melchior de Vogüé (1848-1910), who devoted a chapter to Dostoevsky in his book *Le roman russe* (1886). De Vogüé offered the Russian novelists as an antidote against the French naturalists, praising Turgenev and Tolstoy in particular. He contrasted the Russians' ethical pathos and Christian charity with the deterministic pessimism of a Zola. But he treated Dostoevsky with an oddly distant, almost puzzled air. *"Voici venir le Scythe, le vrai Scythe,"* are the first words of the chapter, and phrases such as "the Jeremiah of the jail," "the Shakespeare of the lunatic asylum" set the tone of startled apprehension at Dostoevsky's outlandish "religion of suffering." De Vogüé spoke perceptively of *Crime and Punishment*, but all the later novels seemed to him "monstrous" and "unreadable." So strongly did they offend his sense of French form and style that he even doubted they should be called *romans:* he wanted a new word, such as *"roussan."* Almost simultaneously there appeared an essay (1885, reprinted in *Ecrivains françisés,* 1889) by the brilliant young critic, Emile Hennequin (1859-88), which also concentrated on Dostoevsky's rejection of reason, his exaltation of madness, idiocy, and imbecility, and totally ignored his ultimate outlook. The versatile and influential Danish critic, Georg Brandes (1842-1927), whose *Impressions of Russia* (1889) appeared simultaneously in English translation in New York, went no further: Dostoevsky preaches the "morality of the pariah, the morality of the slave."

It was pure chance that the lonely German philosopher Friedrich Nietzsche (1844-1900) discovered Dostoevsky. In February, 1887, Nietzsche picked up a French translation of *Notes from the Underground* and immediately recognized a kindred mind: "the only psychologist from whom he had anything to learn" about the psychology of the criminal, the slave mentality, and the nature of resentment. Nietzsche went on to read *The Insulted and the Injured* and *Crime and Punishment,* which had been a success in Germany since its translation in 1882. But Nietzsche was soon to lose his reason: his discovery of Dostoevsky had come too late to make any discernible impression on his thinking. In any case, he saw Dostoevsky only as another decadent and could not perceive the real nature of his religious and philosophical position.

The pattern of Dostoevsky criticism established in the nineteenth century continued, substantially unchanged, into the twentieth. In Russia the main ideological division became even more accentuated. Around the turn of the century the leading Russian symbolist, Dmitri Merezhkovsky (1865-1941), began to elaborate his series of comparisons between *Tolstoy and Dostoevsky* (1901), Tolstoy, the pagan, "the seer of the flesh," with Dostoevsky, the Christian, "the seer of the spirit." Merezhkovsky argued against the "radical" critics that Dostoevsky is not a realist but a symbolist. Dostoevsky does not describe a social situation but presents tragedies of ideas: he is a prophet of a new religion embodied in works of art. But the image is schematized and conventionalized: the antitheses are drawn too sharply, the features of Dostoevsky assume a decadent and Nietzschean tinge. Nevertheless, Merezhkovsky was the first to realize Dostoevsky's full historical and artistic importance —the first to free him from the simple political judgment of the radical critics and the literal-mindedness of his immediate disciples. Merezhkovsky's book, soon translated into the principal European languages, profoundly influenced all later criticism. His interpretation was supported, but also modified, by Leo Shestov's frequent comments. Leo Shestov (actually Schwarzmann, 1866-1938) made an early confrontation between *Dostoevsky and Nietzsche* (1903) and his later writings proclaimed a radical irrationalism which sought support in *Notes from the Underground.* Shestov's interpretation anticipates that of existentialism: Dostoevsky's utopianism and optimism is ignored in favor of his apocalyptic vision of catastrophe and decay. Both writers exalted Dostoevsky as the representative of a new defiantly antirationalist, antiscientific religion. The other side, understandably, saw Dostoevsky as an enemy. In 1905 Maxim Gorky (1868-1936) attacked Dostoevsky as "Russia's evil genius," a reactionary and apologist of passive surrender to oppression. After the October Revolution, Dostoevsky was dethroned from his position as a rival of Tolstoy and was discussed by Marxist critics with great reservations. During the years of Stalinist orthodoxy, Dostoevsky was almost forbidden fare. A comfortable distinction was established which is still used in Soviet Russia: there was the "good," progressive, humanitarian Dostoevsky (up to and including Crime and Punishment), and there was the "bad," reactionary, religious Dostoevsky of the later years. The early works were reprinted in cheap editions for mass consumption, while The Possessed and The Brothers Karamazov were available only in sets or small editions. Soviet writers today can sympathize with Dostoevsky as a critic of Tsarist Russia and a prophet of the Revolution, but they ignore or condemn him for his later political views and dismiss his religion and philosophy as "mysticism" and "irrationalism." They can admire him as a realistic reporter on Russian life and as a creator of social types, but they disparage or ignore his symbolism and his constant deviations from the conventions of nineteenth-century realism. Even so sophisticated a Marxist as the Hungarian György Lukács (born 1885) can, in his essay on Dostoevsky (1943), utilize a simple dichotomy between Dostoevsky's instinctive sympathies and his overt ideology, and ignore vast stretches of his work that not only carry his deepest emotional and intellectual commitments but also succeed most triumphantly as art.

In spite of this official attitude, historical scholarship in Soviet Russia has contributed a great deal toward the understanding of Dostoevsky. "Stavrogin's Confession," the suppressed chapter of The Possessed, was discovered and published (1922); Dostoevsky's letters were collected and edited by A. A. Dolinin (in spite of all delays put in his way), the writer's notebooks were unearthed and analyzed—even though some of the comment could be published only in Germany. Much was done to shed light on Dostoevsky's involvement in the Petrashevsky conspiracy and his position among his contemporaries and predecessors. Leonid Grossman (born 1888) may be singled out as probably the most eminent of the Russian specialists on Dostoevsky.

The results, though highly valuable, often entail a kind of immunization, a cold storage of Dostoevsky's meaning. Much in Russian scholarship asks us to accept the view that Dostoevsky belonged only to a specific historical situation, that he represented certain class interests of the time, and that his challenge can today be safely ignored. This also seems to be the view of the few Soviet scholars who, in the wake of the

Formalist movement, studied Dostoevsky's techniques and stylistic devices. M. M. Bakhtin, in his ingenious *Problems of Dostoevsky's Writings* (1929), argued that Dostoevsky developed a special kind of "polyphonic" novel: a novel of many voices, none of which can be identified with the author's own. He comes to the patently false conclusion that "all definitions and all points of view are made part of dialogue. There is no final word in the world of Dostoevsky."

Although the theories of "socialist realism" are obviously not receptive to Dostoevsky's art, almost all twentieth-century Russian literature reflects his influence. Not only the decadents and symbolists, such as Bryusov, but also some prominent Soviet authors, such as Leonid Leonov, show the imprint of Dostoevsky's mind and art.

In recent years Dostoevsky has been reprinted more widely and Soviet scholars have discussed even the later books and the hostile ideology with greater comprehension. A more deliberate attempt is being made to reinstate Dostoevsky among the canon of Russian classics, to assimilate him into the general tradition of realism and social humanitarianism. It can succeed only partially and at the expense of the most original and seminal of Dostoevsky's characteristics: his psychology, his antinihilism, his religion, and his symbolism.

While social, historical, and formal questions were being debated in Soviet Russia, the Russian emigrants adopted Dostoevsky as a prophet of the apocalypse and a philosopher of orthodox religion. Nikolay Berdyaev (1874-1949) and Vyacheslav Ivanov (1866-1949) exalted Dostoevsky to dizzying heights. In *The World View of Dostoevsky* (Prague, 1923), Berdyaev concludes: "So great is the worth of Dostoevsky that to have produced him is by itself sufficient justification for the existence of the Russian people in the world: and he will bear witness for his countrymen at the last judgment of the nations." Berdyaev, unquestionably, has a profound grasp of the theological and philosophical implications of Dostoevsky's views, and is by no means uncritical of some of his teachings: he does not, for example, consider him "a master of spiritual discipline" but rather tries to make the concept of freedom, the choice between good and evil, the center of Dostoevsky's thought—as it is of his own thinking. Whereas Berdyaev almost ignores Dostoevsky the novelist, Ivanov—himself an eminent symbolist poet—interprets the novels in his essays (collected in English as *Freedom and the Tragic Life,* 1952) as a new genre: "the novel-tragedy," and tries to define its peculiar norms. Actually Ivanov's emphasis falls on the myths in Dostoevsky's writings: he sees the novels as vast allegories prophesying the new reign of saints. While these two great men often forced Dostoevsky's meaning to fit their own purposes, more detached Russian émigré scholars studied his thought and art very closely. The fine scattered work of Dmitri Chizhevsky (born 1894) has thrown much light on the psychology and ethics of Dostoevsky as well as on the relations of the novelist with the history of thought and literature. The essay, "The Theme of the Double" (1929), happily combines an insight into philosophical problems with a knowledge of historical relationships. The same scholarly spirit pervades the work of V. V. Zenkovsky (born 1881), whose ample *History of Russian Philosophy* (1948) compares Dostoevsky's thought with that of his predecessors and contemporaries. Konstantin Mochulsky's *Dostoevsky* (Paris, 1946) also keeps close to the actual texts. This long book is enlightened by a warm sympathy for symbolism and orthodox religion and concludes by associating Dostoevsky with the great Christian writers of world literature—Dante, Cervantes, Milton, and Pascal. Mochulsky meticulously interprets figures, scenes, and meanings actually present in the novels. L. A. Zander's *Dostoevsky* (1942), on the other hand, presses Dostoevsky's metaphors and symbols too hard into the mold of myths. Dostoevsky ceases to be a novelist or even a publicist: he becomes the propounder of an elusive wisdom about the good earth and the heavenly bridegroom, a mystic in the Russian Orthodox tradition.

Thus the opposed interpretations of Dostoevsky in Russian criticism remain divided by an insuperable gulf. The compassionate painter of Petersburg misery confronts the prophet of "the paradise around the corner." The Marxists wrongly dismiss Dostoevsky's central preoccupations, but the émigré writers—who correctly perceive the religious and mystical inspiration of Dostoevsky's work—also misunderstand its nature if they extract a message from it, a system of doctrines and precepts.

There were many religious philosophers and political prophets in nineteenth-century Russia who are almost totally unknown today in the West, though they eloquently expressed many of the ideas which Dostoevsky embraced. But they wrote treatises and dissertations, not novels. Dostoevsky's ideas come alive in his characters: the Christian humility of Prince Myshkin and Alyosha Karamazov, the Satanic pride of Raskolnikov and Ivan Karamazov, the dialectical atheism of Kirilov, or the messianic Slavophilism of Shatov. In Dostoevsky at his best, ideas incandesce, concepts become images, personalities, symbols, or even myths. Had Dostoevsky merely presented a picture of Russian slum-life in the nineteenth century or propounded a peculiar version of mystical speculation and conservative politics, he would not be read all over the world today.

In the West, where Dostoevsky is not a political issue, the divergence of interpretations is less marked. It is possible to avoid the fierce commitments of the Russians, to speak of Dostoevsky dispassionately, to make compromises, to combine approaches, to suggest shadings of meaning. Much of the Western criticism has been handicapped, however, by its ignorance of Russian scholarship on Dostoevsky and, even worse, by vague conceptions of the Slavic world and of Russian intellectual and social history. To cite a flagrant example, Thomas Mann's essay "Dostoevsky—in Moderation" (1945) alludes in awe-struck terms to "Stavrogin's Confession" as "unpublished" though it had been available in Eng-

lish since 1923 and in German since 1926. Mann confuses the chronology
of Dostoevsky's stories and mistakenly disparages a late short novel, *The
Eternal Husband* (1870), as early and "immature." Even more damage
has been done by loose generalizations about the "Slavic soul," which
Dostoevsky is supposed to represent, and by the determined blindness of
many Western writers who insist on seeing Dostoevsky as completely
outside the Western tradition—as chaotic, obscure, and even "Asiatic"
or "Oriental." Without denying his allegiance to the Eastern Church or
his attachment to a nationalist ideology, and without minimizing his
powerful originality, one cannot ignore his literary association with the
traditions of the European novel: particularly that of Balzac, Dickens,
Hugo, and E. T. A. Hoffmann. Nor can his ideology be detached from
the Western tradition of Christian and nationalist thought. His tremendous stress on the substantial unity of mankind is a version of Franciscan
Christianity that conceives of man and nature—and even animals and
birds—as ultimately united in love and universal forgiveness. The
"saint's life" of the Elder Zosima, which Dostoevsky considered his final
and telling answer to the blasphemous "revolt" of Ivan Karamazov, de-
scends directly from an eighteenth-century Russian writer, Tikhon
Zadonsky, who in turn was saturated with the sentiments and ideas of
German pietism. There appear in Dostoevsky versions of Romantic his-
toricism and folk worship that came to Russia with the great vogue of
Schelling and Hegel in the generation immediately preceding Dostoevsky's. Even Dostoevsky's depth psychology, with its interest in the life
of dreams and the splitting of personality, is heavily indebted to the
theories of Romantic writers and doctors, such as Reil and Carus. Dostoevsky's conscious attitudes toward Europe were often ambiguous; but
as an artist and thinker he is part of the stream of Western thought and
Western literary traditions.

Still, there have been divergences in Dostoevsky criticism in the main
Western countries. In France, the early interest was in Dostoevsky's psy-
chology. Only in the changed atmosphere of the twentieth century, when
Romain Rolland, Paul Claudel, Charles Péguy, and André Gide redis-
covered the life of the spirit, could Dostoevsky become a master. In 1908,
Gide (1869-1951) saw that Dostoevsky had taken the place of Ibsen,
Nietzsche, and Tolstoy: "But one must say that a Frenchman feels un-
comfortable at the first contact with Dostoevsky—he seems to him too
Russian, too illogical, too irrational, too irresponsible." Gide himself
overcame this discomfort. His own *Dostoevsky* (1923) emphasizes Dostoevsky's psychology, ambiguity, and indeterminism, and seeks support
for Gide's own central concern with human freedom, with the *acte gra-
tuit.* Jacques Rivière (1886-1925), the editor of *La Nouvelle Revue Fran-
çaise,* voiced his suspicion of Dostoevsky's mysteries in a brief essay (1923):
"In psychology the true depths are those that are explored." Marcel
Proust protested that Dostoevsky's "genius—contrary to what Rivière

says—was for construction"; but in the well-known passage of *La Prison-nière,* Proust confesses that Dostoevsky's "preoccupation with murder is something extraordinary which makes him very alien to me." Surprisingly, there is little French criticism on Dostoevsky: the early book by André Suarez (1913) can be dismissed as a flamboyant rhapsody on Dostoevsky as a mystical sensualist and sufferer. The attacks on Dostoevsky by Denis Saurat and Henri Massis must be seen in the context of the "defense of the West" against the forces of Eastern chaos, anarchy, and irrationalism which Dostoevsky was supposed to represent.

In French existentialism, Dostoevsky appears as a forerunner and crown-witness. "Every one of us is responsible for everyone else, in every way, and I most of all": the teaching of brother Markel, who asked even the birds for forgiveness, is almost a slogan for these writers. Sartre's *Huis clos* is a counterpart of Dostoevsky's "Bobok." In Camus' *Myth of Sisyphus* (1942) Kirilov's dialectic is used to support the thesis of the absurdity of creation, and in *L'Homme revolté* (1952) Ivan Karamazov becomes the proponent of metaphysical rebellion. Dostoevsky's influence on such diverse writers as Charles-Louis Philippe, Malraux, Mauriac, Sartre, and Camus is incalculable. It has hardly begun to be studied. But, in general, most French writers seem to misunderstand Dostoevsky's final position. The existentialists see only the "underground" man in Dostoevsky and ignore the theist, the optimist, and even the Utopian who looked forward to a golden age—a paradise on earth—while disparaging the socialist dreams of a collective Utopia as a monstrous "anthill" or Tower of Babel.

The Germans have produced by far the largest body of Dostoevsky interpretation and scholarship outside Russia. Karl Nötzel wrote a fully documented *Life* of Dostoevsky (1925) and there are any number of German studies of Dostoevsky's thought. The most conscientious is Reinhard Lauth's *Die Philosophie Dostojewskis* (1950), which thoroughly analyzes Dostoevsky's psychology, ethics, aesthetics, and metaphysics, and treats all his sayings as if they formed a coherent exposition of a consistent system. The basic assumption seems mistaken, but the book is the best and most objective result of a long debate among theologians and philosophers. Eduard Thurneysen was the first (1921) to interpret Dostoevsky with the concepts of the "theology of crisis" deriving from Karl Barth, the Calvinist theologian. But Paul Natorp, a prominent member of the Neo-Kantian movement, described Dostoevsky (1923) as a pantheist: "He accepts the world unreservedly: he loves the immediacy of each lived moment. Everything lives, only life exists." Hans Prager, in the well-known *Dostoevsky's World-view* (1925), saw him chiefly as a philosopher of nationalism: God is to Dostoevsky only "the synthetic personality of a nation." Romano Guardini, a German Jesuit scholar of Italian origin, meditated eloquently and sensitively on Dostoevsky's religious characters (1951), deeply worried by his hostility to the Roman Catholic Church. A Lithuanian, Antanas Maceina, gave a careful reading of the *The Grand Inquisitor* (1952) as a scheme of a philosophy of history. Hans Urs von Balthasar, in the second volume of *Apokalypse der deutschen Seele* (1939), discusses Dostoevsky's theology with a profound insight into his extremism, his faith in the *salto mortale:* "Dostoevsky, granting almost everything to the enemy [atheism] in order to defeat him with the ultimate weapon, bets everything on one last card, religion." In rejecting the socialist dream because of his knowledge of man's depravity, Dostoevsky embraces instead the religious dream, which finally fuses with the atheistic dream of a golden age. Urs von Balthasar also understands Dostoevsky's view of a community of guilt. There is no lonely guilt; each man shares in all guilt; and hence the Church is necessary as the redemption from guilt in the incarnation of Christ. No doubt these discussions often attempt to use Dostoevsky as a support for personal convictions, but they contain an insight into the theological and philosophical problems and display a knowledge of Russian intellectual history that is often lacked by purely literary or social critics in the West.

From central Europe comes another influential interpretation of Dostoevsky: the psychoanalytical method. Sigmund Freud (1856-1939) devoted to Dostoevsky an essay (1928) that derives his epilepsy (or rather epileptoid hysteria) and his gambling mania from the basic Oedipus complex. Much is made of the trauma Dostoevsky suffered at the murder of his father, and of the central theme (parricide) of *The Brothers Karamazov*. But the evidence for Freud's reduction of Dostoevsky's views—even his political ones—to a desire of submission to the Father seems very tenuous: the chronology of Dostoevsky's epileptic fits is totally obscure and no proof can be adduced that Dostoevsky felt guilty for the killing of his father by peasants while he was away in engineering school. Ivan's famous outcry (not cited by Freud) at the trial—"Who of us does not desire his father's death?"—is rather a recognition of universal guilt. Parricide is for Dostoevsky the highest symptom of social decay, a disruption of human ties that contradicts the obligation to universal forgiveness and the promise of resurrection in the flesh with which *The Brothers Karamazov* concludes. The Freudian view (elaborated by later writers) has favored the reduction of Dostoevsky's novels to autobiographical documents and has emphasized the morbid, and even the pathological and criminal themes in Dostoevsky.

Dostoevsky's effect on creative German literature was hardly less than his effect on the French. Rilke's *Malte Laurids Brigge* (1912) is imbued with Dostoevsky. The German expressionist poets welcomed him enthusiastically as a prophet of universal brotherhood. In a curious painting of the Expressionist group, Max Ernst portrayed himself as sitting on the lap of Dostoevsky. After the First World War Dostoevsky became extremely fashionable: in 1921 alone over 200,000 copies of his novels were sold. But the complete edition of the Piper Verlag in Munich, with introductions by Arthur Möller van den Bruck and other apocalyptic interpreters of the Russian soul, did as much to spread a distorted image of the author as to spread a knowledge of the texts. Kafka certainly learned from Dostoevsky (though he learned more from Gogol and Tolstoy); Jakob Wassermann wrote virtual imitations of Dostoevsky's novels; and something of Dostoevsky's spirit of compassion and universal brotherhood permeates the novels of Franz Werfel. Hermann Hesse (born 1877) shows the imprint of Dostoevsky in *Steppenwolf* (1927) and elsewhere, though a pamphlet, *Blick ins Chaos* (1920), expresses his fear of Dostoevsky's Slavic murkiness. Thomas Mann expounds the view of Dostoevsky as a combination of criminal-and-saint and asks for "moderation" in one's admiration; but surely Adrian Leverkühn's Devil in *Dr. Faustus* (1947) comes straight and undisguisedly from Ivan Karamazov's shabby visitor.

Dostoevsky was very late in reaching the English-speaking world. *The Brothers Karamazov* was translated by Mrs. Constance Garnett only in 1912, when she began the complete translation of Dostoevsky's novels that is still standard and unsurpassed (in spite of a few errors and a few lapses into Victorian prudery). *The House of the Dead* had been translated in 1881 (as *Buried Alive*) and *Crime and Punishment* in 1886. De Vogüé's book was translated in the following year and seems to have been the source of much early critical reaction to Dostoevsky in England. R. L. Stevenson expressed enthusiasm (in a letter, 1886) for *Crime and Punishment,* which he had read in French translation—and he remembered some of its details in writing *Markheim* (1885), a story of the killing of a pawnbroker. In 1882, Oscar Wilde praised *The Insulted and the Injured* as not inferior to *Crime and Punishment.* George Moore disparaged Dostoevsky as a "Gaboriau [an early French crime novelist] with psychological sauce," but oddly enough wrote a laudatory preface to a translation of *Poor People* (1894). George Gissing noted the affinity between Dickens and Dostoevsky and was one of the first to appreciate Dostoevsky's humor. But Henry James referred to Tolstoy's and Dostoevsky's "baggy monsters" and "fluid puddings," their "lack of composition, their defiance of economy and architecture," even while he recognized the "strong, rank quality" of their genius. Dostoevsky aroused violent distaste in Joseph Conrad and John Galsworthy. Conrad called *The Brothers Karamazov* ". . . an impossible lump of valuable matter. It's terrifically bad and impressive and exasperating. Moreover, I don't know what D. stands for or reveals, but I do know that he is too Russian for me. It sounds like some fierce mouthings of prehistoric ages." Galsworthy, who could not have shared Conrad's Russophobia, complained about "incoherence and verbiage" and thought Tolstoy and Turgenev far greater. The attitude of academic critics was similarly hostile. George Saintsbury, in his *History of Nineteenth Century Literature* (1907), mentions only *Poor People* and *Crime and Punishment* and finds Dostoevsky "unattractive and 'such as one could have done without.' " In the United States, William Lyon Phelps, in his *Essays on Russian Novelists* (1911), devoted his chapter on Dostoevsky to lamentations about morbidity and lack of form: he regarded even *Crime and Punishment* as "abominably diffuse, filled with extraneous and superfluous matter, and totally lacking in the principles of good construction." The more serene art of Tolstoy and Turgenev appealed much more strongly to the taste of the time.

Apparently only the experience of the First World War aroused a new appreciation of Dostoevsky, although there were a few murmurs of praise earlier. Maurice Baring's *Landmarks in Russian Literature* (1910) contains the first really perceptive appraisal of Dostoevsky by an Englishman: he sees no absurdity in placing Dostoevsky "equal to Tolstoy and immeasurably above Turgenev," recognizes the relevance of *The Possessed* in the light of the 1905 revolution, and appreciates the religious inspiration of the great novels. Dostoevsky's books are "a cry of triumph, a clarion peal, a hosanna to the idea of goodness and to the glory of God." Arnold Bennett, one of the reviewers of Baring's book, joined in praise for *The Brothers Karamazov,* which he had read in French, as "containing some of the greatest scenes ever encountered in fiction."

But the first full-length English book, Middleton Murry's *Fyodor Dostoevsky* (1916) extravagantly exalted Dostoevsky as the prophet of a new mystical dispensation. According to Murry, Dostoevsky's "Christianity is not Christianity, his realism is not realism, his novels are not novels, his truth is not truth, his art not art. His world is a world of symbols and potentialities which are embodied in unlivable lives." With similar recklessness Murry interprets Svidrigailov as the real hero of *Crime and Punishment* and allegorizes *The Brothers Karamazov.* "It may be there really was no Smerdyakov as there really was no devil, and they both had their abode in Ivan's soul. But then who did the murder? Then of course it may have been Ivan himself, or, on the other hand, there may have been no murder at all." Still, D. S. Mirsky's harsh words about Murry's "Pecksniffian sobstuff" are not justified. Murry is surely right in his principal claim: that Dostoevsky's belief in the regeneration of mankind presupposes a miracle. In his opinion, however awkwardly labored, Dostoevsky "contemplated and sought to penetrate into a new consciousness and new mode of being which he said was metaphysically inevitable for mankind." Murry proudly felt that "the objective 'pattern' of Dostoevsky had declared itself, through me as instrument," though we should recognize the influence of both Merezhkovsky and Shestov. Murry's conception of Dostoevsky as the "archhierophant of intellectual self-consciousness" explains the violence with which D. H. Lawrence, who then lived in close association with Murry, reacted to the worship of Dostoevsky. "I don't like Dostoevsky. He is like the rat, slithering along in hate, in the shadows, and in order to belong to the light, professing love, all love." Lawrence thinks that Dostoevsky, "mixing God and Sadism," is "foul." In two letters to Murry his dislike becomes shrill vituperation of what he considers Dostoevsky's mania to be "infinite, to be God." "The whole point of Dostoevsky lies in the fact of his fixed will that the individual ego, the achieved I, the conscious I, shall be infinite, God-like, and absolved from all relation." The novels seem to Lawrence great parables, but false art. "They are only parables. All the people are fallen angels—even the dirtiest scrubs. This I cannot stomach. People are not fallen angels, they are merely people." When Lawrence received Murry's book he indulged in a paroxysm of disgust. Dostoevsky "can nicely stick his head between the feet of Christ, and waggle his behind in the air." But when Lawrence had managed to depict Murry and Katherine Mansfield as Gerald Crich and Gudrun in *Women in Love* and to find an antidote to Dostoevsky in the Russian philosopher Rozanov and the novels of Verga, his view of Dostoevsky became more detached and tolerant. The introduction he wrote to a translation of *The Grand Inquisitor* in the year of his death (1930) shows a fine understanding of the argument and its implication, though Lawrence misreads the end when he speaks of Jesus "giving the kiss of acquiescence to the Inquisitor." Surely Jesus Christ does not accept the arguments of the Grand Inquisitor: he answers them in the only way religion can answer atheism—by silence and forgiveness. The Inquisitor is refuted by the silent kiss. Alyosha immediately afterwards kisses Ivan, as Christ did the Inquisitor, forgiving him for his atheism, answering his "revolt" by Christian mercy. Ivan knows this when he says: "That's plagiarism. You stole it from my poem."

The Murry–Lawrence dialogue is symptomatic of the tremendous emotional reaction to Dostoevsky in England during and shortly after the First World War. A Dostoevsky cult existed for a few years and certainly many English novelists show that they have read him and have tried to evoke his mood or draw Dostoevskean characters. The novels of Russia by Hugh Walpole (1884-1941)—*The Dark Forest* (1916) and its sequel, *The Secret City* (1919)—may serve as examples. A figure such as Spandrell in Aldous Huxley's *Point Counter Point* (1928) is inconceivable without Stavrogin and Svidrigailov. But English critical literature on Dostoevsky rather reflects a reaction against the apocalyptic interpretation of Murry and the Russians (Berdayev and Ivanov) who were then translated into English. E. H. Carr's biography (1931) may be characterized as excessively sober and detached; and D. S. Mirsky's widely read *History of Russian Literature* (1927) treats Dostoevsky very coolly as "an absorbingly interesting novelist of adventure," and accepts, on the whole, Shestov's emphasis on his nihilism. Mirsky was a Russian prince temporarily settled in England, who imported the attitudes of the Russian Formalists: their distrust of all ideology, their emphasis on formal virtues, their love of Pushkin, Lermontov, and Tolstoy. The deft little psychological study of *Dostoevsky and His Creation* (1920) by Janko Lavrin, or the pedestrian survey of *Characters of Dostoevsky* (1950) by Richard Curle, cannot be accused of extravagance. The fine essay by Derek Traversi (1937) may seem even oversevere in criticizing Dostoevsky's mysticism as "baseless and false" and in drawing such sharply critical consequences for Dostoevsky's art from his dualism between spirit and flesh, God and the world. Mr. Traversi sees only the anti-Catholic polemics and ignores Dostoevsky's paradoxical defense of the Orthodox Church. Recently the Continental concern with Dostoevsky's theology and what may be called the existential concept of man have begun to appear in English criticism, too. Martin Jarrett-Kerr has expounded Dostoevsky's agony of belief in *Studies in Literature and Belief* (1954); Colin Wilson, in *The Outsider* (1956), used Dostoevsky's heroes as examples of the quest for identity and perceptively linked him with Blake. D. S. Savage brilliantly discussed *The Gambler* (in *The Sewanee Review*, 1950), though oddly enough ignoring the striking figure of the gambling grandmother; and Michael H. Futrell studied the relation between "Dostoevsky and Dickens" (in *The English Miscellany*, ed. Mario Praz, Vol. 7, 1956) with meticulous care and common sense. But, on the whole, Dostoevsky criticism in England has definitely quieted down since the hectic excitement of Middleton Murry's days.

The situation in the United States is somewhat different: because the impact of Dostoevsky came much later, its greatest effect seems to coincide with the Second World War rather than the First. Dostoevsky's influence on American writers has hardly begun to be explored, partly because it is difficult to isolate it from that of many intermediaries. Dreiser's *American Tragedy* (1925), for example, revolves around the same moral problem of the guilty, guiltless murderer as does *The Brothers Karamazov.* There are echoes of *Crime and Punishment* in Faulkner's *Sanctuary,* and the atmosphere of many of Faulkner's novels may strike us as Dostoevskean. Faulkner himself has acknowledged Dostoevsky's influence. In 1941, Carson McCullers drew the parallel to Southern literature in very general terms: "In this approach to life and suffering the Southerners are indebted to the Russians. The technique is briefly this: a bold and outwardly callous juxtaposition of the tragic and the humorous, the immense with the trivial, the sacred with the bawdy, the whole soul of man with a materialistic detail."

American criticism of Dostoevsky was hardly existent, however, before the Second World War. James Huneker's essay (in *Ivory Apes and Peacocks,* 1915) still echoes De Vogüé and still considers Dostoevsky "infinitely inferior to Turgenev." There was a good biography by Avrahm Yarmolinsky (1934) which was preceded by a study of Dostoevsky's ideology (a Columbia dissertation, 1921). Yarmolinsky tells his story with sympathy, shunning both the raised-eyebrow manner of Carr and the strained hagiographical tone adopted by many Russians and Germans. With E. J. Simmons' *Dostoevsky, The Making of a Novelist* (1940), Americans received a reliable digest of Russian and German scholarship and a clear account of Dostoevsky's career as a novelist rather than a person or philosopher.

Increasingly, American critics have turned to a discussion of Dostoevsky. The three articles by R. P. Blackmur (in *Accent*, 1942, in *Chimera*, 1943, and in *The Hudson Review*, 1948) are meditations in the style of the later Henry James and progressively lose contact with the texts. George Steiner's *Tolstoy or Dostoevsky: An Essay in the Old Criticism* (1959) brilliantly and sweepingly restates the old contrast between the two writers but spoils its effect by perversely reading *The Grand Inquisitor* as an "allegory of the confrontation between Dostoevsky and Tolstoy." Dostoevsky occurs prominently in many contexts: in Eliseo Vivas' *Creation and Discovery* (1955), in Renato Poggioli's *The Phoenix and the Spider* (1957), in Irving Howe's *Politics and the Novel* (1957), in Murray Krieger's *The Tragic Vision* (1960), and in Albert Cook's *The Meaning of Fiction* (1960). A series of articles by Philip Rahv (in the *Partisan Review*, 1936, 1954, and 1960) are particularly satisfying as they are nourished by a knowledge of the Russian discussions and animated by a central vision. Joseph Frank (in the *Sewanee Review*, 1961) gives a preview of what promises to be a distinguished critical study of Dostoevsky's work.

Since the Second World War, and with the development of academic studies in Russian literature, Americans have produced an increasing number of papers, articles, and even monographs on specific aspects of Dostoevsky's ideas, techniques, imagery, and use of quotations. Ralph Matlaw's listing of Dostoevsky's recurrent imagery of insects (in *Harvard Slavic Studies*, Vol. 3, 1957) and his pamphlet, *The Brothers Karamazov: Novelistic Technique* (The Hague, 1957); Robert L. Jackson's *The Underground Man in Russian Literature* (The Hague, 1958), which traces the influence of Dostoevsky's negative hero on subsequent Russian literature; and the scattered papers of George Gibian, may be cited as encouraging testimonies to the burgeoning vitality of American Dostoevsky scholarship. Certainly the materials for considered criticism are at hand. Americans are exempt from the dire dilemma of choosing between Marxist and Orthodox interpretations. They can see Dostoevsky for what he primarily is: a novelist, a supreme creator of a world of imagination, an artist with a deep insight into human conduct and the perennial condition of man.

\*          \*          \*

Many important books on Dostoevsky are now available in cheap editions: *e.g.*, Yarmolinsky, Simmons, Gide, Berdyaev, and Ivanov. There seems no point in reprinting extracts from them. The selections which follow contain four essays by contemporary American critics, each treating one of the four great novels: Philip Rahv, "Dostoevsky in *Crime and*

*Punishment"*; Murray Krieger, "Dostoevsky's *Idiot:* The Curse of Saint-liness"; Irving Howe, "Dostoevsky: The Politics of Salvation"; Eliseo Vivas, "The Two Dimensions of Reality in *The Brothers Karamazov."* I have included D. H. Lawrence's introduction to the *The Grand Inquisitor* and Freud's pioneering essay on "Dostoevsky and Parricide." Dmitri Chizhevsky's study of "The Theme of the Double," here translated from the Russian for the first time, cuts through Dostoevsky's work from a point of view which could be called existentialist. The Orthodox theological point of view is represented by V. V. Zenkovsky's chapter; the Marxist outlook, by Lukács' essay, which has not been translated before. Finally, the English critic Derek Traversi puts the case against Dostoevsky's art in a little-known piece now reprinted for the first time. Thus a wide spectrum of approaches to Dostoevsky is represented.

# Dostoevsky in
## *Crime and Punishment*

## *by Philip Rahv*

> When thought is closed in caves
> Then love shall show its roots in deepest hell
> —William Blake

Is this the type of narrative nowadays called a psycho-thriller? Yes, in a sense it is, being above all, in its author's own words, the psychological account of a crime. The crime is murder. But in itself this is in no way exceptional, for the very same crime occurs in nearly all of Dostoevsky's novels. Proust once suggested grouping them together under a single comprehensive title: *The Story of a Crime.*

Where this novel differs, however, from the works following it is in the totality of its concentration on that obsessive theme. Virtually everything in the story turns on Raskolnikov's murder of the old pawnbroker and her sister Lizaveta, and it is this concentration which makes the novel so fine an example of artistic economy and structural cohesion. Free of distractions of theme and idea, and with no confusing excess or over-ingenuity in the manipulation of the plot, such as vitiates the design of *A Raw Youth* and reduces the impact of *The Idiot, Crime and Punishment* is the one novel of Dostoevsky's in which his powerful appeal to our intellectual interests is most directly and naturally linked to the action.

The superiority of this work in point of structure has been repeatedly remarked upon, but what has not been sufficiently noted is its extraordinary narrative pace. Consider the movement of Part I, for instance. In this comparatively short section (coming to eighty-four pages in Constance Garnett's translation), we get to know the protagonist fairly well, to know the conditions of crushing poverty and isolation under which he lives and the complex origins of his "loathsome scheme"; we see him

"Dostoevsky in *Crime and Punishment.*" From *Partisan Review*, XXVII (1960), 393-425. © 1960 by Philip Rahv. Reprinted by permission of the author.

going through a rehearsal-visit to the victim's flat; we listen to Marmeladov's sermon in the pothouse, to the recital of his domestic woes, including the circumstances that forced his daughter Sonya to become a prostitute; we witness the drunken old man's homecoming and the hysterical violence with which he is received by his wife; then we read with Raskolnikov the long letter from his mother, learning a good deal about his family situation; we dream with him the frightful dream, looking at once to the past and to the future, of the beating to death of the little mare; finally, after several more scenes of the strictest dramatic relevance, we are brought to a close-up of the double murder, probably the most astonishing description of its kind in fiction, and watch the murderer returning to his lodgings where, after putting back the axe under the porter's bench, he climbs the stairs to sink on his bed in blank forgetfulness.

Thus in this first section of seven chapters a huge quantity of experience is qualitatively organized, with the requisite information concerning the hero's background driven into place through a consummate use of the novelistic device of foreshortening, and with the swift narrative tempo serving precisely as the prime means of controlling and rendering credible the wild queerness of what has been recounted. For this wild queerness cannot be made to yield to explanation or extrinsic analysis. To gain our consent—to enlist, that is, our poetic faith—the author must either dramatize or perish, and for full success he must proceed with the dramatic representation at a pace producing an effect of virtual instantaneousness. To have secured this effect is a triumph of Dostoevsky's creative method—a triumph because the instantaneous is a quality of Being rather than of mind and not open to question. As the vain efforts of so many philosophers have demonstrated, Being is irreducible to the categories of explanation or interpretation.

The artistic economy, force and tempo of Part I is sustained throughout the novel. (The epilogue, in which hope and belief play havoc with the imaginative logic of the work, is something else again.) There is no wasted detail in it, none that can be shown to be functionally inoperative in advancing the action and our insight into its human agents. And it is important to observe that the attaining of this fullness and intensity of representation is conditional upon Dostoevsky's capacity to subdue the time element of the story to his creative purpose. Readers not deliberately attentive to the time-lapse of the action are surprised to learn that its entire span is only two weeks and that of Part I only three days. Actually, there is no real lapse of time in the story because we are virtually unaware of it apart from the tension of the rendered experience. Instead of time lapsing there is the concrete flow of duration contracting and expanding with the rhythm of the dramatic movement.

Least of all is it a chronological frame that time provides in this novel. As the Russian critic K. Mochulsky has so aptly remarked, its time is purely psychological, a function of human consciousness, in other words

the very incarnation of Bergson's *durée réelle*.[1] And it is only in Berg-
sonian terms that one can do it justice. Truly, Dostoevsky succeeds here
in converting time into a kind of progress of Raskolnikov's mental state,
which is not actually a state but a process of incessant change eating into
the future and expanding with the duration it accumulates, like a snow-
ball growing larger as it rolls upon itself, to use Bergson's original image.

This effect is partly accomplished by the exclusion from Raskolnikov's
consciousness of everything not directly pertaining to his immediate situation. From beginning to end he is in a state of crisis from which there is
no diversion or escape either in memory or fantasy. The import of what
he thinks, feels, and remembers is strictly functional to the present. Thus
he thinks of his mother, who is involved in the action, with distinct al-
ternations of feelings, while his dead father hardly exists for him. He
belongs to the past, and so far as Raskolnikov is concerned the past is
empty of affect. The one time he evokes his father's figure is in the anguished dream of the beating to death of the little mare, and his appearance in that dream is singularly passive, manifestly carrying with it
no charge of emotion. This dream, enacting a tragic catharsis, is introduced with calculated ambiguity. Is the dreamer actually remembering
an episode of his childhood or is he imagining the memory? In any case,
though the dream is of the past its meaning is all in the present. The
pitiful little mare, whipped across the eyes and butchered by Mikolka
and a crowd of rowdy peasants, stands for all such victims of life's in-
sensate cruelty, in particular such victims as Sonya and Lizaveta whose
appeal to Raskolnikov is that of "poor gentle things . . . whose eyes are
soft and gentle." Also, the mare stands above all for Raskolnikov himself,
and in embracing her bleeding head in a frenzy of compassion it is himself he is embracing, bewailing, consoling. He is present in the dream
not only as the little boy witnessing an act of intolerable brutality but
as at once its perpetrator and victim too. The dream's imagery is entirely
prospective in that it points ahead, anticipating the murder Raskolnikov
is plotting even while exposing it as an act of self-murder. Its latent
thought-content is a warning that in killing the pawnbroker he would be
killing himself too, and it is indeed in this light that he understands his
deed afterwards when, in confessing to Sonya, he cries out: "Did I murder the old woman? I murdered myself, not her! I crushed myself once
and for all, forever." The cathartic effect of the dream is such that upon
awakening he recovers the sense of his human reality, feeling "as though
an abscess that had been forming in his heart had suddenly broken . . .
he was free from that spell, that sorcery, that obsession." But the catharsis
is momentary, and he no sooner hears that the pawnbroker will be alone
in her flat the next evening than he is again gripped by his obsession.

Another instance of the functional character of Raskolnikov's memory

---

[1] *Dostoevskii: zhizn i tvorchestvo* (Paris, 1947), p. 243 ff.

is the way he recalls the invalid girl to whom he had once been engaged. "I really don't know," he says, "what drew me to her then . . . she was always ill. If she had been lame or hunchback, I believe I would have liked her even better." This is a meaningful admission, and it is curious that the numerous commentators on the novel should have unanimously ignored it. It is as if they all wanted to spare Sonya. For what prompts this memory if not his involvement with Sonya, who is in her own way ill too? In the eyes of the world and likewise of Raskolnikov in some of his moods she is a morally deformed creature, an outcast, and "a religious maniac" to boot. Physically too, the description of the invalid girl has much in common with that of Sonya. *yet - whoring does not affect Sonya morally she is above it.*

Yet, for all his living in the present, Raskolnikov wills and acts with his whole past back of him; and it is for a very good reason that we are not permitted to gain a privileged understanding of his past in the sense of entering a series of his mental states anterior to the action. By denying us such intimacy the author effectively prevents us from rationalizing the mystery of the crime and its motive—the mystery which is never really solved but toward the solution of which everything in the novel converges. Now the study of Dostoevsky's manuscripts has shown that he was himself disturbed no end by the indefiniteness and uncertainty of Raskolnikov's motive, and he wrote a note reminding himself that he must once and for all clear up the uncertainty and isolate the "real" motive in order "to destroy," as he put it, "the indefiniteness and explain the murder this way or that way" (*tak ili etak*). Fortunately he was able to forget this injunction as the novel progressed. For his basic idea of his hero's motivation is such as to identify it with the totality of his consciousness, and to have changed that conception to a more conventional one would have led to the withering of that fine insight; and what that insight comes to, in the last analysis, is that human consciousness is inexhaustible and incalculable. It cannot be condensed into something so limited and specific as a motive. The consciousness is ever obliging in generating a sufficiency of reasons, but it is necessary to distinguish between reasons and motives. Not that motives have no existence; they exist, to be sure, but only on the empirical plane, materializing in the actual practice of living, primarily in the commitment of action. Existentially speaking, the acting man can be efficient and self-assured only insofar as his consciousness is non-reflective. Raskolnikov, however, is above all a man of reflection, and his crime is frequently described in the book as a "theoretical" one, "theoretical" not only in the sense of its being inspired by a theory but also in the sense that theory, that is to say abstraction, is of its very essence: no wonder he carries out the murder in the manner of a sleep-walker or of a man falling down a precipice. The textual evidence shows that what his crime mainly lacks is empirical content, and that is what some critics had in mind, I think, in defining it as a pure experiment in self-cognition. Thus it can be said of this murderer that he produces a corpse but no real motive. His consciousness, time and again recoiling upon itself in a sickening manner, consumes motives as fast as it produces them.

*Crime and Punishment* may be characterized as a psycho-thriller with prodigious complications. It is misleading, however, to speak of it as a detective story, as is so often done. It is nothing of the sort, since from the outset we know not only the murderer's identity but are also made to enter into some of his innermost secrets. True, the story is almost entirely given over to detection—not of the criminal, though, but of his motive. Inevitably it turns out that there is not one but a whole cluster of motives, a veritable *embarras de riches,* and if the criminal himself is in his own fashion constrained to take part in the work of detection it is because he is soon lost in the maze of his own motivation. Never quite certain as to what it was exactly that induced him to commit murder, he must continually spy on himself in a desperate effort to penetrate his own psychology and attain the self-knowledge he needs if he is to assume responsibility for his absurd and hideous act. And this idea of him as the criminal in search of his own motive is precisely what is so new and original in the figure of Raskolnikov.

His knowing and not knowing is in a sense the worst of his ordeal. He is aware of several motives that keep eluding him as his thought shifts among them, and there are times when they all seem equally unreal to him. To sustain himself in the terrible isolation of his guilt he must be in complete possession of a single incontrovertible motive representing his deepest self, his own rock-bottom truth. But he no sooner lays hold of this truth than he catches himself in a state of mind that belies it, as, for example, in the scene when right after burying the loot—a purse and some trinkets of jewelry—he suddenly stops in the street to confound himself with a simple and terrifying question: "If it had all really been done deliberately and not idiotically, if I really had a certain and definite object, how is it that I did not even glance into the purse and didn't know what I had there. Then why have I undergone these agonies and have deliberately undertaken this base, dirty and degrading business?" This is but one of several passages in which the abstraction—so to speak —of the crime, its lack of empirical substance, is brought home to us. There is an intrinsic incongruity between this criminal and his crime which is exhibited by the author with masterful indirection, and nowhere to better effect than when Raskolnikov makes his confession to Sonya. In the course of it, though straining as hard as he can to discover and at long last seize the motive that impelled him, he still cannot stop wavering and giving various and contradictory explanations of his act. He begins by stating that he murdered "for plunder," but when Sonya cries: "You were hungry! It was to help your mother? Yes?" he at once retracts that explanation, muttering: "No, Sonya, no . . . . I was not so hungry . . . . I certainly did want to help my mother, but that's not the real

thing either . . . ." A little later he adds that if he had simply killed the
old pawnbroker because of hunger he would be *happy* now, exclaiming
that he really wanted to become a Napoleon and that is why he killed
her. Yet still later we hear him say that the argument from Napoleon is
"all nonsense" as he reverts to the explanation from poverty and simple
need. Soon enough, however, he strikes again the Napoleonic note, ac-
counting for the murder now as a matter of wanting to have the daring:
"I only wanted to have the daring . . . that was the whole cause of it";
he claims that he killed "not to gain wealth and power" but for himself
alone so as to find out quickly whether "he was a louse like everybody
else or a man," whether he was a "trembling creature" or one who has
"the right" to step over barriers. Still another cause, more immediately
psychological in bearing, is introduced when he speaks of his airless cupboard of a room, that room where he turned sulky and sat "like a spider,"
where he would not work but simply lay for hours thinking. It is chiefly
this perpetual thinking, this desperate resort to sheer reflection, which
is the source of the mystifications that torment him. Though it is his
consciousness which did him in it is to his empirical self that he absurdly
looks for the justification it cannot supply; so that in the end, for all the
keenness with which he explicates his act to Sonya, we are still left with
a crime of indeterminate origin and meaning. indeterminacy the point
    The indeterminacy is the point. Dostoevsky is the first novelist to have
fully accepted and dramatized the principle of uncertainty or indeterminacy in the presentation of character. In terms of novelistic technique
this principle manifests itself as a kind of hyperbolic suspense—suspense
no longer generated merely by the traditional means and devices of fiction, though these are skillfully brought into play, but as it were by the
very structure of human reality. To take this hyperbolic suspense as a
literary invention pure and simple is to fail in comprehending it; it
originates rather in Dostoevsky's acute awareness (self-awareness at bottom) of the problematical nature of the modern personality and of its
tortuous efforts to stem the disintegration threatening it. Thus Raskolnikov, like Stavrogin and other protagonists of Dostoevsky's, is represented throughout under the aspect of modernity (the examining magistrate Porfiry Petrovich sees him very specifically as "a modern case")
understood as spiritual and mental self-division and self-contradiction.
It is in this light that the search for the true cause of the crime becomes
ultimately intelligible, the search that gives the novel at once its form
and meaning, taking us where no psycho-thriller before or after *Crime
and Punishment* has even taken us, into a realm where only the sharpest
psychological perception will see us through and into still another realm
where our response to ideas is impetuously solicited: ideas bearing on
crime and its relation to psychic illness on the one hand and to power
and genius on the other; ideas about two kinds of human beings, ordinary
and extraordinary, with the former serving as mere material for the latter

who arrogate to themselves the right "to overstep the line" and remove moral obstacles at will; ideas concerning the supernal value of suffering and the promise of deliverance in Christ.

The principal characters (Raskolnikov, Svidrigailov and others) are the carriers of these ideas, and if we are not to sever the unity of thought and action, theory and practice, prevailing in the Dostoevskean world, it is necessary to take their ideas for what they are, without reducing them, with the purely psychological critics, to a species of "interesting" rationalization, or, with the formalistic critics, to mere "fictive matter" drawn fortuitously from the intellectual sphere. That we must first of all regard the ideas as dramatic motivation goes without saying; but that should not deter us from also accepting them as given on the level of thought. "I killed not an old woman but a principle," declares Raskolnikov. What is that principle and why does he want to kill it? The answer to such questions has been much simplified or, worse still, credulously taken for granted.

From the Christian standpoint Raskolnikov is easily enough perceived to be a kind of Lazarus whom Sonya strives to raise from the dead. Yet if he comes forth from the tomb it is only after experiencing the ecstasy and terror of having touched for one moment the secret springs of freedom and power. "What, then, is to be done?" asks Sonya. This is indeed the fateful question which reverberates throughout the whole of Russian literature and to which all the leaders of Russian thought, from Chaadayev to Lenin, sought to provide an answer. Raskolnikov, too, accepts the challenge. "Break what must be broken," he replies, "once and for all, and take the suffering on oneself. . . . Freedom and power! Over all trembling creation and all the antheap! . . . That is the goal, remember that!" No wonder that though apparently renouncing that goal in yielding to Sonya's entreaties that he save himself through penance and submission, he nevertheless remains essentially unrepentant to the end. At the very least it can be said that he remains so deeply divided in his mind as to give himself up more because of confusion and despair than because of any real change of heart. About his regeneration we are told only in the epilogue, when at long last the pale sickly faces of the murderer and the saintly prostitute become "bright with the dawn of a new future." But this happy Siberian aftermath is the beginning of something altogether new and different. As the author observes in the last paragraph of the text, it "might be the subject of a new story but our present story is ended." [2] We, as critical readers, cannot overmuch con-

---

[2] It might indeed have been the subject of a new story. However, Dostoevsky, as a number of critics have noted, appears to have been incapable of carrying out his declared intention to depict the renewal of life on Christian foundations. On this score the late Leo Shestov made one of the most sardonic notations: "*Crime and Punishment* ends with the promise to picture the Christian rebirth of the hero. His words sound as if he were binding himself with a sacred vow. And, in point of fact,

cern ourselves with such intimations of ultimate reconcilement and salvation. Our proper concern is with the present story, with the story as written.

Dostoevsky wrote the first of his four great novels in monthly installments for the *Russky Vestnik,* where it ran serially between January and December, 1866. He was following his usual course of producing a long work under the immediate pressure of editors and printers. In this instance, however, he appears to have encountered very few difficulties in meeting the magazine's schedule. And the ease with which he accomplished the actual composition may have been partly due at least to the fact that the narrative mode he had adopted after considerable experimenting and much vacillation, the mode, that is, of telling the story from the standpoint of the "omniscient author," justified itself in practice, allowing him to make the most of his material without strain or hindrance.

The strain had indeed told on him in the late months of 1865, when while living in Wiesbaden he had written an incomplete draft of the novel in the form both of a diary and of a murderer's confession. Those versions turned out to be so unsatisfactory, chiefly because of the cramping effects of the method of narration in the first person, that he was forced to scrap them. The economy of interest he had been trying to enforce by means of that method proved to be too much of a good thing, and he now took exactly the opposite tack, expanding the interest where formerly he had compressed it. Into the new expansive scheme he introduced the figures of Svidrigailov and Porfiry Petrovich, who have nothing in common besides the fact that both represent possible attitudes toward Raskolnikov, viewpoints or perspectives enabling us to see at once more clearly and more variously the significance of his case. Dostoevsky also

as a professed teacher of humanity, was not Dostoevsky in duty bound to let us in on the secret of the new reality and fresh possibilities that opened up to Raskolnikov? Yet our preceptor never managed to fulfill that sacred vow. The same promise is encountered again in his foreword to *The Brothers Karamazov,* where we are told that in order to portray his real hero, Alyosha, he would need to write still another volume, as if the existing book with its thousand pages lacked sufficient space to accommodate the 'new life.' In the three novels he produced after *Crime and Punishment* there is no mention of the sacred vow. Prince Myshkin cannot be taken into account here. If he is the one representing the 'renewal' awaiting mankind . . . then there is no point whatever in looking toward the future. . . . No, compared to Dostoevsky's other heroes Prince Myshkin is a misfit. This novelist understood only restless, fractious, struggling people whose search is never ended. No sooner did he undertake to show us a man who has found himself and achieved tranquility than he fell into fatal banalities. One thinks, for instance, of the elder Zosima's dreams of 'the coming wonderful union of men.' What is this 'wonderful union' if not another of those idyllic pictures of the future which even the socialists—so maliciously ridiculed in his cellar by the narrator of *Notes from the Underground*—have by now learned to do without?" *Dostoevskii i Nitsshe: filosofiya tragedii* (St. Petersburg, 1903).

introduced into his revised scheme the basic elements of a tale, entitled *The Drunkards,* which he had just sketched out in outline and in which he was proposing to enter into "all the ramifications" of the then rather topical subject of alcoholism rampant among the city poor, with the emphasis falling on "the picture of a family and the bringing up of children under such circumstances." It is in this somewhat fortuitous manner, or so it would seem on the face of it, that the Marmeladov sequence, so reminiscent of the author's earlier vein in its pathos of indigence and harrowing exposition of the Petersburg misery, as the Russians are wont to call it, came to be included in the account of Raskolnikov's crime.

But the fortuitousness is more apparent than real. There is an inner logic, both of content and structure, in his combination of subject matter from which the novel gains enormously—and this can be said even while conceding that the rather stagey woes of the Marmeladovs are inducive of some moments of weariness. A somewhat Dickensian family with deviations toward Russian intensity, they are of course the very embodiment of the Petersburg misery. But Raskolnikov is also a child of that misery, patently belonging to the world of the insulted and injured, though in him the humility and submissiveness of that world's human mixture are turned inside out. He is the first of its inhabitants to attempt its redemption by making a bid, in however futile and hideous a fashion, for freedom and power.

Intrinsically his figure is a composite of the typical protagonists of Dostoevsky's earlier and later fiction. Morbidly estranged as he is from life and ceaselessly brooding in his cupboard of a room, he at once brings to mind certain traits of *the* underground man as well as of the daydreaming recluse portrayed in such stories of the 1840's as *The Landlady* and *White Nights*—the recluse who, suffering from nearly pathological depression and nameless guilt-feelings, keeps to himself and lives a life of wishful fantasy. At the same time Raskolnikov represents a startling departure from the recluse type in that, having overcome the latter's masochistic need for self-abasement, his aggression is no longer turned inward but outward. He is quite as much a fantast as the daydreaming recluse, but his fantasy has left behind it all *Schwärmerei* and noble aspiration *à la* Schiller: it has taken on the color of blood. A complete egoist on one side of his nature at least and a surprisingly candid one at that, he is filled with the wrath of outraged pride and a furious impatience to break out from his trapped existence even at the risk of self-destruction. Moreover, to see him from this angle of vision, as the Dostoevskean hero in process of evolution, is to note another new element in him, namely, that he is an intellectual *pur sang,* recklessly yielding himself to the passion of thought and caught at last in the toils of an idea, mastered by it to the point of monomania. Thus the novel of which he is the protagonist has a double aspect. In virtue of its carryover of the theme of the Petersburg misery, it brings to a close the series of so-called social narratives which, from *Poor Folk* to *The Insulted and Injured,* is dominated by a consistent motif that has been aptly defined as that of "the impotent protest of powerless people." In its second aspect, however, the novel throws off the limitations of the earlier theme, attaining the higher goals of its author's greater or ultimate period.

Raskolnikov's involvement with the Marmeladov clan enabled Dostoevsky to solve what must have been his main compositional problem: How to portray with entire cogency a hero who is a solitary and monomaniac acting throughout in a mood of "morbid irritability" verging on madness without succumbing to him, that is to say, without letting him take the lead to the degree of making the world over in his image? This is but another way of formulating one of the principal difficulties which forced Dostoevsky to abandon the first versions of the book. For to have permitted Raskolnikov, as first-person narrator, to absorb the story unto himself would surely have resulted in its impoverishment, producing an impression of life closing in, a claustrophobic effect diminishing the hero's stature in our eyes and turning him into an altogether special case.[3] And this is where the Marmeladovs come in exactly, that for all the grimness of their situation and its grotesque features they still somehow exist within the bounds of the normal, whereas Raskolnikov is decidedly outside it; hence their presence adds considerably to the story's quota of circumstantial realism, helping to overcome the hazard implicit in Raskolnikov's malaise. For we must keep in mind that his story, which on one side is an account of a crime open to explanation on the seemingly objective grounds of material need and a sinister "nihilistic" theory, is converted on the subjective side into an analysis of an extreme pathological condition or soul-sickness, if you will.

The episodes dealing with Svidrigailov, the would-be seducer of Raskolnikov's sister Dunya have an engrossing interest of their own, but they also serve the same functional purpose of reducing the protagonist's remoteness from the common human measure. In order to heighten the dramatic tension and explore to the end the complex meanings of Raskolnikov's plight, it was positively necessary to involve him in intimate human associations, notwithstanding the feeling of absolute aloneness, or "agonizing, everlasting solitude," into which he is plunged by his murderous act. It is a feeling brought on by the guilt he refuses to acknowledge and strains every nerve to repress; and what better way was there of dramatizing the struggle within him between guilt and scornful

---

[3] The special or clinical case is precisely what no master of the narrative medium will let himself in for. Dostoevsky did let himself in for it once, in the early nouvelle, *The Double,* which, for all its startling effects, cannot be rated otherwise than as a failure. He never repeated that youthful error. In lesser talents, however, this error becomes habitual, for in coping with the extremes of morbidity or irrationality they are frequently lured into betraying the shared sense of human reality.

pride than by showing him entering almost in spite of himself into relations with people who for reasons both good and bad are intent on
penetrating his isolation? Sonya, his "chosen bride" and Christian men-
tor, is of course the chief agent of this turn of the plot, but so in his
own paradoxical fashion is Svidrigailov. The latter, however, is so fascinating a character in his own right, exercising an appeal nearly match-
ing that of the hero, that at times he threatens to run away with the
story; certainly the scene of his suicide and of the dream-haunted night
that precedes it are perfectly realized incidents and among the marvels
of the book. It must have called for the nicest management on the author's
part to hold him to his subordinate position. But that was only part of
the task Dostoevsky set himself in undertaking to unify the three thematic
elements at his disposal: the major theme of Raskolnikov's crime and its
consequences and the strongly contrasted minor themes of the lowly and
good Marmeladovs on the one hand and of the wealthy immoralist
Svidrigailov on the other. And it is the achieved integration with its fine
contrapuntal effects which makes for verisimilitude of a higher order,
for novelistic truth and density, and for structural cohesion.

But though the Svidrigailov sequence is successfully integrated into
the main action, there is no denying that he is invested with an originality
and expressive power that invite comment. It will not do to see him,
in the fashion of most critics of Dostoevsky, as being merely Raskolnikov's
double, representing the pole of self-will in his character. The formal
abstractness of this traditional approach to Svidrigailov cannot do him
justice; and so far as the element of self-will is concerned, Raskolnikov,
like all "the children of darkness" in Dostoevsky, has more than enough
of it in himself and is in no need of Svidrigailov's services. No, the latter
has an independent existence in the novel though his position in it is
structurally subordinate; his function is not simply that of ministering
to its hero. There is no innate relationship between the two, no affinity
of the mystical order such as is posited in so many Dostoevsky studies.
Actually Svidrigailov enters the novel by way of the external plot or
intrigue (his pursuit of Dunya), yet once he is in it he provides the story
not only with an additional perspective on Raskolnikov but also with the
psychosexual vitality which it otherwise lacks, for both Raskolnikov and
Sonya are singularly sexless. Svidrigailov exemplifies a distinct character-
type in Dostoevsky, the type of the nihilist in the realm of sensuality. He
is a more elaborate and refined version of the rather coarse-grained liber-
tine Valkovsky in *The Insulted and Injured* and he anticipates the figures
of Stavrogin and the elder Karamazov in the later novels (like Stavrogin
he is guilty of outraging a little girl). In this character-type, sensuality
becomes a flight from the vertiginous consciousness of freedom and from
a kind of ennui which has gone beyond the psychological and has ac-
quired a metaphysical status. Thus Svidrigailov believes in ghosts who
"are as it were shreds and fragments of other worlds" and who appear

only to people whose psyche is prepared to receive them. He rejects all dogma, including that of the atheists, as he is given to relativizing all possible ideas, whether of belief or unbelief. Whereas Raskolnikov does not believe in a future life, Svidrigailov speculates that perhaps the future life does exist but that there are only "spiders there or something of that sort." "We always imagine eternity as something beyond our conception, something vast, vast! But why must it be vast? Instead of all that, what if it is one little room, like a bathhouse in the country, black and grimy and spiders in every corner, and that's all eternity is?" As for vice, he chides Raskolnikov for his moral prejudices, contending that in sexual vice "there is at least something permanent, founded indeed upon nature and not dependent on fantasy, something present in the blood like an ever-burning ember, forever setting one on fire and maybe not to be quickly extinguished even with years. You agree that it's an occupation of a sort." Admitting that it is a disease, like everything that exceeds moderation, he defends his indulgence in it by claiming that to give it up would mean that he would be forced to shoot himself. Clearly, his métier is not the simple-minded villainy of melodrama but a species of objective cruelty (as in his doing away with his wife and driving his footman to suicide) which is in a sense a form of meditation upon life beyond good and evil translated into practice. Therefore he is at the same time capable of acts of sympathy and kindness, as when he helps the Marmeladov orphans and lets Dunya go after cornering her. Good and evil are never ends to him but simply the available, even if sometimes redundant, means of convincing himself that it is possible to continue living. Hence the actions he performs strike one as transpiring somewhere outside himself, for they are at bottom experiments conducted by a self which is itself an experimental projection.

It has been observed often enough that every literary artist genuinely an innovator creates his own audience. This is certainly true of Dostoevsky, in whose sphere we have now learned to move without undue strain but who shocked his contemporaries by his open and bold reliance on melodrama and by the seeming fantasticality of his characters. The Russian reader had learned by that time to identify the unhurried, equable, lifelike realism of writers like Turgenev, Goncharov and Tolstoy with the higher norms of the novel; and what those writers scrupulously avoided above all was the sensational and excessive. Dostoevsky was hard put to it to persuade the reader that he too, despite his startling deviations from the newly-established norms, was a realist. Hence while writing *Crime and Punishment* he fretted over the thought that his story would gain no credence from the public; and since he had long been trying to defend himself against the charge of insufficient regard for the real, he was pleased to note, shortly after the appearance of the first installment of the novel, that a crime curiously similar to the one he was describing had been committed by a Moscow student and reported in the newspapers. He at once seized upon this item as confirming his own "special view" of the relation between art and actuality. "What the majority call fantastic and exceptional," he wrote to the critic Strakhov, "sometimes signifies to me the very essence of reality. . . . In every issue of the newspapers you come upon accounts of the most real facts and amazing coincidences. For our writers, who are unconcerned with them, they are fantastic. But being facts they are reality none the less."

But this appeal to actual life—formless, disorderly and inconsequent life with its "most real facts and amazing coincidences"—is unworthy of the genius of Dostoevsky. In spite of his opposition to such radical-minded simplifiers of the relation of art and life as Chernyshevsky, Dobrolyubov and Pisarev, critics exceedingly influential in their time, he was himself far from immune to the idea then prevailing in his intellectual milieu that the work of art was useless and perhaps even immoral in its inutility unless directly validated by life or "reality," understood in the simplest empirical sense of these terms. Dostoevsky was after all a Russian writer of his generation, a generation ideologically inspired to exalt life over art and seeking to justify the latter by citing the gifts of illumination and hopes of betterment it ostensibly brings to life. Where Dostoevsky twisted that common assumption to suit his creative practice was by claiming to discern the essence of reality not in its typical everyday manifestations but in the exceptional and fantastic. He was unable to go beyond that formula toward the assertion of a symbolic rather than literal correspondence between life and the fictive worlds of his own devising. Hence the speciousness of his argument from life in his literary apologetics, as in his pointing to life's "amazing coincidences" in the letter to Strakhov quoted above. The fact is that no coincidence copied from life can make in the least plausible the kind of coincidences, even the minor ones, you find in *Crime and Punishment,* such as the prosperous and respectable bourgeois Luzhin turning up in the same slum-lodging with the starving Marmeladov family or Svidrigailov, a rich man, finding no better place to stay in Petersburg than in the very same house where Sonya lives, a house in which his flat adjoins the room where she practices her trade and conducts those incredible conversations with Raskolnikov upon which he eavesdrops with the greatest relish. It is plain that Svidrigailov is situated where he is in order to make it possible for him to learn Raskolnikov's secret at the same time as he confides it to Sonya; an important turn of the plot depends on it. This is a calculated coincidence different in kind from those, however improbable, that life offers. It belongs to the stock-in-trade of melodrama, and Dostoevsky learned the use of it in his assiduous reading of Hoffmann, Dickens, Balzac, Sue, and a host of lesser authors of crime-thrillers and adventure stories.

It is in literature rather than in unprocessed life that you find some of the sources of this novel, including its major plot-element of a murder

Raskol. *as a Russian Julien Sorel!*

committed by someone who stands in no personal relation to the victim. Also, the Napoleon motif, on which so many changes are rung by Dostoevsky, is clearly transposed by him to a Petersburg setting from mid-nineteenth-century French fiction, Balzac and Stendhal in particular, both of whom glorified Napoleon (the former covertly and the latter overtly) and justified their ambitious plebeian heroes by appealing to his illustrious example. Thus Raskolnikov may be seen as a Russian version of Julien Sorel and Eugène de Rastignac—the young man on the make who comes to the capital from the provinces intent on a career and a conquest. It is especially Balzac's *Le Père Goriot* that suggests an influence in the design of Raskolnikov's story. In his essay on Dostoevsky[4] Georg Lukács mentions the anecdote of the Chinese mandarin in Balzac's novel as containing the hint that the Russian writer might have developed. The revelant passage is worth citing in full. It occurs in a dialogue between Rastignac and his friend the medical student Bianchon:

> "What makes you look so serious?" asked the medical student, taking his arm [Rastignac's] to walk up and down in front of the palace with him.
> "I am bothered by troublesome thoughts."
> "Of what kind are they? You know that thoughts can be cured."
> "How?"
> "By yielding to them."
> "You are laughing at me, without knowing what I mean. Have you read Rousseau?"
> "Do you remember the place where he asks the reader what he would do, if he could become rich by killing an old mandarin in China, by the sole act of his will, without stirring from Paris?"
> "Yes."
> "Well?"
> "Pooh! I have already come to my thirty-third mandarin."
> "Don't joke. Come, suppose you knew it were possible, and that a nod from you would do it, should you consent?"
> "Is he a very old mandarin? But young or old, sick or well, my goodness —the deuce. No, I shouldn't."

And Bianchon concludes his argument in favor of sparing the Chinaman by warning Rastignac against a rash solution of the problem posed at "the entrance of life," against the attempt to cut that Gordian knot with his sword. "If you mean to act thus," he says, "you must be an Alexander or else you will be sent to the gallows." Unlike Rastignac, however, Dostoevsky's hero confides in no one and sets out to cut the Gordian knot without in the least resembling an Alexander or a Napoleon, though hoping that his crime might possibly prove him to belong to their superior breed.

It seems to me, too, that Dostoevsky drew on *Le Père Goriot* for far more than the germinal anecdote of the Chinese mandarin. Svidrigailov's posture vis-à-vis Raskolnikov is in certain respects strongly reminiscent of Vautrin's relation to Rastignac in Balzac's novel. We know that Svidrigailov is missing from the early drafts of *Crime and Punishment*, and it is not improbable that when it came to composing the final version Dostoevsky decided to introduce a character playing Vautrin to his own Rastignac. Consider that both Vautrin and Svidrigailov are older men who assume the role of mentors in the ways of the world, that both have insinuating manners and appear cheerful and obliging when it suits them, that both are sexual deviants (the Frenchman is a homosexual and the Russian has very special tastes in underage girls), and that both are predatory types who make no secret of their immorality. Moreover, some of the ideas that Vautrin communicates to Rastignac turn up in Raskolnikov's thought virtually without modification, as if he had absorbed the lesson addressed to his French prototype. Vautrin declares, for instance, that there are but two courses open to a man, blind obedience or open revolt, and that he can make his way in the world either "by the splendor of genius or the adroitness of corruption. He must burst like a cannon-ball into the ranks of his fellow-men, or he must move among them like the pestilence. Honesty is of no use. Men yield to the power of genius; they hate and calumniate it . . . but they yield to it if it persists, and kneel to it when they find that they cannot suppress it." There is a remarkable parallel between this formulation and Raskolnikov's view, passionately expounded to Sonya, that "whoever is strong in mind and spirit will have power over men. Anyone who is greatly daring is right in their eyes. . . . I divined that power is only vouchsafed to the man who dares to stoop and pick it up. There is only one thing, one thing needful: one has only to dare." Clearly, Vautrin's genius who bursts like a cannon-ball among his fellow-men bears an uncommon resemblance to Raskolnikov's criminal of genius who dares assert the right inherent in his superiority and whose criminality is soon forgiven or forgotten as he becomes a lawgiver and leader among men. However, in constructing Raskolnikov's theory of the relation between power and genius, Dostoevsky borrowed from more than one source; Balzac is but one of them.

It is possible to speak if not of a school then surely of a Petersburgian genre in Russian literature, of which Dostoevsky is in fact the leading practitioner. Pushkin's *The Bronze Horseman* is doubtless the outstanding poem of that genre, as Gogol's "The Overcoat" is the outstanding story and *Crime and Punishment* the outstanding novel. One must be aware of its author's profound response to Petersburg and of the masterly way in which he appropriated it to imaginative purposes in order to perceive that as the scene of Raskolnikov's crime the city is one of the essential constituents of the story, more foreground than background, a unique urban setting charged with multiple meanings, of which one of the more

urgent emerges from Dostoevsky's preoccupation with the Petersburg
misery and his depiction of it in a manner demonstrating his solidarity
with its victims. As a novelist of the modern metropolis he was of course
in the line of Balzac and Dickens, by whom he was greatly influenced,
though there is a marked difference in his representation of the city and
theirs. Balzac's Paris, as Arnold Hauser has remarked, is still a romantic
wilderness, "a theatrical setting painted in chiaroscuro contrasts, a fairy-
land in which dazzling riches and picturesque poverty live side by side," [5]
whereas Dostoevsky describes the metropolis in somber colors, taking us
into its reeking taverns and coffin-like rooms, bringing to the fore its petty-
bourgeois and proletarian types, its small shopkeepers and clerks, students,
prostitutes, beggars and derelicts. True as this is, there is also something
else in Dostoevsky's vision of Petersburg, a sense not so much of romance
as of poetic strangeness, a poetic emotion attached to objects in themselves
desolate, a kind of exaltation in the very lostness, loneliness and drabness
which the big city imposes on its inhabitants, as is so poignantly brought
out in the scene when in an evening hour Raskolnikov stops on a street
corner to listen to a sentimental song ground out on a barrel-organ and
sung by a girl in a cracked and coarsened voice:

> "Do you like street music?" said Raskolnikov, addressing a middle-aged
> man standing idly by him. The man looked at him, startled and wondering.
> "I love to hear singing to a street organ," said Raskolnikov, and his man-
> ner seemed strangely out of keeping with the subject. "I like it on cold,
> dark, damp evenings—they must be damp—when all the passers-by have
> pale green, sickly faces, or better still when the wet snow is falling straight
> down, where there's no wind—you know what I mean? and the street
> lamps shine through it. . . ."
> "I don't know. . . . Excuse me. . . ." muttered the stranger, frightened
> by the question and Raskolnikov's strange manner. . . .

Catching Raskolnikov talking to himself on the street, Svidrigailov
says to him: "This is a town of crazy people. . . . There are few places
where there are so many gloomy, queer influences on the soul of man as in
Petersburg." There is indeed something peculiarly Petersburgian about
Raskolnikov, and not merely in the sense that he belongs to its "proletariat of undergraduates." The crime he commits—in the idea of it,
namely, which is so strange an amalgam of the abstract and artificial with
the sheerly fantastic—corresponds intrinsically to the character of this
city, frequently described in exactly such terms.[6] It is in the heat and

[5] *The Social History of Art* (New York: Alfred A. Knopf, Inc., 1952), Vol. 2, p. 854.
[6] The ambiguity of Petersburg in its odd blending of the real and the unreal is
what Dostoevsky tried mainly to capture. In *A Raw Youth* there is an especially suggestive passage in which young Arkady speaks of a Petersburg morning as being at the
same time infinitely prosaic and infinitely fantastic: "On such a wild Petersburg morn-

stench of its slums, as he wanders endlessly through the streets, that Raskolnikov spawns his idea, which he himself likens to "a spell, a sorcery, an obsession." And afterwards, having carried his idea to its terrible conclusion, though not at all in the bravura manner of a Napoleon but rather like a man deprived of reason and will power by mental illness, on the very next day he resumes his wanderings about the city in a state more often than not bordering on delirium.

St. Petersburg was far more the capital of the Russian empire than of the Russian land. It was erected on the Finnish marshland with cruel haste and at the cost of many lives by the edict of Peter the Great, who undertook, with the savage rationality typical of belated and alien converts to progress, to transform his backward domain all at once into an efficient state militarized along modern lines. The self-will and precipitate style of this operation brought into being a city without roots in the past or in the vast rural hinterland, the center of alienation and of everything novel and foreign violating the national traditions and the patriarchal mode of life. It was in Petersburg that in a fashion peculiar to it the imperial bureaucracy exerted itself to westernize the country from above while the turbulent and seditious "proletariat of undergraduates," impelled by other motives and a nobler vision, strove to effect the same end from below. Thus the material brutality of the caste pressing down upon society from the top met its counterpart in the tragic spiritual brutality of the dissident intelligentsia forcing the issue lower down.

No wonder the Slavophils hated Petersburg. Khomyakov, a leading ideologue of their faction, spoke of it as a city of dead beauty, where "all is stone, not only the houses but the trees and inhabitants as well." The Marquis de Custine, visiting the capital in 1839, could not believe that it would endure. "I have seen no place that is more penetrated with the instability of human beings," he wrote. Penetrated with the instability of human beings—a marvelously apt phrase which we can apply to the Dostoevskean world as a whole with but a slight shift of context. You will

ing, foul, damp and foggy, the wild dream of some Hermann out of Pushkin's 'Queen of Spades' (a colossal figure, an extraordinary and regular Petersburg type . . . the type of the Petersburg period) might, I believe, strike one as a piece of solid reality. A hundred times over, in such a fog, I have been haunted by a strange and persistent fancy: 'What if this fog should part and float away? Would not all this rotten and slimy town go with it, rise up with the fog, and vanish like smoke, and the old Finnish marsh be left as before and in the midst of it, perhaps, to complete the picture, a bronze horseman on a panting, overdriven steed?' "

The bronze horseman is Falconet's statue of Peter the Great, but implicitly the reference is of course to Pushkin's famous poem of that title. Hermann is the protagonist of Pushkin's story "The Queen of Spades," in whom some scholars have discerned an early model of Raskolnikov. For like Dostoevsky's hero, Hermann is under the spell of Napoleon and he too, daring all on one throw, kills an old woman in an attempt to wrest from her the secret that will make his fortune. What the two characters share, basically, is the Petersburgian power-urge combined with the peculiar Petersburgian dreaminess.

find this singular instability in Raskolnikov, to be sure, but you will also find in him more than a trace of that savage rationality characterizing the champions of the Petersburg period in Russian history and subsequently the revolutionary elite. He emerges from that "literate world of reckless youth," as Bakunin called it, in which the latter professed to see the hope of the revolution, and he is the epitome of those traits of which Alexander Herzen gave an account of incomparable precision in his *Memoirs.* "We are greatly given," he noted, "to theoretical pedantry and argumentativeness. This German propensity is in us associated with a special national element—which we might call the Araktcheyev[7] element—a ruthlessness, a passionate rigidity, and an eagerness to dispatch their victims. To satisfy his grenadier ideal, Araktcheyev flogged living peasants to death; we flog to death ideas, arts, humanity, past leaders, anything you like. In dauntless array we advance step by step to the limit and overshoot it, never sinning against logic but only against *truth;* unaware, we go on further and further, forgetting that real sense and real understanding of life are shown precisely in stepping short before the extreme. . . ."

In truth Raskolnikov is one of those young men whose coming was foreshadowed with fear by Joseph de Maistre, the author of *Soirées de St. Pétersburg,* when he observed, in discussing the peasant uprisings of the eighteenth century, headed by such leaders as Emelian Pugachev, an obscure and illiterate Cossack, that if another such revolt ever took place in Russia it would be headed by a Pugachev "armed with a university degree." But the hour of the university Pugachevs had not quite struck when Raskolnikov set out entirely on his own, cut off from any social effort or collective historical action, to remove "certain obstacles." Proclaiming the necessity of breaking once and for all what must be broken, in other words, of killing not simply an old woman but the principle of authority bolstered by the moral law, he yet proceeds to commit not an act of political terror but another crime altogether that inevitably stamps him as no more than a common criminal, a criminal from egoism. He is a dissenter and rebel *(raskol,* the word from which his name derives, means *schism* or *dissent),* in essence the type of revolutionary terrorist of that period, whose act of terror is somehow displaced unto a private object. The terrorist is a political criminal, and if he is to be vindicated at all it is by an appeal to historical necessity; no such appeal is open to Raskolnikov.

Of course he has at his disposal a theory justifying his crime, and I have already indicated one source of it in Balzac. Another and more important source, to my mind, is Hegel's concept of the historic hero (the agent of the World-Spirit) and his victims. The enormous influence of the Hegelian philosophy in Russia during the late 1830's and the 1840's

---

[7] Alexis Araktcheyev (1769-1834), a high official and trusted adviser of Alexander I in the closing years of his reign, put into effect such inordinately cruel administrative practices as to give rise to the dread term *Araktcheyevchina.*

is well known; the period of this influence coincides with Dostoevsky's youth and it would have been impossible for him to escape it. But that he was in fact concerned with it is shown, moreover, by his letter (of February 22, 1854) from Siberia to his brother Mikhail asking that he send him, among other books, Hegel's *Philosophy of History*.[8] It is strange that this source, far from esoteric, should have been overlooked. I imagine that scholars and critics have been so carried away by the apparent analogy between Raskolnikov (in his theory of himself, that is) and Nietzsche's Superman as to have missed a more substantial likeness, though one which is more in the nature of a caricature than an exact replica. It is only in the vulgarized popular version of the Superman that Raskolnikov's theory reminds us of him; so far as Nietzsche's actual idea of the Superman goes, as a product of a mutation of the human species, there is no resemblance. It is in Hegel rather that we discover a direct and obvious source of Raskolnikov's notion of inferior and superior men, the superior ones having the right to commit breaches of morality while inferiors are obliged to mind their business, which is to stay put in the common rut. Now what Dostoevsky has done in devising Raskolnikov's justification is to convert into a theory of human nature what is in Hegel not a psychological theory at all but a theory of men as subjects and objects of history. Hegel's world-historical individual—such as Alexander or Caesar or Napoleon, the very names invoked by Dostoevsky's protagonist—performs the grandiose tasks set for him by the *Weltgeist* irrespective of moral considerations; he can do no other, for, as Hegel puts it, "the history of the world moves on a higher level than that of morality." These heroes may "treat other great and even sacred interests inconsiderately—a conduct which subjects them to moral reprehension. But so mighty a figure may trample down many an innocent flower, crush to pieces many things in its path." Thus as the subject of history he rides roughshod over its mere objects or victims. Dostoevsky gives us a parody-version of Hegel's theory of two types of men by abstracting it from its historical logic. This enables him to entangle Raskolnikov in what is in truth a comedy of mistaken identity: an obvious victim of the historical process—a small man in search of personal security and happiness—laughably taking himself for its hero. In this sense he is no better than a clown, and he does indeed laugh at himself from time to time. "One sudden idea made him laugh. Napoleon, the pyramids, Waterloo, and a wretched skinny old woman, a pawnbroker with a red trunk under her bed. . . . It's too inartistic. A Napoleon creep under the old woman's bed! Ugh, how loathsome!"

However, though Raskolnikov refuses the historical action of the political rebel, and, instead of throwing a bomb at a general or even the

[8] "Send me the Koran, and Kant's *Critique of Pure Reason*, and if you have the chance of sending me anything not officially, then be sure to send Hegel, particularly Hegel's *Philosophy of History*. Upon that depends my whole future."

Czar himself, crushes the skull of an old woman with an axe, there is still something in his deed, for all its weird abjectness and ugliness, which in some sense comes through to us as a protest against the Petersburg misery and the ethics justifying it. One cannot but agree with Alberto Moravia's statement in his essay "The Marx-Dostoevsky Duel" that though "Raskolnikov had not read Marx and regards himself as a super-man beyond good and evil, he was already, in embryo, a people's com-missar." [9] Moravia is one of the very few Western commentators on the novel who has not overlooked its aborted political meaning, which emerges again and again, as when Raskolnikov dissociates himself from his friend Razumikhin's abuse of the socialists. He understands very well that rebellion can take another form, the collective form advocated by the socialists. After all, what the socialists want, he remarks to himself, is the happiness of all. As it happens, however, he is not the one "to put his little brick into the happiness of all," for what he wants is to live properly here and now. Into his manuscript Dostoevsky inserted the fol-lowing passage (later deleted) into a speech of Raskolnikov's: "What care I what will come to pass in the future? Is it possible to live at present? I cannot pass by with indifference all these horrors, this suffering and misery. I want power." Power for what purpose? Presumably to do good, to alleviate the suffering and misery. He is in a state of fatal self-contra-diction, however, in that he attempts to further a common end of an al-truistic character with egoistical and purely private means. In order to test his strength he needs more than anything else the support of a social faith. This is plainly seen by the examining magistrate, Porfiry Petrovich, who is the one figure in the story who can be said manifestly to speak for the author, and it is he who says to Raskolnikov: "You made up a theory and then were ashamed that it broke down and turned out to be not at all original! It turned out something base, that's true, but you are not hopelessly base! . . . How do I regard you? I regard you as one of those men who would stand and smile at their torturer while he cuts their en-trails out, if only they have found faith or God." It is significant that the phrase is "faith *or* God," not faith *in* God, as if to say that there are other faiths besides the traditional one.

That Raskolnikov stands in an inauthentic relation to his crime is thus confirmed by the author's spokesman in the novel. The crime does not truly belong to him, and that is the reason he affects us as being almost ludicrously inadequate to his deed, as when he faints in the police station the day right after the murder, even though there is as yet no sus-picion attached to him, and calls attention to himself in other ways too. In spite of all his protestations to the contrary, he is prostrate with guilt and the yearning for punishment. It is not that he lacks the strength to kill and bear the responsibility for it to the end, but that he killed for

yearning for punishment

himself alone, deranged by unconscious urges and over-conscious theories, rather than for the common cause to which his "nihilistic" generation was dedicated; and that is also the secret of Sonya's hold on him. There is no social substance in his anarchic individualism, as there is none in Sonya's idea of Christian salvation.

Sonya, "the eternal victim so long as the world lasts," is a small thin girl of eighteen, every feature of whose face reflects "a sort of insatiable compassion." Raskolnikov turns to her in his need because, as he tells her: "We are both accursed, so let us go together." She is the very embodiment of meekness and humility (far more so than Myshkin or Alyosha), and only Dostoevsky, with his uncanny powers of representation, could have brought her to life without blundering into mawkish sentimentality. But though he so brilliantly persuades us of her reality as a novelistic creation, this in itself in no sense constitutes a "proof" of her idea of Christian salvation. She proves quite as much the Nietzschean negation of it. It appears to me that it is precisely in his characterization of Sonya, rather than of Raskolnikov, that Dostoevsky's insight coincides with that of Nietzsche; the fact that the Russian arrives at that insight by way of assent, and the German by way of dissent, is scarcely to the point here. Thus Nietzsche speaks in his *Antichrist* of "that queer and sick world into which the Gospels introduce us—as in a Russian novel, a world into which the scum of society, nervous disorders, and 'childlike' idiocy seem to be having a rendezvous." Sonya is truly an inhabitant of that world, and she has the stirring charm of the mixture it exhibits—"a mixture of the sublime, the sickly and the childlike." Nowhere in literature do we find so striking a confirmation of Nietzsche's idea of the evangelical type as in the figure of Sonya. What is that type? It is one in whom "the incapacity for resistance becomes morality," who experiences "any resistance, even any compulsion to resist, as unendurable *displeasure* . . . and finds blessedness (pleasure) only in no longer offering any resistance to anybody, neither to evil nor to him who is evil—love as the only, as the *last* possible way of life." Significantly, Sonya's faith is not one that has been attained through struggle. When Raskolnikov challenges her faith, she answers with simple pathos: "What should I be without God?" This is the kind of faith which, as Nietzsche said, "has been there from the beginning; it is as it were an infantilism that has receded into the spiritual." [10] Plainly, Sonya's faith is of a sort that offers no solution to Raskolnikov, whose spiritual existence is incommensurable with hers. No wonder that the epilogue to the novel, in which he finally seems to be preparing himself to accept her outlook, has struck many readers as implausible and out of key with the work as a whole.   *epilogue*

A few weeks after Dostoevsky's death in January 1881, a terrorist of the People's Will party by the name of Andrey Zhelyabov took part in

[10] *The Portable Nietzsche,* edited by Walter Kaufmann (New York: The Viking Press, Inc., 1954), p. 602 ff.

the successful attempt on the life of Alexander II. He was caught and brought to trial, and this is what he had to say to the court: "I was baptized in the Orthodox Church but I reject Christianity, although I acknowledge the essential teaching of Jesus Christ. This essential teaching occupied an honored place among my moral incentives. I believe in the truth and righteousness of that teaching and I solemnly declare that faith without works is dead and that every true Christian ought to fight for the truth and for the rights of the oppressed and the weak, and even, if need be, to suffer for them. Such is my creed." Evidently the blood he shed did not weigh on Zhelyabov's conscience, for he went to his death on the gallows calm and impenitent. Raskolnikov, cheated of Zhelyabov's fate, goes to a Siberian prison in the same state of perplexity and outrage with which he undertook to carry out his "loathsome scheme." But, then, it was a hideous old harpy he killed, not the Czar of all the Russias.

Whatever the manifest theme of the novel, its latent theme is not that of crime as such or the criminal's innate need of punishment but the right to violent rebellion. It was the violence that Dostoevsky condemned, even as he was secretly drawn to it, fearing that if let loose it would tear down the authority both of heaven and earth, and Raskolnikov goes down to defeat to prove his creator right.

In its aspect as a polemic against the radical generation of the 1860's —whose obscurantist rationalism and notion of enlightened self-interest as the motive-force of human conduct Dostoevsky began satirizing in *Notes from the Underground*—the novel depends on the sleight-of-hand of substituting a meaningless crime for a meaningful one. But if that were all, *Crime and Punishment* would not be the masterpiece it undoubtedly is. The very substitution of one type of crime for another set problems for Dostoevsky which he solved brilliantly by plunging his hero into a condition of pathology which ostensibly has nothing to do with the "heroic" theory by means of which he justifies himself. In his article "On Crime" Raskolnikov wrote that the perpetration of a crime is always accompanied by illness, and that is an exact description of his own case, though he believes himself to be another kind of criminal altogether, one acting from rational calculation and in the interests of a higher idea; the irony of his self-deception is among the finest effects of the book. And it is astonishing how well Dostoevsky was able to preserve the unity of his protagonist's character, to present him as all of a piece in spite of the fact that we are dealing not with one but with several Raskolnikovs. There is Raskolnikov the altruist and there is Raskolnikov the egoist, "a despot by nature"; there is the crypto-revolutionary Raskolnikov and there is the self-styled genius who demands power as his right and as the guaranty of his freedom; then of course there is the neurotic who acts out his illness through a murder intellectually rationalized but inexplicable except in terms of an unconscious drive. After all, he conceives an "insurmountable repulsion" to Alyona Ivanovna, the old moneylender, weeks before

several Raskolnikovs

he elaborates his murderous plan. Dostoevsky confronted the hazard of these contradictions with unequalled mastery. His capacity to combine them creatively in a single brain and a single psyche, while staving off the danger of incoherence at one end and of specious reconciliation at the other, is the measure of the victory scored in this novel by the imaginative artist in him over the ruthless polemicist.

# Dostoevsky's "Idiot":
# The Curse of Saintliness

## by Murray Krieger

If Pierre has committed the unique sins, Dostoevsky's Myshkin is guilty
of the unique follies—in their way, perhaps, as destructive in their consequences. The critic cannot begin to talk about the problem of Myshkin
without citing Dostoevsky's famous claim, "My intention is to portray
a truly beautiful soul." And this claim would seem clearly to remove
Myshkin from consideration as a tragic visionary in my sense. It would
rather argue that Dostoevsky has here transcended the tragic vision and,
in portraying a true saint, has reached to a considerably more sublime
vision. It would argue consequently that the inevitable half-darkness in
which I have seen all these extreme protagonists to be wandering may be
unequivocally and divinely lightened, that the duality which characterizes
their moral life may—given enough innocence and purity—reach a higher
reconciliation. In arguing for this exalted affirmation, it would, in other
words, argue against my claim for the inescapability of the tragic vision
within the conditions of extremity and the aesthetic and existential demands for authenticity, as our crisis-novelists have conceived these. And
since one can hardly dispute Dostoevsky's passion for extremity or the
fierce candor of his authenticity, I must find a place for even his sublim-
est work or else qualify my general contention considerably. I have chosen
*The Idiot,* then, as the most difficult of his works to bring within my
context and as perhaps the most crucial of all novels from the standpoint
of my dialectic. I see it as the case against my view *a fortiori,* with its
protagonist at the end of the spectrum toward which I have been shading
constantly, the seemingly angelic end farthest removed from the open
demons with which I started. It remains to be seen whether this spectrum
returns upon itself so that, as our intermediate novels seemed to be

prophesying, we end much where we began and moral progression is finally illusion.

In this one case, then, I must use this second novel of the chapter, not as a nontragic (or a less tragic) analogue, but as an even more critical example of the tragic. Not, of course, that any sensible reader could even for a moment see Myshkin as being transformed into a demoniacal creature. He is surely not to be confused with Pierre. Both are self-sacrificing enthusiasts, but while Pierre's dedication to virtue stems from a prideful and highly self-conscious assumption of righteousness, Myshkin takes up the burdens of humanity with a humility that makes no pretensions for his role—indeed that would deny any which others would make for him. Pierre is a self-appointed Jesus while Myshkin would shrink from any such imputation, although his actions, combining personal disinterestedness with lack of pronouncement, based on love of persons rather than love of principle, seem far more Christ-like. Thus this comparison would suggest that, as Dostoevsky intended, Myshkin approaches the Christ parable without its obvious perversion into parody—a perversion we have frequently witnessed, if nowhere more forcefully than in *Pierre*. But if I know better than to try to transform Myshkin into one of that rebellious group of visionaries of whom Pierre is our most recent and most extreme example, neither can I allow his goodness to remain unquestioned by casting all blame for his unhappy end upon a fallen and uncomprehending world that cannot tolerate the divine simplicity of innocence. I must hope it is not merely the cold unyielding eye of Plinlimmon I am using as I claim to find the novel casting some of the blame on Myshkin through the very presumption upon the rest of humanity that his humility inversely asserts.

It may of course be that Dostoevsky did not totally succeed in his attempt "to portray a truly beautiful soul" or at least it seems likely that he was not totally satisfied with the results. If he were satisfied, would he have felt the need to pursue the problem of saintliness and worldliness in the more careful and qualified way he did with Zosima and Alyosha in *The Brothers Karamazov*? Zosima's saintliness seems unquestionable, but it is dramatically inconclusive in that he had to retire from the world to achieve it. He is transfigured from a licentious worldling only through the monastery, which is the safeguard against extreme situations because it forbids human involvement. Zosima appears to recognize as much in summoning Alyosha to a more difficult saintly mission:

> . . . this is not the place for you in the future. When it is God's will to call me, leave the monastery. . . . I bless you for great service in the world. Yours will be a long pilgrimage. And you will have to take a wife, too. You will have to bear *all* before you come back." [1]

[1] From *The Brothers Karamazov*, translated by Constance Garnett (New York: The Macmillan Company, 1912), p. 76.

It seems, then, that Dostoevsky may have felt some sense of failure with Myshkin, leading him to try again with Alyosha to explore the possibilities of sainthood operating with the necessary limitations of its human agent within a fallen world. And Dostoevsky was too much of a Christian not to insist that the fallen world would somehow have to be reflected in its saintly but human intruder, and that the intruder would have the humility to accept and assert this fact. So Zosima sends forth Alyosha to a danger and a suffering perhaps beyond what he could trust himself to undergo. The story as regards Alyosha was left unfinished by Dostoevsky and, although the children are cheering him at the close of the novel, many doubts are left about how he would have made out in the unwritten sequel—with the Aglaya-like, sick figure of Lise lingering in the background casting many of them. Given his Karamazov name and Dostoevsky's honesty—as well as my own theory about the tragic—I remain at least as skeptical as Eliseo Vivas is in his essay[2] whose persuasiveness allowed me to turn back to *The Idiot* with confidence. I am skeptical finally because all I have really to go on is the earlier failure of Myshkin, a failure Dostoevsky took seriously enough to try again in *The Brothers Karamazov,* even if he could not bring Alyosha far enough for us to judge whether he can do better, indeed whether man can do better. So it still must be Myshkin's career we examine to find Dostoevsky's detailed study of the consequences of man as Jesus.

There is Zosima as well as Alyosha in Myshkin. His retirement in the Swiss sanitarium both before and after the action of the novel is clearly his withdrawal from human involvement, his monastery where his modest sanctity goes its way in peace. He is, like the saint, unfit for society, which will not understand him, labels him "idiot," and keeps him apart in forced solitude. When he recovers enough superficial similarity to his fellows to get by, he returns to society where his essential position remains the same, his ideas "idiotic" and his language gibberish. But his involvement brings the darkest of troubles to others and himself, and he shall have to withdraw again to his sanctuary where he can safely commune with himself and make literal the symbolic distance between himself and the world.

During his worldly trials also the impulse to retreat is alive in him. When his difficulties managing with people seem insuperable, he has a "terrible longing . . . to leave everything here and to go back to the place from which he had come, to go away into the distance to some remote region, to go away at once without even saying good-bye to any one" (291).[3] Or: "Sometimes he longed to get away, to vanish from here

[2] "The Two Dimensions of Reality in *The Brothers Karamazov*," by Eliseo Vivas, in *Creation and Discovery* (New York: Noonday Press, 1955), pp. 47-70.

[3] From *The Idiot*, translated by Constance Garnett (New York: Random House, Inc., 1935). Copyright by The Macmillan Company. All page references are to the Random House edition.

altogether. He would have been positively glad to be in some gloomy, deserted place, only that he might be alone with his thoughts and no one might know where he was" (329). But at this stage of his career he must not take the way of Zosima. We are told, after the first of these passages, that he did not consider his "terrible longing" "for ten minutes; he decided at once that it would be 'impossible' to run away, that it would be almost cowardice, that he was faced with such difficulties that it was his duty now to solve them, or at least to do his utmost to solve them" (291). And after the second of these passages he turns back to the world to look into those taunting wild eyes of Aglaya. True to his Christ-like decision to mix with the affairs of the world, he must confess to Ippolit that he has "always been a materialist" (368) in a statement that Ippolit wisely considers significant. A very special sort of materialist, it goes without saying.

There is much else about Myshkin that is divided. Whatever duality we find in him is evidence of his humanity, his imperfection, his similarity to the lesser people about him. For example, Keller, with Lebedyev the basest and most obviously "underground" creature in this story that is filled with them, has been confessing to Myshkin the confusion in him of the noble and the base, the undercutting of every noble intention by an insidiously base countermotive: he ashamedly admits that he had decided to make a full confession of sins to Myshkin and then, even while still feeling this need profoundly, had thought of turning it to profit by asking Myshkin for money. Indeed, he is even using this novel form of double confession as a new way of extorting money from Myshkin. And surely Myshkin knows this, although he cheerfully allows Keller to succeed. Myshkin tries to account to Keller for the following of the noble by the base, the impulse to confess by the impulse to extort:

> "But most likely that's not true; it's simply both things came at once. The two thoughts came together; that often happens. It's constantly so with me. I think it's not a good thing, though; and, do you know, Keller, I reproach myself most of all for it. You might have been telling me about myself just now. I have sometimes even fancied," Myshkin went on very earnestly, genuinely and profoundly interested, "that all people are like that; so that I was even beginning to excuse myself because it is awfully difficult to struggle against these *double* thoughts; I've tried. God knows how they arise and come into one's mind." (293)

In part, of course, this is God's humble man seeing in himself the weaknesses of others in order not to be the self-righteous judge. But Myshkin is indeed concerned about his own "double thoughts." Only a few pages earlier we were told, "of late he had blamed himself for two extremes, for his excessive 'senseless and impertinent' readiness to trust people and at the same time for his gloomy suspiciousness" (285).[4]

[4] One could point out, as evidence of Myshkin's less than angelic inconsistency, his bitter attack on Roman Catholicism (518) in that wild engagement party that cul-

There is also Myshkin's conviction of the momentary ecstasy allowed by his epilepsy in the moment of pure light that preceded his fits. In phrases that sound like Mann in his more dangerously *"spirituel"* moments, Myshkin debates the ambiguities of disease and health with himself:

> . . . he often said to himself that all these gleams and flashes of the highest sensation of life and self-consciousness, and therefore also of the highest form of existence, were nothing but disease, the interruption of the normal condition; and if so, it was not at all the highest form of being, but on the contrary must be reckoned the lowest. And yet he came at last to an extremely paradoxical conclusion. "What if it is disease?" he decided at last. "What does it matter that it is an abnormal intensity, if the result, if the minute of sensation, remembered and analysed afterwards in health, turns out to be the acme of harmony and beauty, and gives a feeling, unknown and undivined till then, of completeness, of proportion, of reconciliation, and of ecstatic devotional merging in the highest synthesis of life?" (214)

We may be reminded of his earlier performance before the Yepanchin women, his existential psychoanalysis of the executed criminal, which concluded with his speculation about the hearing of the clang of iron at the last moment or about that brief (and yet unending) all-significant moment in which the head may know it has been cut off. Alexandra's reaction to Myshkin's recital can serve for the later dialogue with himself as well, and perhaps for Myshkin's more than simple temperament generally: "That's nothing like quietism, certainly" (61).

I have claimed that it was Myshkin's ability to return to enough of a superficial similarity to his fellows that enabled him to return to society, but that his continuing difference from them got him and them into trouble. The examination of his divided temperament has revealed that much of him was capable of being truly similar to those around him, all too similar. Thus his difficulties may be traced primarily to his incom-

---

minates in the breaking of the vase and his second fit. His fervent partisanship, his avid hatreds, might be looked upon as humanizing elements that bring him away from the world of love and closer to the world of principle and to Pierre. However, anxious as I am to make my case, this evidence seems unconvincing. For one thing, Myshkin, hopelessly out of place on this hopeless and even absurd occasion that is designed to domesticate him, is just talking and cannot stop—with an urgency and a compulsive panic that lead to the epileptic fit which may already have sent out its forerunners. For another, when Dostoevsky gets off on the problems of Roman Catholicism and of Russian-ness, he seems to lose all aesthetic presence and ventriloquizes freely. I cannot, then, take this passage seriously, as being more than an errant insertion in this book that is so full of them. Always uninhibited by formal considerations, Dostoevsky never lets himself go more recklessly than in *The Idiot*. Thus Myshkin's momentary invective is just one of many inconsistencies and excursions in this difficult, often confusing and imperfect novel.

pleteness in any direction, to his being only half-saint (or half-"idiot") and half-man, half out of the world but half committed to it. It is this doubleness that misleads Aglaya and results in both their falls. With this in mind we can trace the development of their relationship. We may note at the outset that Myshkin himself undergoes a significant development, a fact that argues for his all-too-human imperfections and complexities. Myshkin moves from saintly to human attitudes; and then, after Aglaya has been partly persuaded to trust his human emotions, he reverts to the saintliness that must desert her for a wider obligation of love.

Myshkin's initial championing of Nastasya is clearly presented to us in the framework of Quixotism. Aglaya puts his first note to her in a book which turns out to be *Don Quixote,* and in the poem she recites about the "poor knight"—the title she both admiringly and scornfully applies to Myshkin—she inserts Nastasya's initials as those the knight, inspired by "an all-consuming fire" (238), inscribes in blood upon his shield to defend in battle. The perceptive Yevgeny, in that all-important dialogue with Myshkin at the end, corroborates the notion that Myshkin's chivalry in behalf of Nastasya was caused by "the first glow of eagerness to be of service" (553), which accompanied Myshkin's return to Russian society. Myshkin, "a virginal knight" "bewitched" by Nastasya's "demoniacal beauty," was "intoxicated with enthusiasm" (553), the word that returns us to the universe of *Pierre*. Yevgeny's claims remind us of Aglaya's definition of the poor knight as "a man who is capable of an ideal, and what's more, a man who having once set an ideal before him has faith in it, and having faith in it gives up his life blindly to it" (235). She leaves no doubt that she means the ideal to be a lady, the lady whose initials he carries. And she terms the poor knight the serious equivalent to Quixote.

Myshkin's feelings for Nastasya partly confirm the diagnosis. He urges Rogozhin not to consider him as a rival for Nastasya even though Myshkin repeatedly takes her away from him. Denying that he and Nastasya ever lived together, Myshkin says, "I explained to you before that I don't love her with love, but with pity. I believe I define it exactly" (196-197). But the kind of love Myshkin is capable of is to change. On the eve of his birthday, despite Rogozhin's account of Nastasya's most recent aberrations, Myshkin is able to claim cheerfully, "my new life has begun to-day" (348). Rogozhin himself acknowledges this fact by noting the remarkable change in Myshkin. The cheerful change is that he is able to believe in his personal and domestic future as this is related to his personal and normally human love for Aglaya. So he can tell Aglaya of his feelings for Nastasya, ". . . I only pitied her, but . . . I . . . don't love her any more" (413). We cannot help noting that in his "new life" love and pity have become separate entities: he has dropped the saint's *Agape* to pick up the humanizing *Eros*. He can go on to tell Aglaya, "I can't love her now . . . I can't sacrifice myself like that, though I did want to at one time" (415).

It seems, then, that Myshkin is becoming Aglaya's knight rather than Nastasya's, the medieval knight-errant of the lady fair with amorous obligations rather than Spenser's allegorical, dehumanized knight in the arduous service of holiness. After all, we have only Aglaya's word for it that Myshkin was carrying Nastasya's initials. We may remember that in the poem, before hurling himself into battle, the knight shouted, *"Lumen coeli"* (238). And we are told several times that it is Aglaya who represents the light-principle to Myshkin. Nastasya's ambiguous letters to Aglaya are full of Myshkin's assertions that Aglaya is a "ray of light" (432) to him; and Myshkin himself has told her, after denying his ability any longer to sacrifice himself for Nastasya, "In my darkness then I dreamed. . . . I had an illusion perhaps of a new dawn" (415). No wonder the vaguest prospect of a possible future with Aglaya prompted Myshkin to dream of beginning a "new life." So perhaps it is to be Aglaya's light rather than Nastasya's darkness that our poor knight must serve—which would mean that he would also be serving himself. For he would be lightening his own darkness instead of trying, however fleetingly, to bring the irrevocably lost Nastasya "to seeing light round her once more" (413).

Despite his continuing feelings of obligation to the spiritual burdens of Nastasya which he has helped to amass, Myshkin appears to have persuaded Aglaya that he has made a moderate return to humanity. Not a complete return to normality, since it is the "poor knight" in him that the fiercely romantic Aglaya loves. A childlike enthusiast herself, she must have something of quixotic dedication in Myshkin, but must have it sufficiently stripped of its most obvious idiocies to be undeserving of her bitterest contempt. And of course she must have it hers and not another's, despite any claim to misfortune that deserves a champion. But Myshkin has promised more than he can deliver at the due date. His partial saintliness that recalls him to duality will not allow him to sustain his "new life," and it leads him, as Yevgeny makes abundantly clear, to be false to obligations to Aglaya as sacred and at least as seriously undertaken as those earlier ones to a *caritas* that embraced Nastasya. When the mad Rogozhin, knowing Myshkin's weakness only too well, speaks of Nastasya's companion madness and of their doomed future together, he challenges Myshkin to say whether he can still be happy. " 'No, no, no!' cried Myshkin with unspeakable sadness" (436). Perhaps he already knows that he cannot keep his back turned and that his hopes for a new life were founded on self-deception. And when, as we know he must, he chooses Nastasya over Aglaya in that harrowing scene of mutual lacerations, we know he has returned to self-sacrificing enthusiasm. By the time of his final conversation with Yevgeny—during which the latter tells him that Aglaya loved him "like a woman, like a human being, not like an abstract spirit" (556)—he is able to assert once again that despite his fears he loves Nastasya "with all my heart" (556). When we are told that "in his love for her there was an element of the tenderness for some sick,

unhappy child who could not be left to shift for itself" (562), we know
that love and pity have become identified for him again and finally.
We may wonder whether there may not be considerable truth in Yevgeny's accusation: ". . . didn't you deceive that adorable girl [Aglaya]
when you told her that you loved her?" (554). As for Aglaya herself,
Myshkin has destroyed her, has converted her childlike idealism into
fraudulent and decadent romanticism, and has brought her incipient
demonism into the open. When we learn that she marries a swindling
Polish count and ends by converting to Catholicism, we should know
Dostoevsky's prejudices well enough to be provided with incontestable
evidence of the unhappy disposition he has made of her.

It is difficult to witness her fall and, seeing its relation to Myshkin's
rejection of her, not to ask with Yevgeny, "And where was your heart
then, your 'Christian' heart? Why, you saw her face at that moment:
well, was she suffering less than *the other,* that other woman who has
come between you? How could you have seen it and allowed it? How
could you?" (554). But of course Myshkin is responsible for more than
this. It seems that it was he who continually drove Nastasya into Rogozhin's murderous hands and who at the same time whipped Rogozhin into
the frenzy needed to turn homicidal. And Myshkin is painfully aware of
it. His analysis of Nastasya's madness, for example, is brilliant in its prob-
ing accuracy. He understands why again and again she has deserted
Rogozhin after promising to marry him, in order to run off with Myshkin,
only to be even more terrified of her feelings of guilt with the little saint
whom she must in turn desert to seek her fated death once more at the
hands of Rogozhin. Her final turn—and she knows it is to be the last one
—is to Rogozhin. After the murder Rogozhin tells Myshkin, "it was you
she was afraid of" (579). She feared death with Rogozhin less than life
under Myshkin's all-discerning, all-forgiving eye. Myshkin's earlier analysis prepares us for all this:

"That unhappy woman is firmly convinced that she is the most fallen, the
most vicious creature in the whole world. Oh, don't cry shame on her, don't
throw stones at her! She has tortured herself too much from the consciousness of her undeserved shame! And, my God, she's not to blame! Oh, she's
crying out every minute in her frenzy that she doesn't admit going wrong,
that she was the victim of others, the victim of a depraved and wicked man.
But whatever she may say to you, believe me, she's the first to disbelieve it,
and to believe with her whole conscience that she is . . . to blame. When
I tried to dispel that gloomy delusion, it threw her into such misery that
my heart will always ache when I remember that awful time. It's as though
my heart had been stabbed once for all. She ran away from me. Do you
know what for? Simply to show me that she was a degraded creature. But
the most awful thing is that perhaps she didn't even know herself that she
only wanted to prove that to me, but ran away because she had an irresistible inner craving to do something shameful, so as to say to herself at once,

'There, you've done something shameful again, so you're a degraded creature!' Oh, perhaps you won't understand this, Aglaya. Do you know that
in that continual consciousness of shame there is perhaps a sort of awful,
unnatural enjoyment for her, a sort of revenge on some one. Sometimes
I did bring her to seeing light round her once more, as it were. But she
would grow restive again at once, and even came to accusing me bitterly of
setting myself up above her (though I had no thought of such a thing) and
told me in so many words at last, when I offered her marriage, that she
didn't want condescending sympathy or help from anyone, nor to be ele-
vated to anyone's level." (412-413)

Yet Myshkin must persist, with what consequences we know, going
on to condemn himself for the suspiciousness revealed by his acute per-
ceptions. This leads him to insist with inner shame on his own unworthiness. Almost immediately before Rogozhin's assault upon him,
Myshkin has been upbraiding himself for harboring dark thoughts about
Rogozhin: "Ah, how unpardonably and dishonorably he had wronged
Rogozhin! No, it was not that 'the Russian soul was a dark place,' but
that in his own soul there was darkness, since he could imagine such
horrors!" (218) Immediately before the young nihilistic invaders slander
him mercilessly before his friends, Myshkin senses their ruthless intention but turns angrily upon himself:

> . . . he felt too sad at the thought of his "monstrous and wicked suspicious-
> ness." He felt that he would have died if anyone had known he had such
> an idea in his head, and at the moment when his guests walked in, he was
> genuinely ready to believe that he was lower in a moral sense than the low-
> est around him. (244)

But of course his least generous thoughts about others are always his
most accurate ones. *forgiveness harder than anger to accept .*
Myshkin is of course always ready to blame himself for the sins of
others, a proper saintly attitude. But it seems to drive his more sinful
fellows to ever more desperate crime. When Yevgeny concedes that he is
willing to forgive Ippolit his behavior, Myshkin, unsatisfied, suggests this
is not enough: "You ought to be ready to receive his forgiveness too"
(324). He is answered rather skeptically by Prince S. (and wouldn't it be
more appropriate if these lines were spoken by the shrewd Yevgeny
himself?) that reaching paradise on earth poses more difficulties than
Myshkin will face. His translation of this Zosima-like notion into action
infuriates far more seriously those who have offended him. He very
nearly treats Rogozhin as the wronged party when he meets him for the
first time after the attempted knifing: "We were feeling just the same.
If you had not made that attack (which God averted), what should I
have been then? I did suspect you of it, our sin was the same, in fact"
(346-347). Rogozhin's scornful laugh promises that he feels dared to do

still worse. Myshkin's youthful tormentors are also frustrated by the impossibility of offending him, so that he drives them to exceed their viciousness moment by moment while he takes the blame for it. The ill and sensitive Ippolit softens momentarily and seems ready for conversion. Instead, there is reversion, and Myshkin, all-seeing once more, admits he has been expecting it, although he has done nothing to head it off.

> Suddenly Ippolit got up, horribly pale and with an expression of terrible, almost despairing, shame on his distorted face. ". . . if I hate anyone here . . . it's you, Jesuitical, treacly soul, idiot, philanthropic millionaire; I hate you more than every one and everything in the world! I understood and hated you long ago, when first I heard of you; I hated you with all the hatred of my soul. . . . This has all been your contriving. You led me on to breaking down! You drove a dying man to shame! You, you, you are to blame for my abject cowardice! I would kill you if I were going to remain alive! I don't want your benevolence. . . ." (282-283)

We have seen, then, how through his Christian humility with Nastasya, Rogozhin, and Ippolit, Myshkin has refused to give his beloved humanity the human privilege of sinning, of being offensive and arousing moral indignation. Myshkin has the keenness to understand what he is driving them to do, and yet he cannot do otherwise himself. Instead of easing and consoling them in their raging "underground" ambivalences, he is making their way infinitely more difficult. His irrational Christlike transcendence of mere ethical judgment turns deadly. He knows it and persists, becoming dangerously offensive himself. By assuming himself worse than others, he gives them a greater moral burden than in their human weakness they can carry. They break under it and become worse than without Myshkin they would be—partly in order to spite him. But there is no stopping Myshkin, laboring as he is under the psychosis of humility, perhaps in its own way not much less blameworthy than Pierre's psychosis of pride.

This sprawling novel is made up of several long, climactic, and calamitous scenes, well spaced and interspersed with digressions and minor movements. The calamities increase until the final catastrophe, and, as we have seen, much of the responsibility for all of them must be borne by Myshkin. What is so destructive in him is the sense others must get from his infinite meekness that they are being judged. Of course, Myshkin knows the sin of pride that is involved in judging and so carefully refrains, condemning himself instead. But this very inversion of the process constitutes a form of judgment too for the guilty, in many ways a more painful one than conventional judgment. Thus Aglaya can tell him, "I think it's very horrid on your part, for it's very brutal to look on and judge a man's soul, as you judge Ippolit. You have no tenderness, nothing but truth, and so you judge unjustly" (406). Myshkin charges her

*(margin note: judgment unjust — "no tenderness, nothing but truth")*

with being unfair to him, and perhaps she is. But there is some justice in her claim that Myshkin's unerring depth of moral perception makes it impossible for him to miss the slightest failing in others, however quick he may be to condemn his own suspiciousness and to ask forgiveness. The relentlessness of his moral candor makes any subsequent involutions all the more painful to bear.

Aglaya's judgment of his judgment seems more profoundly to the point than that of unworthies like Keller and Lebedyev. For these, Myshkin's refusal to play the judge, as in the case of Keller's "double thoughts" in the passage I have examined, seems most effective; for with their lackey baseness they find it useful, indeed profitable. Keller responds to Myshkin's confession of his own similar guilt rapturously: "Even the preacher, Bourdaloue, would not have spared a man; but you've spared one, and judged me humanely! To punish myself and to show that I am touched, I won't take a hundred and fifty roubles; give me only twenty-five, and it will be enough!" (294). Dostoevsky emphasizes the point by having Lebedyev walk in even before Keller has left and begin the same routine, closing with another celebration of the prince's power to "judge humanely" (294). As these creatures shriek their abjectness throughout the novel, using their self-condemnation as their major weapon, we cannot help seeing in them a parody of Myshkin's own devout humility, a parody that perhaps strikes a resounding note in the monologue of that other buffoon, Clamence, in Camus' *The Fall.*

It is Myshkin's rational inversion in matters of moral judgment that Yevgeny appears to be referring to in speaking of his "lack of all feeling for proportion" (553), his power of "exaggeration that passes belief" (554) in their late dialogue to which I have referred several times. He must wonder "whether there was natural feeling or only intellectual enthusiasm" (554) in Myshkin's extraordinary actions in behalf of Nastasya. He indicates the nature of Myshkin's enthusiasm by adding: ". . . in the temple the woman was forgiven—just such a woman, but she wasn't told that she'd done well, that she was deserving of all respect and honor, was she?" (554). Compassion is admirable, but senseless inversion that inflicts pain on the more blameless is another matter. Contemplating the wreck of Aglaya, Yevgeny asks, "What will compassion lead you to next?" (554). Here as elsewhere in this conversation Myshkin miserably cries out that he is to blame. Yevgeny answers pointedly and "indignantly": "But is that enough? . . . Is it sufficient to cry out: 'Ach, I'm to blame!' You are to blame, but yet you persist!" (554). Precisely—he persists to the end. As we watch Myshkin preparing for his marriage with Nastasya, we are advised: "As for protests, conversations like the one with Yevgeny Pavlovich, he was utterly unable to answer them, and felt himself absolutely incompetent, and so avoided all talk of the kind" (563).

The conversation with Yevgeny has furnished us with crucial commentary throughout. It is significant that Dostoevsky seeks to make certain that we take Yevgeny seriously, in part at least as his spokesman. For the book, like all of Dostoevsky's, is filled with the pompous prattle of fools, especially fools who try to be rational. But there seems to be no irony in the credentials our author gives Yevgeny, who in the key conversation speaks "clearly and reasonably" and "with great psychological insight" (552). The narrator admits strongly: "Altogether, we are in complete sympathy with some forcible and psychologically deep words of Yevgeny Pavlovich's, spoken plainly and unceremoniously . . ." (550). Of course it is possible that our author is posing as a worldly, sensible narrator who cannot help but sympathize with Yevgeny—although Dostoevsky is hardly the sort of novelist who plays tricks with "point of view." It is true that some of Yevgeny's analysis reveals the limitations of the somewhat cold-blooded realist and skeptic that he is. He was the fellow introduced, ironically, into the midst of the recital and discussion of the "poor knight" and described there as having "a fine and intelligent face and a humorous and mocking look in his big shining black eyes" (237). Unlike Myshkin, he is often ironic and uncharitable, especially with Ippolit, but like Myshkin he is usually right. Although Dostoevsky is frequently cruel to his more rational characters—and Yevgeny betrays no "underground," no great internal life—he treats Yevgeny well at the close, even if Yevgeny knows "he is a superfluous man in Russia" (584). He becomes an influence on Kolya, takes charge of Myshkin's future, and is deeply moved by Myshkin's unlikely prospects. The author acknowledges that "he has a heart" and even gives him one of his most lovable and delicate creations, Vera Lebedyev. I think Yevgeny has won enough of Dostoevsky's approval for us to conclude that he is there to help us judge Myshkin rather than to be judged through Myshkin.

Yevgeny, neither a creature of the "underground" nor a proponent of a political or philosophical program, holds a unique position among the important figures in the novel. One of the major forces in it is what we might call a kind of Benthamite liberalism or, more simply, the "modern idea." Most forcefully—and brutally—represented by the group of young people surrounding "the son of Pavlishchev," it receives in several places Dostoevsky's usual and powerful attack that reduces it to the cannibalism that eliminates all moral questions. But the primary inadequacy we witness in this mechanical reduction of the human is that it fails to account for the very complexity of motive among those who hold it. Thus among several of Myshkin's assailants, notably Ippolit, we see the intrusion of the unpredictable "underground" elements that demoniacally counteract the push-button principle of self-interest. So the demoniacal is a second major force, most purely represented by Nastasya and Rogozhin. But as there are "underground" elements within the "liberal," so there are angelic elements within the demonic. In the portrait of Nastasya, after all, Myshkin saw "something confiding, something wonderfully simple-hearted" associated with the "look of un-bounded pride and contempt, almost hatred" (74). The duality we see in Myshkin, that Myshkin sees in himself, he does indeed share with those around him, even down to Keller and Lebedyev. And, of course, the third major force would appear to be the purely angelic, with Mysh-kin its representative—except that we have had reason enough to worry about whether he really does not fall back into the second group. The final alternative is that of the withdrawn and unattached, the always uncommitted because skeptical, Yevgeny. It is from this position, the only one with which the narrator expresses any identification, that the third is made most persuasively to appear illusory, a self-deceived version of the second. One prefers not to be left with Yevgeny and suspects that Dostoevsky would have preferred someone more throbbing. But the alternatives come at a high price, and Yevgeny's presence as well as Myshkin's failure proves it.

Like so many others, *The Idiot* is a novel of the desperate struggle for personal human dignity in a world that finds endless ways of de-priving man of it. In the major action, in the minor actions like Ippolit's "Explanation" and mock suicide or like General Ivolgin's pitiable end at the hands of the pitiless Lebedyev, in the countless minor tales that are related to us along the way, always it is the beseeching human cry that asks that one may really matter and may be cherished for mattering. The youthful, deluded "liberals" demand dignity with such ferocity and spite that we are assured of the savage sickness that speaks through them and their program. Our openly demoniacal creatures have a purity and an integrity of demand so intense that, given the alloyed nature of what we can be given at best in life, they can be satisfied only when their life itself has been refined away to the nothingness they have sought. Mysh-kin seeks only to give dignity to each, even—or rather especially—at the cost of his own. But the bizarre enthusiasm of his relentless efforts ap-pears as an inversion that, perhaps more surely than any alternative, would deny dignity to others through its very magnanimity. Thus he too must be rejected. And Yevgeny, the retiring critical intelligence that knows the futility of the problem too well to bother confronting it, helps us reject Myshkin's kind of offer as the others do. Myshkin retires to his wretched safety, and we are sorry to see him go—as is Yevgeny who really "has a heart." For we are left with no further alternative possibilities—where can one go beyond Myshkin?—since Yevgeny's way is also the way of retirement.

Or is there not another possibility, however imperfect, after all? The last words in the novel are spoken to Yevgeny and not by him. They are spoken by one of Dostoevsky's most magnificent creations, Lizaveta Yepanchin, the general's wife and Aglaya's mother. Totally Russian and totally winning, if perhaps not totally sane, she is complaining about the unreality of Europe: ". . . all this life abroad, and this Europe of yours is all a fantasy, and all of us abroad are only a fantasy" (586). She is always a vigorous force for life, however messily she runs it. Even the ruin of Aglaya cannot long deter her. She must return to pick up her reality at home and must speak to the expatriate Yevgeny "almost wrathfully" and in warning against withdrawal. For Myshkin has not spoken the last word, although he has spoken the most extreme word. Whatever word is spoken beyond this is not spoken out of the tragic vision.

# Dostoevsky: The Politics

# of Salvation

## *by Irving Howe*

## I

In nineteenth-century Russia the usual categories of discourse tend to break down. Politics, religion, literature, philosophy—these do not fall into neat departments of the mind. Pressed together by the Tsarist censorship, ideas acquire an extraordinary concentration; the novel, which in the West is generally regarded as a means of portraying human behavior, acquires the tone and manner of prophetic passion. Not till the rise of the Symbolists at the end of the century does the cult of estheticism, with its tacit belief in a fragmenting of experience, prosper in Russia; for the most part Russian thought is seized by that "mania for totality" which is to become characteristic of our time. Where ideas cannot be modulated through practice, they keep their original purity; where intellectuals cannot test themselves in experience, they must remain intransigent or surrender completely. For the subtler kinds of opportunism, such a society offers little provision. The seriousness we all admire in Russian literature is thus partly the result of a social impasse: energies elsewhere absorbed by one or another field of thought are here poured into the novel. "Literature in Russia," writes the critic Chernyshevsky, "constitutes almost the sum total of our intellectual life." And that is why, in dealing with the Russian novel, one is obliged to take religion as a branch of politics and politics as a form of religion. The school of criticism which treats the novel mainly in terms of social manners will consequently face grave difficulties when confronted with a writer like Dostoevsky, for whom the act of creation invariably means an act of prophecy.

During Dostoevsky's lifetime the intelligentsia multiplies at an astonishing rate. A belated seepage from Western thought, the frail beginnings

"Dostoevsky: The Politics of Salvation." From *Politics and the Novel,* by Irving Howe (New York: The Horizon Press, Inc., 1957). © 1957 by Irving Howe. Reprinted by permission of the author and The Horizon Press, Inc.

of capitalist production in the cities, the decay of both serfdom and communal peasant holdings in the countryside—these are but a few of the reasons. It is an intelligentsia of a kind found only in "backward" countries: ablaze with activity yet brutally confined in its power to communicate, brimming with the boldest ideas yet without a tradition of freedom, aspiring to independence yet reduced to an appendage of the city poor.

The problem which more than any other obsesses the Russian intellectuals is their relationship to the people, the dark unsounded mass of peasants on top of whom has formed a skim of proletarians only yesterday peasants. One may read nineteenth-century Russian history as a series of attempts by the intellectuals, frequently desperate and always pathetic, to make contact with the people. That fashionable disdain for the masses which in the latter part of the century arises among Western literary men is virtually unknown in Russia, for there the intellectuals, deprived of even a marginal independence, sense that their fate is bound up with the fate of the people. Political discussions repeatedly focus on the question: How can we awaken the peasants? And so long as this question remains unanswered, there will always be some who despair of answering it and decide to do the job themselves—to force history by sacrifice and terror.

Dostoevsky once wrote that Russian literature was "a literature of landowners." Despite its touch of malice, his remark is extremely acute. A great many Russian writers, from Griboyedov to Turgenev, are disaffected noblemen. Both Tolstoy and Turgenev owe a large debt to Aksakov, an author whose pastoral chronicles flow with the evenness and fullness of the Russian seasons. Some of the loveliest passages in Tolstoy and Turgenev are nostalgic in tone, romantic turnings to eighteenth-century manorial life which seems to them, at least from a distance, relatively stable and free from modern troubles. Dostoevsky shares their tendency to romanticize the peasant, but like Gogol before him and Leskov beside him, he represents a decisive break from the literature of landowners; he is a creature of the city, his writing beats with the rhythms of urban life, his greatest achievement is to penetrate the problematic moods and ideas of homeless intellectuals.

Only superficially does it seem odd that the rise of an urban intelligentsia should coincide with the flourishing of Slavophile ideas. Though themselves men of the city, the Slavophiles placed their faith in the Russian peasants; they believed that Russia could and should avoid the path of the West; and from their vantage-point in the social rear they were able to see the terrifying consequences of the atomistic individualism that had sprung up in the West—though in their disdain of the liberal ideal they were far less perceptive. Their faith in the peasants is a sign of their distance from the peasants, their belief in a special Russian destiny a sign of their helplessness before the problems of Russia.

Popular opinion often assumes that the Slavophiles were a gang of reactionaries brewing fantastic theories about the Russian soul, but while such Slavophiles no doubt existed, it would be a mistake to suppose the movement to have been consistent and homogeneous. One can find traces of its influence in the thought of almost every Russian writer and thinker of the time, including such "Westernizers" as Herzen and Turgenev, who wished to copy from the West but were repelled when they looked too closely at their models. *Narodnikism* (from *Narod, folk* or *peasant*), a populist movement aiming for a non-industrial socialism based on the *mir* (peasant commune), bears the Slavophile stamp. And so does Bolshevism—for while desiring an industrialized Russia, the Bolsheviks did not suppose that it had to retrace each step of Western history. Slavophilism may therefore be divided into at least three main tendencies: the pan-Slavists who provide a rationale for Tsarist imperialism; a middle group which fluctuates between its desire to retain Russian distinctiveness and its desire to reform Russian society within the framework of a constitutional monarchy; and the radicals who aspire toward a peasant democracy. Now the key—at least one key—to Dostoevsky is that he managed, with varying degrees of emphasis and clarity, to hold all three perspectives at once.          *D. and Slavophiles*

The dominant formal theme in his work is a conception of Russian destiny. Everything characteristically Russian, he wrote, "everything that is ours, preëminently national (and therefore, everything genuinely artistic)—is unintelligible to Europe." For Dostoevsky Russia was inseparable from the Orthodox Church, the unsullied vessel of Christianity in which alone was preserved "the Divine image of Christ." But Russia was also a world power with imperial ambitions, and Dostoevsky shouted: "Sooner or later Constantinople will be ours."

A disturbing though not unusual paradox: the writer whose most sacred image is that of Christ turning the other cheek demands the conquest of Constantinople, the almost craven apostle of humility exalts the use of brute power. Part of the truth about Dostoevsky is that this extraordinarily sensitive man who trembles for the slightest creature can also be a coarse and brutal reactionary.

For there *was* something coarse and brutal in Dostoevsky. He knew it perfectly well, hence his desperate straining for love and humility. The love-seeker or God-seeker is particularly vulnerable to self-torment if he inwardly believes that he seldom experiences true love and that instead of embracing God he merely celebrates his own ego. This is a central ambivalence of neurotic character—one is almost tempted to say of modern character; and it is nowhere more spectacularly illustrated than in Dostoevsky, whose spiritual imago is Alyosha Karamazov, but whose life is tainted by the lust of Dmitri, the skepticism of Ivan, the emotional torpor of Stavrogin.

At least in part, Dostoevsky's politics is a function of his psychology, that is, of his struggle to heal his moral fissure and of his horrified recoil from the sickness he finds in all men. Dostoevsky dreaded the autonomous intellect, the faithless drifting he had himself experienced and was later to portray in Ivan Karamazov; he feared that the intellectual, loosed from the controls of Christianity and alienated from the heart-warmth of the Russian people, would feel free to commit the most monstrous acts to quench his vanity. <u>Once man is free from responsibility to God, what limit can there be to his presumption?</u>—an argument that might be more convincing if there were evidence that believers as a group have been less arrogant than skeptics. Together, it should be noticed, with the messianic strain in his religion, there is an element of coarse "pragmatism": God as celestial overseer.

Though a tendentious moralist, Dostoevsky was an entirely honest novelist, and in his novels he could not but show that while the will to faith is strong in some modern intellectuals, it seldom leads them to the peace of faith. His God-seekers, like Shatov in *The Possessed,* are men peculiarly driven by anguish: the more serious their desire for God, the more must they acknowledge the distance separating them from Him— and the more they are tempted, in the manner of the radical Slavophiles, to assimilate God to the people. Since the quest of such characters is partly motivated by an intense dislike for commercial civilization, they often find themselves in unexpected conflict with society. Their ideas, it is true, have little in common with socialist doctrine, but their values lead them to an uneasy kinship with socialism as a critical activity.

Yet they cannot accept socialism. Dostoevsky despised it as "scientific," a bastard of the Enlightenment and the twin of rationalist atheism; he rejected it, also, because he feared that man might barter freedom for bread. No political system which located salvation in the secular world could have been acceptable to him, and in a sense R. P. Blackmur is right when he says that Dostoevsky's politics were those of a man "whose way of dealing with life rested on a fundamental belief that a true rebirth, a great conversion, can come only after a great sin." It is even profitable to think of Dostoevsky's novels as rituals of rebirth, with a series of plebeian heroes (in *The Possessed,* it is Shatov) reenacting the drama of the Resurrection. But Blackmur's observation is not complete, a counter-term is needed.

Dostoevsky's politics were indeed, as Blackmur says, "nonsocial" and hence apocalyptic, but they were also colored by an intense fascination for the social politics of his time. Though he despised the ideas of the revolutionary intellectuals, he had been soaked in the atmospheres that nourished them, and as a result, his intellectual divergence signified less than his temperamental affinities. He "translated" the political radicalism of the 1840's, the radicalism of fraternity and utopia, into Christian terms—highly unorthodox and closer in spirit to primitive Christianity

than to any church of his or our day. At times he verged on the heresy—
I am not enough of a theologian to identify it—that every man is or
can be Christ. This heresy, which may involve a rejection of the Last
Judgment except insofar as it occurs every day, is in radical opposition
to Catholicism, since it denies the Church, and in milder opposition to
Protestantism, since it depreciates the Word; it is closer to Rousseau than
to Paul. In his brilliant study of *The Possessed,* Philip Rahv is entirely
right in saying that Dostoevsky's idea of salvation comes to "little more
than an anarcho-Christian version of that 'religion of humanity' which
continued to inspire the intelligentsia throughout the nineteenth century and by which Dostoevsky himself was inspired in his youth, when
. . . he took for his guides and mentors such heretical lovers of mankind
as Rousseau, Fourier, Saint-Simon and George Sand."

Repelled by the present, distrustful of those who claimed the future,
Dostoevsky had but one recourse—to construct an ideal society based
on an idyllic version of the Russian past. (In *A Raw Youth* the major
character Versilov has a dream of "A Golden Age," which is to be "the
earthly paradise of man . . . The Golden Age is the most unlikely of all
the dreams that have been, but for it men have given up their life and
all their strength, for the sake of it prophets have died and been slain,
without it the peoples will not live and cannot die. . . .") The idyllic
past was the communal life of the Russian peasant, whose greatness of
soul, wrote Dostoevsky, was revealed in a "craving for suffering, perpetual and unquenchable suffering." Ignorant and debased though the
peasant may be, he is superior to the intellectual in that he knows, at
least, from whom to beg forgiveness. That Dostoevsky himself was entirely
urban in habit and psychology, merely widened the gap between his experience and his ideas. Everything in his work implies an exalted vision
of the peasants yet he is one of the few Russian masters who barely
touches on their life.

Now it should be recognized that Dostoevsky's peasant was as much
an idealized figure as the proletarian of the cruder Marxists, that his
ideal Russia had about the same relation to the actual Russia as T. S.
Eliot's "idea of a Christian society" to the existing Christian states. And
his celebration of the peasant's desire for suffering, apart from its dubious accuracy, must be related to the fact that in his own life he could
not always distinguish between ecstasy and humiliation. Dostoevsky's
ideal Russia was a "projection backwards," in which the bureaucracy
of the Orthodox Church was made to enclose the utopian dreams of his
youth. For the novelist such a "projection backwards" is both advantage
and danger: it stimulates the most powerful criticism of the present but
also tempts him into confusing reality and desire.

## II

*The Possessed* is drenched in buffoonery. This itself is a major reason for the atmosphere of violent negation which hangs over the book. Dostoevsky's buffoonery means that while he takes seriously the problems raised in his novel he cannot do as much for the people who must face them; unwittingly, his book becomes a vote of no-confidence in society—both the seething Russian underworld and the stiffening overworld. Not one character is spared his ridicule, which seems more corrosive than Swift's because more local, intimate and viciously jolly. A novelist who proclaims himself the partisan of order and then mocks and lacerates everyone within his reach, is entirely subversive in effect. By the time he came to write *The Possessed,* at the age of 50, Dostoevsky's opinions had turned reactionary but his temperament remained thoroughly revolutionary.

Buffoonery is appropriate to *The Possessed* because the characters are mainly pretenders. Stepan Trofimovich is a liberal pretending to heroism, a liberal who trembles before his shadow and is so lost in rhetoric that he cannot separate what he says from what he thinks. Stavrogin is called Ivan the Tsarevitch, the false Tsar who will reign once the nihilists have triumphed. This description is provided by Pyotr Verkhovensky, himself a pretender who speaks in the name of socialism yet admits he is a fraud with no call to speak in the name of anything. The upper strata of the novel—Lembke, the brackish Governor; his wife Yulia, a prototype of the wealthy woman who dabbles in the causes of interesting young men; Karmazinov, the famous writer who toadies before the revolutionaries because he wishes to be praised by everyone—these too are pretenders. And so are Shatov and Kirilov, the most serious people in the book, for they pretend to a clarity and resoluteness they seldom enjoy, and must therefore struggle with the unrealizable images they have constructed of themselves. Every character is a mockery of his own claims, a refutation of his own ideas; all are self-alienated in conduct and feverishly erratic in thought: even the saintly Father Tikhon suffers, suggestively, from a nervous tic.

A tone of buffoonery, a cast of pretenders—and a setting of provincial meanness. Though Dostoevsky despised Turgenev and in the character of Karmazinov assaulted him with the utmost ferocity, his view of Russian manners is quite similar to that which Turgenev will express a few years later in his most Westernized novel, *Smoke.* Dostoevsky's provincial town becomes emblematic of the smugness and ignorance, the moral coarseness which Turgenev's Potugin charges against all Russia. The society of *The Possessed* is a society gone stale from lack of freedom.

seedy from lack of cultivation. Dostoevsky hammers at this theme throughout the book, scoffing, for example, at the Russian "men of science" who have "done nothing at all"—though, he wryly adds, "that's very often the case . . . with men of science among us in Russia." When Pyotr Verkhovensky, in the midst of preparing to murder Shatov, stops at a cafe and calmly devours a raw beefsteak, his grossness seems completely typical of the Russian milieu. And still more revealing is the passage in which the clerk Lyamshin, who plays the jester to Stepan Trofimovich's enlightened circle, improvises on the piano a musical duel between the *Marseillaise* and *Mein Lieber Augustin,* with the "vulgar waltz" obliterating the French hymn. Lyamshin intends this as a parody of the Franco-Prussian war but one feels that it is also a parody of all the Lyamshins, that Dostoevsky means to say: this is what happens to our provincial Russia, we start with the pretensions of the *Marseillaise* and end with the sloth of *Mein Lieber Augustin.*

Tone, character, setting—all depend on Dostoevsky's conception of the book. "I mean to utter certain thoughts," he wrote, "whether all the artistic side of it goes to the dogs or not. . . . Even if it turns into a mere pamphlet, I shall say all that I have in my heart." Fortunately the "artistic side of it" could not be suppressed and the book takes us through areas of experience never accessible to pamphleteers. Dostoevsky begins by wishing to sound a warning, he will rouse the educated public to the dangers of Western radicalism and atheism. But this wish so disturbs him, it raises such ambiguous memories and feelings that he can never decide what—other than a fiery incarnation of the Antichrist— the enemy really is. On one level of action radicalism seems a poison rushing through the veins of society, on another level a mere schoolboy prank, a rude fabrication without social basis or intellectual content. This uncertainty of response is typical of Dostoevsky, himself split between God-seeking and God-denying, pan-Slavic reaction and Western radicalism; and it is responsible, as well, for the violent changes which his central idea—the idea of salvation—undergoes in *The Possessed.* Even as he warns against radicalism and scorns liberalism, they repeatedly penetrate his thought; the problem of ideology, which other writers objectify in an imaginary action, is for him a personal torment.

Some critics have used the politics of *The Possessed* to point lessons and draw analogies; to these I shall return shortly; but here I would remark that to read Dostoevsky primarily as a religious or political prophet—and one with a formulated prophecy—is invariably to rob him of those tensions which are the bone and blood of his art. Other critics complain that his treatment of radicals is malicious, a caricature of the facts. This is quite correct, and Dostoevsky has brought such complaints upon himself by writing Alexander III that *The Possessed* was an historical study of Russian radicalism. But while correct, such criticism is of secondary interest; a caricature of the facts may reveal truth, and it is precisely as caricature—what I have called buffoonery—that the book must be read.

Revolutionists cannot help being tainted by the societies they would overthrow. The followers of Pyotr Verkhovensky are exactly what one might expect to find in the airless depths of autocratic Russia: they are petty bureaucrats turned inside out, provincial louts in need of fresh ideas and clean linen. And even at his most malicious Dostoevsky knows this; knows that the Stavrogins, Shigalovs and Verkhovenskys are an integral part of the Russia he exalts. The sores are on *his* back.

Dostoevsky's conception of the Russian radicals is clearly limited: he knows next to nothing about the populist-terrorists of the *Narodnaya Volya* or about the incipient Marxists just beginning to appear in Russia at the time he wrote his book. But in however distorted a way, he does draw upon Russian history and his personal experience for the circle of plotters in *The Possessed*.

In his youth Dostoevsky had belonged to a St. Petersburg discussion group, called after its leader the Petrashevsky Circle, which met to consider utopian schemes for the regeneration of society. Dostoevsky was more deeply involved in these conversations than is generally supposed, and when several members of the Circle formed a secret revolutionary society he joined it. Everyone knows the sequel: police arrests, humiliating sham executions, years in Siberia. Upon his return to St. Petersburg ten years later Dostoevsky, his spiritual features lacerated and transformed, was no longer a radical, though neither was he the vitriolic reactionary of his last years. From his acquaintance with the Petrashevskyists he drew first an acute sense of the distance between grand talk and social impotence: in *The Possessed* he is always teasing the radicals with this; and, secondly, an insight into the monomania which afflicts or fringes every political movement: few things in the novel are funnier or more pathetic than the rosy-cheeked girl forever ready, whether at a radical meeting or the Governor's fete, with her set speech: "Ladies and gentlemen, I've come to call attention to the sufferings of the poor students . . ."

After the Petrashevsky affair Russia became an intellectual graveyard, and not until the 1860's did active political opposition appear. Inevitably, part of this opposition, weighed down by a sense of its futility, turned to terror. The most extraordinary figure of this period is Sergey Nechaev, a déclassé intellectual of plebeian descent. Insignificant as a socialist or anarchist theoretician, Nechaev made his mark by taking for his own the ethics of the Tsarist police, together with a few flourishes from Machiavelli and Loyola; his famous *Catechism of the Revolutionist* is a classical exposition of amorality as a method of politics. It begins with the striking sentence, "The revolutionist is a doomed man," and continues with a list of tactics he must employ: terror, arson, duplicity, spying on comrades. A belated Jacobin who has neither roots nor confidence in the people and is utterly scornful of "the gentlemen playing at liberalism," Nechaev elevates despair into an ideology. But he is also a man of great courage, and his life is filled with remarkable escapes, frauds, and sacrifices, climaxed by ten years of solitary imprisonment during which he never once breaks down.

In 1869, while forming some revolutionary groups, Nechaev found that one of his disciples, Ivanov, doubted his claim to be the Russian representative of a revolutionary Secret Committee. Ivanov was right, Nechaev was shamming in order to give himself an air of authority; but it cost the doubter his life. To dispose of Ivanov and bind the other followers with a chain of guilt, Nechaev arranged for the murder of Ivanov. This is the incident which stirred Dostoevsky to compose the political part of *The Possessed.* Pyotr Verkhovensky is Nechaev's double, a double in whom monstrous courage has been deflated into farce.

And indeed, as long as Russia remained both autocratic and isolated, what could it produce but Nechaevs? Russian rebellion had always been cut from the cloth of despair. Even in the Decembrist revolt of 1825, a movement among officers and nobles to prod the Tsar into granting a constitution, there had appeared an extreme wing called the Southern Society which in some respects anticipated Nechaev. Its leader, Pestel, had developed a program calling for a military dictatorship to replace the Tsar, and had planned his organization as a strict hierarchy with three classes of members, ranging from top conspirators to obedient drones.

These incidents of Russian history became particularly important for Dostoevsky by the time he wrote *The Possessed,* for he believed they illustrated that fatal isolation from the people which drove intellectuals to the error of socialism. Yet it would be false to say that his early radicalism was replaced by reaction. He did not change his ideas as much as add onto them; the radicalism did not disappear, it became encrusted with layers of reaction. Entirely plebeian in outlook, instinctively sympathetic to the complaints of the *lumpen* intelligentsia, Dostoevsky could never become a dull conservative. He still knew what it meant to be hungry and homeless, miserable and lonely; and if he could not always distinguish between alienation from other men and alienation from God, he never forgot that in whatever form alienation is a curse. He was the political opposite of Stendhal, for where Stendhal was a liberal but not a democrat, he was a democrat but not a liberal. Behind his radical Christianity and his mystic populism there is always a sense of being one with the insulted and the injured. The whole of *The Possessed* seems evidence of this, but perhaps it will be more useful to look at an incidental passage:

Stavrogin stands with Captain Lebyadkin, his brother-in-law and the most buffoonish of Dostoevsky's buffoons. It is raining. Stavrogin offers

Lebyadkin an umbrella. In an oversweet voice Lebyadkin asks, "Am I worth it?" Stavrogin replies, "Anyone is worthy of an umbrella." And then Lebyadkin suddenly pours out: "At one stroke you define the minimum of human rights . . . ." Such a passage, deepening buffoonery into tragic statement, is the unique mark of Dostoevsky, possible only to the writer who had once said, "Man is a crook—and a crook is he who says so."

## III

Stavrogin is the source of the chaos that streams through the characters; he possesses them but is not himself possessed. In the first part of the novel, where Dostoevsky plants several clues to his meaning, Stavrogin is likened to Pechorin, the Byronic protagonist of Lermontov's *A Hero of Our Time* who has lost the capacity for identifying or acting upon his emotions. Like Pechorin, Stavrogin seeks excitement because nothing excites him, experiments in sensuality because he wishes to *become* sensual. His tragedy is that he can replace the sense of cosmic fear only with the sense of cosmic void: the awareness of human limits which Dostoevsky regards as essential to life he entirely lacks. A "subtle serpent" who is one of the Devil's party, though from metaphysical despair rather than a Faustian bargain, and a typically modern personality haunted by the "demon of irony," Stavrogin suffers from *acedia,* that torpor of the spirit which provides the greatest resistance to God because it lacks the power to resist anything. Repeatedly Dostoevsky declares the atheist only a step from the perfect believer: the atheist, unlike Stavrogin, exercises moral choice and thereby demonstrates, whether he means to or not, the freedom of his will.

Stavrogin lives below, not beyond, good and evil; naturally so, for in the absence of desire, morality can hardly matter. The Nietzschean vision of "beyond good and evil" implies a harmonious resolution of desires to the point where moral regulation becomes superfluous; Stavrogin, by contrast, is on *this* side of morality. Yet it is no mere perversity on the part of his friends that they look upon him with awe, for in his wasted energies they see the potential of a Russia equally disordered and distraught. People expect Stavrogin to lead, he himself "seeks a burden." Though he never attends the fete, it becomes an occasion for the full display of his chaos; the intellectual saturnalia that occurs there, from "the women who were the embodiment of the women question" to Lebyadkin's vulgar verses and the rumor that Karmazinov will recite in the costume of a governess, is a public release of all that Stavrogin represents. Yet he is never so far gone as Pyotr Verkhovensky, for there are a few moments when he judges himself by standards implicitly Christian. Because he still thinks of his fate in "ultimate" terms, he moves within the orbit of Christian metaphysics. But even from a secular standpoint the distance between the two men is very large: Stavrogin cannot tolerate his condition while Verkhovensky relishes his; Verkhovensky is a *reductio ad absurdum* of rootless individualism, while Stavrogin would immediately understand Bakunin's typically Russian cry, "I do not want to be I, I want to be We."

In a sense he is We: all but one of the major characters are his doubles. Pyotr is his social double, Liza the Byroness his emotional double, and Marya, the cripple he has married, his double in derangement. Fedka the peasant murderer is a double through the link of the intellectual Kirilov, while Lebyadkin and Liputin are doubles in the dress of burlesque. The most important doubles are Kirilov and Shatov, who act out the two sides of Stavrogin's metaphysical problem. There is a significant political reason, though Dostoevsky would not accept it as a basic one, for the impasse in which these two find themselves. They have tried radicalism and recoiled, Shatov into hostility and Kirilov into indifference. Together they have journeyed to America, symbol of the new capitalism, and have left it in hatred. Now they return to what Dostoevsky regards as philosophical bed-rock: Shatov to the problem of God, Kirilov to the problem of man. But this very turn may itself be seen as a token of political despair: when the problems of the social world seem insoluble, as they did in Dostoevsky's Russia, men feel an insidious temptation to "transcend" them.

Though at opposite poles ideologically, Shatov and Kirilov are in close emotional dependence, functioning as the split halves of an hypothetical self. Living in the same house yet tacitly avoiding each other, they represent in extreme form the issues thrown up by Stavrogin and debased by Verkhovensky. Both are appalled by their intellectual isolation, Shatov developing a Christian heresy to overcome his and Kirilov lapsing into a gentle indifference to escape from his. Shatov believes in a God who is a man, Kirilov in a man who will be God. Both revere Christ, but Shatov is not sure he believes in God and Kirilov thinks it unworthy to believe in God. Shatov hungrily pursues God, Kirilov admits that "God has pursued me all my life." A man of pride, Shatov worships humility; a man of humility, Kirilov develops an ethic of pride. Both yearn for sacrifice, Shatov through immersion in the Russian people, Kirilov through immersion in a neutral universe. Neither can tolerate the conditions of existence, Shatov despairing over his distance from God, Kirilov protesting against the edict of Nature which keeps men in the certainty of death. Shatov desires a second reformation to cleanse Christianity of its bourgeois defilement, Kirilov yearns to become the Christ of atheism, sacrificing himself to assert man's freedom and to destroy a God who is nothing but "the pain of the fear of death." To Shatov is assigned Dostoevsky's most cherished idea, to Kirilov his most intimate sickness. Shatov suffers from an excess of self, Kirilov from ideas that can only destroy the self. The two are bound together by a thousand dialectical ties, neither has meaning without the other; Dostoevsky's image of the ideal man implies a unity of Shatov and Kirilov, followed by an act of heroic self-transcendence.

For a moment—it is one of the most exalted in all literature—this unity is almost realized. When Shatov's wife returns to have her baby, he begins to glow with a beautiful, a holy excitement, to which even Kirilov responds. The two men are quickly reconciled, Shatov telling Kirilov that if only he were rid of his atheistic ravings "what a man you'd be," and Kirilov replying with his native sweetness, "Go to your wife, I'll stay here and think about you and your wife." Under the stress of a great experience, ideology is brushed aside and the two men stand together, merely and completely two men—though it is a mark of Dostoevsky's greatness that the purer response is not assigned to his *alter ego* Shatov.

Kirilov is one of Dostoevsky's most brilliant ideological projections but not, I think, an entirely satisfactory one. Is it really true, as Dostoevsky seems to assert, that the highest expression of the will is suicide? One would suppose that a higher heroism of the will might be a choice to live, a choice made with full awareness of the knowledge Kirilov has reached. In any case, Kirilov, having spontaneously helped Shatov, has lost his "right" to commit suicide, for by his act of help he has recognized a human obligation: he is no longer alone, he has acknowledged a "thou," he has granted the world a claim upon his life. And surely a man with his intellectual acuteness would recognize this. Still more troublesome is his readiness to take responsibility for the murder of Shatov. No doubt, Dostoevsky meant to suggest here that Kirilov's ideas make him indifferent to the fate of his friends and indeed of all men, but Dostoevsky himself has shown us otherwise: he could not help presenting Kirilov as a good man. For once—it does not happen very often—Dostoevsky the novelist has been tripped up by Dostoevsky the ideologue.

Shatov is conceived with greater consistency and depth. As he tells his wife, he is a Slavophile because he cannot be a Russian—which is another of Dostoevsky's marvelous intuitions, this one lighting up the whole problem of the intellectual's estrangement and the strategies of compensation by which he tries to overcome it. When Stavrogin presses him, Shatov stammers his faith in Russia, in her orthodoxy, in the body of Christ—and in God? "I . . . I will believe in God," which is to say: I do not yet believe. Shatov defines God as "the synthetic personality of the whole people," and when Stavrogin justly charges him with reducing deity "to a simple attribute of nationality," he replies with still another heresy: "On the contrary I raise the people to God . . . The people is the body of God." Whichever it may be, Shatov cannot accept—he cannot even face—man's distance from God; in Kierkegaard's dictum that "between God and man there is an infinite, yawning, qualitative difference," he would have found a dreadful confirmation of the lovelessness, the "Christlessness" of Protestantism.

In Shatov's mind, as in Dostoevsky's, God figures as a national protector rather than a universal mover, Christianity is seen as a radical morality committed equally to the extremes of ecstasy and suffering, and paradise, being realizable on earth, approaches the prescription Nietzsche offered for the good life. Before Nietzsche wrote, "What is done out of love always takes place beyond good and evil," Dostoevsky had written, "There is no good and bad." When Shatov declares the people to be the body of God, he offers a refracted version of nineteenth-century utopianism with its dream of a human fraternity that will dispense with the yardsticks of moral measurement. Together with this utopian faith, which cannot easily be reconciled with most versions of Christianity, Dostoevsky had a strong sense of the conservative and authoritarian uses of organized religion. (Pyotr Verkhovensky tells an anecdote which slyly reinforces the story of the Grand Inquisitor: A group of liberal army officers "were discussing atheism and I need hardly say they made short work of God. . . . One grizzled old stager of a captain sat mum, not saying a word. All at once he stands up in the middle of the room and says aloud, as though speaking to himself: 'If there's no God, how can I be a captain then?' ") In only one respect is the anarcho-Christian vision of Dostoevsky incomplete: like most primitive Christians he cannot find a means of translating his radical impulses into concrete politics.

Politics is left to Pyotr Verkhovensky, whose role in the book, as a Nechaev turned buffoon, is to bring the fantasies and fanaticisms of the Russian intelligentsia into visible motion. He reduces Kirilov's metaphysical speculations to petty problems of power, acts upon Stavrogin's nihilism by spreading confusion through all levels of society, and deflates the liberal rhetoric of his father, Stepan Trofimovich, to mere political maneuver. Under Verkhovensky's grotesque guidance, politics becomes a catalyst speeding the moral break-up of Russia; it is a sign of the national derangement, chaos made manifest, the force which sets into motion those latent energies of destruction which Dostoevsky finds beneath the surface of Russian life ("every Russian," he bitterly remarks, "is inordinately delighted at any public scandal and disorder").

Simply as a character in a novel, Verkhovensky is somewhat nebulous. What does he believe? Does he believe anything at all? Which of the many motives suggested for him are we to credit? How much sincerity, how much guile, can we allow him? Is he a revolutionist, a police spy or both? Twice he describes himself as "a scoundrel of course and not a socialist" —which is to imply that a socialist is something other than he, something other than a scoundrel. One would suppose that Verkhovensky has begun as a vague, muddled revolutionist, become entangled with the police and now continues on his own, deceiving the secret service, his comrades and himself. Though Dostoevsky is often most remarkable for the life-like fluidity of his characterization, Verkhovensky is allowed to become too fluid, perhaps because Dostoevsky was never quite sure what to make of him. Certainly as a thinker Verkhovensky is absurd, and the implication that he "represents" Russian radicalism is vicious.

Yet once noted, these strictures may be put somewhat to the side. For we have learned to know political types at least as ambiguous as Verkhovensky, men so confused in belief, so devious in affiliation, so infatuated with intrigue that they themselves could hardly say which cause, if any at all, they served. Verkhovensky is not merely the *agent provocateur* to the provocation born, he also foreshadows the adventurers who will soon spring up in the unswept corners of all political movements, ready to capitalize on victories and betray in defeat.

Toward the wretched little circle of plotters which revolves about Pyotr Verkhovensky, Dostoevsky shows no sympathy: *he does not need to,* he is their spiritual brother, his is the revilement of intimacy. Mocking and tormenting them with fraternal violence, Dostoevsky places each of the radicals exactly: Liputin, a cesspool of a man, frothing with gossip and slander, yet sincere in his reforming zeal; Virginsky, a pure enthusiast whom the latest apostle of the most advanced ideas will always be able to lead by the nose; Erkel, a fanatical youth searching for a master to worship and finding him in Verkhovensky; and Shigalov, a superb caricature of the doctrinaire. As portraits of radical personality, all of these are malicious, slanderous, unjust—and rich with truth about human beings, particularly human beings in politics. The "old Nechaevist" Dostoevsky—so he called himself and he did not lie—knew them all like the fingers of his own hand: they *were* the fingers of his own hand. Dostoevsky could have said, to paraphrase a remark of Henry James: "Where extremism is, there am I." [1]

Still, we should be wary of those critics who claim a neat correspondence between Verkhovensky's followers and recent political movements, if only because all efforts to find real-life models for characters in a work of art are inherently dubious. To identify Verkhovensky with, say, the Leninist personality is to shed the most uncertain light on either *The Possessed* or the Russian Revolution. Between Verkhovensky and the Leninist type there is the difference between intellectual chaos and a rigorous, perhaps too rigorous, ideology; conscious cynicism and an idealism that frequently spills over into fanaticism; contempt for the plebes and an almost mystical faith in them. Given the continuity of Russian

---

[1] Dostoevsky has never received the critical attention from Russian Marxists that Tolstoy has, but in the early years of the revolution, before it was strangled by Stalinism, his genius was often appreciated. Lenin is said to have called *The Possessed* "repulsive but great," and Lunacharsky, the first Commissar of Culture, praised him as "the most enthralling" of Russian writers. In a memorial published in 1920 for the hundredth anniversary of Dostoevsky's birth there appears this generous tribute: "Today we read *The Possessed,* which has become reality, living it and suffering with it; we create the novel afresh in union with the author. We see a dream realized, and we marvel at the visionary clairvoyance of the dreamer who cast the spell of Revolution on Russia. . . ."

history from Alexander II to Nicholas II, there are of course bound to be certain similarities: Verkhovensky, for example, anticipates the dangerous Leninist notion of a "transitional generation," one which molds its conduct from a belief that it is certain to be sacrificed in a revolutionary maelstrom. And Shigalov personifies those traits of dogmatism to be found among the Russian radicals, indeed, among most Russian intellectuals, who were forced by their intolerable position to drive all opinions to extremes. But even these similarities, while real enough, should not be pressed too hard.

Somewhat more plausible, though also limited in value, is the comparison frequently made with the Stalinists. Verkhovensky's vision of a society in which all men spy on one another and "only the necessary is necessary" has largely been realized in Stalinist Russia, but his "movement," in both its political bewilderment and intellectual flux, bears little resemblance to Stalinism. Dostoevsky's characters are profoundly related to reality, but they exist only in Dostoevsky's novels. His radicals are men of wildness, creatures of extreme individuality, largely cut off from social intercourse; the Stalinist functionary, by contrast, is a machine-man, trained to servility, and rooted in a powerful state. Verkhovensky himself would not last a week in a Stalinist party, he would immediately prove too erratic and unreliable.

"Starting from unlimited freedom," says Shigalov, "I arrive at unlimited despotism. I will add, however, that there can be no solution of the social problem but mine." Familiar as this sounds, it is not quite the blinding anticipation of totalitarian psychology some critics suppose. For Dostoevsky has failed to recognize that side of ideology, in our time the most important one, which consists of unwitting self-deception, sincere masquerade; his scoundrels not only know they are scoundrels, they take pleasure in announcing it to anyone who will listen. In his eagerness to get at the root of things, Dostoevsky has confused the objective meaning of "Shigalovism" with Shigalov's subjective mode of thought. For surely a Shigalov would insist, in accents of utmost earnestness, that he starts with unlimited freedom and, no matter how bumpy the road, ends with a still higher conception of freedom. Between Shigalov's naive frankness and the torturous workings of the totalitarian mind there has intervened a whole epoch of political complication.

Dostoevsky's truly profound insight into politics appears elsewhere, and cannot be appropriated by any political group, for it has to do with ideology in general. From *any* coherent point of view, Dostoevsky's politics are a web of confusion—few fears now seem more absurd than his fear that Rome and socialism would band together against the Orthodox Church; yet he is unequalled in modern literature for showing the muddle that may lie beneath the order and precision of ideology. Himself the most ideological of novelists, which may be half his secret, he also fears and resists ideology, which may be the other half. In our time ideology cannot be avoided: there is hardly a choice: even the most airy-minded liberal must live with it. Dostoevsky knew this, and would have mocked those cultivated souls who yearn for a life "above mere ideas." But ideology is also a great sickness of our time—and this is true despite one's suspicion of most of the people who say so. In all of his novels Dostoevsky shows how ideology can cripple human impulses, blind men to simple facts, make them monsters by tempting them into that fatal habit which anthropologists call "reifying" ideas. No other novelist has dramatized so powerfully the values and dangers, the uses and corruptions of systematized thought. And few passages are as remarkable in this respect as the one toward the end of *The Possessed* in which Shigalov refuses to participate in the murder of Shatov. Here, one hopes, here at last is one man who will not lend himself to this shameful act. But in a moment it becomes clear that Shigalov has left, not because he is revolted by the act itself but because the murder is not required by his scheme. In a sense, he is worse than Pyotr Verkhovensky, for he is neither hot nor cold; for him the man Shatov does not exist; the only reality he acknowledges is the reality of his doctrine. He has become the ideological man in his ultimate, most terrible form.

## IV

I have said that all but one of the major characters is a double of Stavrogin, and that exception is, of course, Stepan Trofimovich, the liberal with heroic memories. Toward him Dostoevsky is least merciful of all; he stalks him with a deadly aim; he humiliates him, badgers him, taunts him, and finally shatters him—and yet, he loves him.

For all that Stepan Trofimovich fancies himself a "progressive patriot," a "picturesque public character" living in "exile," he depends upon the patronage of Varvara Petrovna, an eccentric landowner. In the relationship between these two quarrelsome yet loving creatures—I am aware of the dangers of allegorizing—Dostoevsky seems to suggest the relationship between matriarchal Russia and her errant liberalism. Stepan Trofimovich is Varvara Petrovna's "invention," her "day-dream," but Dostoevsky is too honest not to add that "in turn she exacted a great deal from him, sometimes even slavishness." And in one of his moments of sudden self-awareness, Stepan Trofimovich acknowledges, though not without an edge of bravado, the condition of liberalism: *"Je suis un simple dependent et rien de plus. Mais r-r-rien de plus."*

Though he preens himself on being advanced, he has only a childish notion of social realities: the liberal has been protected too long, he does not realize how much his comfort depends on the indulgence of authority. Stepan Trofimovich really believes he will be arrested for his imaginary political heresies, and each night he hides under his mattress a letter of self-defense concerning a poem several decades old and read by no one at all. In the presence of his friends he becomes boastful and eloquent when recalling his youth, but the thought of the police sets him trembling. When a peasant riot breaks out in the province, he is among the first to call for stern measures: "He cried out at the club that more troops were needed . . ." And indeed, precisely its half-heartedness and cowardice is one of Dostoevsky's major complaints against liberalism.

By making Stepan Trofimovich the protégé of Varvara Petrovna, Dostoevsky destroys the liberal's claim to intellectual independence; by making him the parent of Pyotr, he implies that nihilism is the necessary outcome of liberalism. Yet in both relationships Stepan Trofimovich shows considerable resources. He gratifies Varvara Petrovna's hunger for new ideas, for scraps of Western thought with which to relieve the dullness of Russia, and not least of all, for a consistent if erratic display of affection. Toward Pyotr he behaves with impressive and unexpected dignity. "She [Varvara Petrovna] was a capitalist," sneers the son, "and you were a sentimental buffoon in her service." It is true, it strikes to the heart of the old man's situation, and yet it is not the whole truth, just as the generalized form of Pyotr's indictment is not the whole truth about liberalism.

In his portrait of Stepan Trofimovich, Dostoevsky incorporated every criticism Marx or Nietzsche or Carlyle would make of classical liberalism; and then he transcended them all, for Stepan Trofimovich in his ridiculous and hysterical way is a sentient human being whom one grows to love and long for, so that the actual man seems more important than anything that may be said about him. As the book progresses, Stepan Trofimovich moves through a number of mutations: the liberal as dependent, the liberal as infant, the liberal as fool (in both senses), the liberal as dandy, the liberal who tries to assert his independence, the liberal as spoiled darling of the radicals, as *agent provocateur,* as provincial, as bohemian, as bootlicker of authority, and the liberal as philosopher. (Which are more important, he asks the young radicals, Shakespeare or boots, Raphael or petroleum?) In each of these roles or phases, Stepan Trofimovich demonstrates the truth of Dostoevsky's remark that "The higher liberalism and the higher liberal, that is a liberal without any definite aim, is possible only in Russia."

Yet it is Stepan Trofimovich who is allowed the most honorable and heroic end. Driven to hysteria by the behavior of his son, his patroness and himself, he sets out in his old age on a mad pilgrimage, taking to the road, he knows not where, "to seek for Russia." Since for Dostoevsky salvation comes only from extreme suffering, Stepan Trofimovich begins to rise, to gather to himself the scattered energies of the book, after having been completely broken at the fete. Some two hundred pages earlier, this ending has already been anticipated: "I will end like a knight," says Stepan Trofimovich, "faithful to my lady." His phantasmagorical wanderings inevitably recall Don Quixote, and indeed he becomes a Russian Quixote seeking Russia, truth, love and reality. These are troublesome words perhaps it would be best to turn once more to a small passage. On the road Stepan Trofimovich meets Lise; he rants in his most melodramatic fashion, falls to his knees, weeps, pities himself extravagantly—and then, as the rain continues to fall, he rises "feeling that his knees too were soaked by the wet earth." The "wet earth" is reality, the reality he has begun to find in his quixotic way; his talk is fantastic but his knees are soaked by the wet Russian earth. It is the reward he wins for having remained beyond Stavrogin's grasp, for clinging to a faith, even if it be the hollow faith of old-fashioned liberalism rather than the faith of Christianity. Together, the earth and the faith make possible his redemption.

But another character has also found his redemption: Shatov, in the Christ-like love that has flooded him upon the return of his wife and the birth of her child. Is this not suggestive of the political ambivalence of the book: that the character with whom Dostoevsky identifies most closely and the character he attacks most violently should both come to a kind of apotheosis? And does this not imply the possibility of some ultimate reconciliation? It has not yet occurred, Dostoevsky will not falsify, the two characters stand apart—but Shatov and Stepan Trofimovich, symbolically placed at opposite poles, are now, for the first time, ready for each other.

If we ask ourselves, what is the source of Dostoevsky's greatness, there can of course be no single answer. But surely part of the answer is that no character is allowed undisputed domination of the novel, all are checked and broken when they become too eager in the assertion of their truths. Once Stavrogin has asked Shatov the terrible question, "And in God?", Shatov can never control the book, and even after Stepan Trofimovich has soared to a kind of quixotic grandeur he is pulled down to reality by his old patroness who tells a priest: "You will have to confess him again in another hour! That's the sort of man he is."

Dostoevsky is the greatest of all ideological novelists because he always distributes his feelings of identification among all his characters—though putting it this way makes it seem too much an act of the will, while in reality it far transcends the will. "What decides the world view of a writer," says Arnold Hauser, "is not so much whose side he supports, as through whose eyes he looks at the world." And Dostoevsky looks at the world through the eyes of all his people: Stavrogin and Father Tikhon, Stepan Trofimovich and Shatov, even Lebyadkin and Pyotr Verkhovensky. He *exhausts* his characters, scours all the possibilities of their being. None escapes humiliation and shame, none is left free from attack. In the world of Dostoevsky, no one is spared, but there is a supreme consolation: no one is excluded.

# The Two Dimensions

# of Reality

# in *The Brothers Karamazov*

## *by Eliseo Vivas*

### I

A novelist of the amplitude and depth of Dostoevsky is likely to be
used by his many critics each for his own special purpose. Dostoevsky
has been used by the founder of psychoanalysis and by innumerable
amateur Freudians as an interesting pathological specimen—which of
course he was. He has also been considered as forerunner of Freud in his
own right, as social or political thinker, as religious prophet and as
theologian. To each of these fields Dostoevsky contributed interesting
speculations, often original and important. But he was and always remained a novelist—although he used the newspaper article and, on
occasion, the lecture platform as vehicle of expression.

To say, however, that Dostoevsky was a novelist is not to say that his
ends were "aesthetic." Dostoevsky was not an artist because of the manner
in which he handled his subject matter. Henry James was unfair to him;
it would be difficult, with the single exception of *The Posssessed,* to suggest improvements in the architecture of his major novels, and this ac-
cords with the fact, known from external sources, that he thought long
and deeply over their composition before he began them. But he never
enjoyed the leisure required to bring his work to perfection. He was,
nevertheless, an artist in the immediate, concrete manner in which he
seized the subject matter of experience. His lack of interest in nature has
often been noticed. It is as if he had an eye capable exclusively of spiritual
vision and for which, therefore, the inanimate ambient world could
become visible only insofar as it is helped to disclose the fluid dynamism
of the psychic. He saw human beings as concrete, actual agents of action,

agonists of the drama of actual life. If we contrast him with Kafka, who in some respects is not unworthy of being put on the same plane as the Russian, we see the difference between an eye which is primarily dramatic and one which is metaphysical. Kafka's world is a dynamic world, but its denizens are not genuine human beings but metaphysical hypostatizations representing certain aspects of the spiritual life. And for this reason what Kafka has to say about the soul does not refer to its concrete workings but to its dialectical tensions. As psychologist—in the sense in which the term can be used to refer to a man like Dostoevsky—Kafka was negligible, for we do not learn anything from his novels which we did not already know from either Kierkegaard or Freud. We learn something else no less valuable, but we do not learn anything new about what is behind our social masks. (From Kafka himself, considered as pathological specimen, we may, using his books as diagnostic evidence, learn about a modern neurosis—but for that we do not need Kafka, and the evidence he furnishes is neither reliable nor complete.)

These remarks are not intended to deny that Dostoevsky had a deep interest in social, ethical, and theological "problems." Indeed it is not difficult to isolate from his writings—or even from his novels alone—a body of doctrine to which we can be reasonably certain that he subscribed. But this doctrine, however truly espoused by him, is not representative of his total vision of the world, since it neglects the context of concrete circumstance which is an essential element in the definition of its meaning for him. It is true, of course, that Dostoevsky had strong convictions. He was, for instance, a committed Christian and a political conservative. But to take his Christianity without the careful qualifications forced on us by the dramatic manner in which he conceived human destiny would be to view it falsely; his faith is not a purely intellectual, logically simple, structure: it is an extremely complex and internally heterogeneous mass of living insights—affective, moral, and intellectual—in tension, and ordered not after the manner of the philosopher but of the dramatist. When therefore one asks oneself what were Dostoevsky's views on Christianity, one has to consider (simplifying for the sake of the illustration) not only what we can find out about one character or a class of characters, but what he tells us in the novels as a whole. But what he tells us is a story, in which one character acts and talks in one way and another in another, each in terms of his own convincing logic and psychology. In this picture we will have to choose the truth, as Dostoevsky saw it, from the error. But this distinction cannot be made in the same sense in which one finds it made in a theological or an ethical treatise. Thus for instance, the reader, in putting Zosima and his beliefs and commitments at the center of the picture, will also have to remember that Dostoevsky was able to make the predicament of Shatov perfectly convincing through his conversation with Stavrogin (*The Possessed*, Part II, Chap. 1, vii). The latter presses Shatov for a confession, to which

Shatov can only answer: "I . . . I will believe in God." But Shatov insists on his faith in "The body of Christ, in Russian Orthodoxy," and asserts, at the same time, and not unaware of his difficulty, that "the object of every national movement, in every people and at every period of its existence is only the seeking for God, who must be its own God." We cannot avoid the conviction that Shatov's predicament was something which Dostoevsky had thought through passionately, and must be reckoned with in formulating his "views." But even if we reject the validity of Shatov's views, we cannot leave out of account the fact that it was in the teeth of the latter's assertions that Dostoevsky held his truth. From internal evidence alone one can formulate in abstract terms the philosophy of a good many novelists and among these of some very great ones. But the error of some of the efforts to interpret the meaning of Dostoevsky's novels lies in the assumption that there are "doctrines" or "views" to be found in them—systematic structures of abstract thought involving major affirmations and denials—when what they contain is a dramatic organization of life, which includes characters most of whom are deeply interested in ideas.

All of this is to say that Dostoevsky fulfills the primary function of the artist, which so very few artists fulfill to the same extent. What he does is to organize or, better, to inform experience at the primary level and by means of animistic and dramatic categories. He does not undertake the philosopher's task, which is to abstract from experience already dramatically informed a formal structure in order to test its capacity to meet the exigencies of logical coherence and clarity of the rational intellect. What he does is to make life, insofar as man can do it, to be a poet and to give experience the form and intelligibility required by the whole mind, by the intellect and by the will. Without this primary organization life would either be chaos or instinctual routine. Men can live without philosophy, and not unsuccessfully, and history and anthropology show that for the most part they do. But without poetry human life is not possible.

I have labored this point because critics of Dostoevsky often undertake to give us systematic accounts of ideas and doctrines which Dostoevsky never could have entertained. Consider for instance Berdyaev's analysis. It is certainly one of the most searching, yet the total picture that we gather from it is that Dostoevsky was a theologian—which he was and was not; he was, since he could not view the human drama except as against the far horizon of eternity; but he was not, since a writer who sides with a character who says that the formula that twice two make four does not meet with his acceptance—a thinker who distrusted the intellect as deeply as Dostoevsky did—is not a man who could have systematized his views, even if he had tried.

It has been said that Dostoevsky organized his works in terms of "an idea," but if what I have said is valid this statement cannot stand. Nor can we say, with another of his critics, that Dostoevsky dramatized his ideas. It is closer to the truth to say that in his books, which are pure stories, the story is the idea. However the word "idea" is not being used here in its ordinary sense, but as it is employed in musical aesthetics. His stories, however, pure drama though they are, exhibit two levels or aspects of human reality: the psychological and the metaphysical. The first we have the right to expect of any serious novelist; only, psychologically Dostoevsky gives us considerably more than we are usually given by even the greatest of poets. The second very few readers demand and when they do very seldom get; indeed a number of his readers—particularly the "enlightened," "modern" ones—find it embarrassing and superfluous. When we look at the relationship between these levels we find that the philosophical informs (in the technical Aristotelian sense) the psychological and the latter in turn informs the story. The matter of the story (the object of imitation, in terms of Aristotelian aesthetics) is human experience. But Dostoevsky has informed it twice through his creative activity; and we, his readers, are able with his aid to grasp the constitution of human experience at a depth impenetrable to all but the greatest poets.

2

. The fresh and profound insights which Dostoevsky added to our knowledge of the human soul have been discussed thoroughly and admirably by many of his critics. All that needs to be done, therefore, is to remind the reader summarily of them; effort can be more profitably put into an analysis of the means through which these insights find expression. Thus, it is a commonplace that Dostoevsky anticipated Freud; that he was cognizant of the fact and understood the role of the unconscious; that he had a lucid knowledge of the duality exhibited by the human psyche and of its consequences; that he understood adequately the function of dreams; that he knew how shame leads a man to frustrate the actions through which he attempts to appease it, and how pride is the expression of insecurity and shame; how cruelty constitutes self-castigation, and how injured vanity takes revenge through love. In short, all the insights that have become commonplaces since Freud were clearly his own; nor can I think of any important phenomenological datum furnished by the Viennese scientist which had escaped the observation of the Russian novelist.

But no abstract catalogue of "insights" can do justice to the breadth and depth of Dostoevsky's knowledge of the man that flourished in Europe and Russia in the nineteenth century and whose descendants have merely refined his neuroses. To do justice to his contribution we must view it not merely as the product of his psychological acumen but as the product of his art. In the vast canvas of his major novels—and this is particularly true of the greatest of them, *The Brothers*—one finds a series of "studies" of the various modalities through which certain types of human beings express themselves. The "type" however is gathered by us inductively from his unique specimens and it is not the former but the latter that interest Dostoevsky; nevertheless it is our intuition of the type in the individuals that makes them intelligible, while the individuals enable us to intuit the type, through the interrelationships of a complex system of similarities and contrasts which in this essay we cannot explore exhaustively but must be content to illustrate succinctly.

For illustration let us consider a type of individual with whom Dostoevsky was profoundly preoccupied and which, for lack of a better designation, we shall call "the liberal." In *The Brothers* there are at least five or six fairly complete "studies" of this type: Ivan, Smerdyakov, Miüsov, Rakitin, and Kolya. But we could increase the number by adding some of the lesser characters. A liberal is, in religious matters, either an unbeliever or an agnostic; politically he is a reformist or a socialist; intellectually a "European" or Europeanized; and morally for Christian love he substitutes secular meliorism. Let us start with Ivan. What we know of him directly, by listening to him talk and observing his relation to his brothers and to his father, his feeling for Katerina Ivanovna, his conversations with Smerdyakov, and his illness, is far from exhausting the knowledge imparted about him, which comes to us also indirectly through what we learn of Smerdyakov, Rakitin, and Miüsov—to mention only these. But young Kolya, too, throws a good deal of light on Ivan. Smerdyakov is, if you will allow the expression, an abyss of shallowness, a pure, corrupted rationalist whose shallow intelligence has nothing to express but his pomaded lackey's vanity and trivial, upstart ambition, while Ivan is intelligent and, in an ordinary sense, sincere. But it is impossible to claim a complete understanding of Ivan until we have seen what can happen to his ideas when they are vulgarized by his bastard stepbrother and are put to the test pragmatically. Because Ivan, an intellectual, will not find out what is "the cash value" of his ideas, the visits to the sick lackey before the latter's suicide are a revelation to him of what he himself truly is and of how he, no less than Dmitri, is as much involved in the murder as the "stinking scoundrel." But neither Ivan nor Smerdyakov are fully intelligible until we have considered Rakitin, the theological student. Here is another upstart, trying to conceal his lowly origin; he is dishonorable, egotistical, unscrupulous and evil; he is vain and clever and he is self-deceived. He says he is a liberal and looks toward Europe for the salvation of Russia, but he is a dishonorable scoundrel interested in no one but himself, lacking the greatness and depth which Ivan in a measure has while possessing advantages which Smerdyakov lacks. He is not a physical murderer, but he is much more of a murderer than the brothers Karamazov: they murdered a depraved buffoon, but he murders innocent and naïve souls with the poison of his ideas. Dmitri fears him instinctively and he has already begun to corrupt young Kolya. In the United States today he would have proclaimed himself a "scientific humanist." This is why, with a wisdom which transcends his own intellectual shortcomings, Dmitri calls him a "Bernard," intuitively grasping the evil inherent in Rakitin's trust in science. Thus Rakitin is both a contrast to and a mirror image of Ivan. The latter is honorable and his atheism is anguished. The former is a clever and shallow cad. But this is not all, for Ivan's advanced ideas must be considered by contrast with Miüsov, the Europeanized Russian liberal who liked to give the impression that he had had his turn on the barricades in Paris. Ivan is not irredeemable, because he never loses his roots in the Russian soil, while Miüsov has lost touch with his native Russia. With his wealth, family background, worldly sophistication, there is nothing inside the polished shell. He thinks of himself as a humanitarian but of course he really isn't, as his treatment of his nephew shows. Now each of these characters throws light on the others, and placed in order from Ivan through Miüsov, Rakitin, Smerdyakov, and Kolya (who is a boyish Ivan who has not yet lost the lovableness of childhood) they give us a complete picture of the antireligious, rationalistic "liberal" in his various modalities. Several other series of contrasting modalities of the same type are "studied," for instance that of the monks, with Zosima, Paissy, Ioseff, Ferapont, and the monk from Obdorsk revealing the nature of Christian love, Christian renunciation of the world, and the pathological manifestations to which religion can give rise.

However it is not possible to understand an individual or a type through behavioral observation alone. We have to look into those secret crevices of the soul which ordinarily the individual does not suspect he has. In *The Brothers* we become acquainted with Ivan in the ordinary manner—see him act, hear him express his attitudes and his ideas. In the famous Chapters 4 and 5 of Book V, entitled "Rebellion" and "The Grand Inquisitor," we see the depth of his concern for the religious problem and are given a first look into the nature of his difficulties. But Dostoevsky goes not only beyond Ivan's observed behavior, into his intellectual and moral structure, but into the unconscious double, which the Freudian would call the Id. This dimension of the personality had begun to be suspected in Dostoevsky's day, but not until Dostoevsky himself clarified it does literature begin fully to explore it. Freud's influence of course has made it the ordinary possession of literate men. (It is merely a matter of accuracy to remember, however, that Dostoevsky has not been the only writer before Freud who was aware of the fact that the human soul has a third, hidden dimension. Shakespeare, to take a trite example, used a somnambulistic dream to reveal a hidden sense of guilt. Nor was Freud the first psychologist to look into unconscious motives;

Nietzsche used the method frequently and with tremendous success.) But Dostoevsky's grasp of hidden motives and of instinctual processes which express themselves deviously differs in a very important respect from that exhibited by contemporary novelists who go to Freud for their knowledge of the human soul. Dostoevsky conceives the soul as fluid and he presents it, so to speak, directly for his reader's inspection. Freudians have taught us to conceive of the soul as a stiff mechanism made up of instincts and forces and energies which constitute a lumbering and creaking machine. Again, they have made current the doctrine that the phenomena which are not directly observable can be discovered only by inference. The reading of dreams, the analysis of the true meaning of everyday errors, the discovery of our hidden desires and intentions behind our ostensible discourse and behavior, thus become a silly and rather mechanical puzzling out of facile charades. And the result is that the conception of character of the novelist who has learned his human nature from Freud and not in the world, as Dostoevsky did, becomes the game of planting symbols according to a simple mechanical formula. In Freud, taken within the context of his therapeutic objectives, his analytic technique and his hypothetical constructions have a pragmatic justification. But when these constructions are used by amateurs for *their* purposes, what in the hands of the therapist is a source of insight degenerates rapidly into a shallow technique of obfuscation.

Dostoevsky reveals Ivan's unconscious through the use of a Freudian device—the hallucination or delirium which Ivan undergoes when he is ill and in which he meets the Devil who, he tells us twice, is himself. Through this "visit" we find out that the man who is preoccupied with the relation between church and state, and who clearly grasps the consequence of the denial of freedom to man in favor of happiness, is really, at bottom, a man whose soul is ripped by a contradiction of which he is perfectly aware, but which he is not able to resolve. For while Ivan cannot believe in God he believes nevertheless in evil; but he goes beyond the Manicheans for he gives evil the primacy. The Devil says to Ivan:

"I . . . simply ask for annihilation. No, live, I am told, for there'd be nothing without you. If everything in the universe were sensible, nothing would happen. There would be no events without you, and there must be events. So against the grain I serve to produce events and do what's irrational because I am commanded to. . . ."

Of course the primacy of evil is qualified by the fact that the Devil accomplishes the creative task in obedience to a command, but nevertheless it is he who is the cause of events.

In this same paragraph the "visitor" says to Ivan, "You are laughing—no, you are not laughing, you are angry again. You are forever angry, all

you care about is intelligence. . . ." This is a very important remark to
which we shall have to return. Let us however follow the conversation
a few minutes longer. Ivan, "with a smile of hatred," asks:

> "Then even you don't believe in God?" . . . .
> "What can I say—that is, if you are in earnest . . ."
> "Is there a God or not?" Ivan cried with the same savage intensity.
> "Ah, then you are in earnest! My dear fellow, upon my word I don't
> know. There! I have said it now!"
> "You don't know, but you see God? No, you are not some one apart, you
> are myself, you are I and nothing more! You are rubbish, you are my fancy!"
> "Well, if you like, I have the same philosophy as you, that would be true.
> *Je pense, donc je suis,* I know that for a fact, all the rest, all these worlds,
> God and even Satan—all that is not proved, to my mind. . . ."

Thus it turns out that Ivan, who believes in the primacy of evil, when
you press him, does not know, is an absolute solipsist, and cannot discover proof of the world, of God, or even of Satan. The reason for his
plight has already been given to us by his double: all he cares about is
intelligence. And intelligence by itself is the source of all evil, and
ultimately of despair. This is one of the things that Dostoevsky knew
with the same certainty that Ivan knew that he was because he thought.

Through the delirium Dostoevsky has shown us the depths of Ivan's
personality, but without the need to refer us to the Freudian code-book.
Other devices which Dostoevsky employs in order to reveal the depths of
the soul are not as easy to explain in general terms. One of the ways in
which he does it is by having one character explain or reveal the meaning
of another's actions; another is by having a character behave differently
before each of the other characters with whom he has intercourse. Thus,
Kolya, that delightfully lovable mischief-maker, is quite a different person
with his fellows than he is with Alyosha or with the two children of the
doctor's wife to whom his mother rented rooms. This device gives us the
complexity of a person. But usually in order to reveal the duality of the
soul Dostoevsky conducts the dramatic narrative on two planes, in
such wise that while a character, let us say, is protesting love for another,
he is revealing hatred. As illustration take the manner in which Fyodor
immediately upon entering the Elder's cell reveals through his buffoonery
his deep shame.

> "Precisely to our time," cried Fyodor Pavlovitch, "but no sign of my son
> Dmitri. I apologize for him, sacred Elder!" (Alyosha shuddered all over at
> "sacred elder.")

Before the guests have had time to take in the room, we, the readers, are
plunged into the scene, shameful and comic, in which Fyodor's buffoonery
discloses what it intends to cover, a sick soul consumed with the need

to castigate itself. Or let us recall the chapter entitled "A Laceration in the Drawing Room," although almost any other episode chosen at random would serve as well. In this chapter Katerina Ivanovna, Mme. Khokhlakov, Ivan, and Alyosha discuss Katerina's feeling for Dmitri. In this conversation Katerina tells the others that she does not know if she still loves Dmitri but that she feels pity for him and does not intend to abandon him even if he abandons her for Grushenka. She will not get in his way, she says, she will go to another town, but she will watch over him all her life. In the long run, she is certain to be able to show him that she loves him like a sister who has sacrificed her life to him. The moment that she begins to discuss Dmitri the reader begins to suspect that she is not quite sincere. The lack of sincerity is suggested by Dostoevsky himself through an explanation which he makes of the word "laceration" used by Madame Khokhlakov during the scene with Grushenka the preceding day. But the word "sacrifice" used by Katerina Ivanovna gives her away completely, for her statement contrasts sharply with the picture already presented of her return of the money given her by Dmitri, the way in which she declares her love to Dmitri and asks him to marry her, telling him that she will be his chattel, when we have already seen how proud she really is. Dmitri earlier had told us that she loved her own virtue, not him. Now it becomes clear that Katerina Ivanovna is really after revenge. In order to make Dmitri pay for the humiliations he has inflicted on her she is quite willing to put herself to a great deal of pain and sacrifice. This is fully confirmed by Alyosha's explosion when he tells her in a tone entirely out of harmony with his usual gentleness that she does not love Dmitri and wants to hurt him, and that she loves Ivan and wants to hurt him also. Later, at the trial, after Katerina Ivanovna has given evidence in Dmitri's favor, she becomes hysterical and gives the President of the Court the letter that convicts Dmitri, thus giving full rein to a hatred which until then she had tried to conceal from herself but which Dostoevsky had already clearly revealed to the reader. But no sooner is Dmitri sentenced than she repents and seeks his love, in an oblique way again.

### 3

Dostoevsky, of course, is not equipped to give a scientific explanation of those aspects of the personality which he discovered, nor is he interested in doing so. But he does more than give a mere phenomenological description of psychological processes. Indeed what gives his novels their depth and makes him one of the great thinkers of the modern world is that while positive science and naturalistic philosophy were straining to reduce man to purely naturalistic terms and to deny his metaphysical dimension in empirical terms, Dostoevsky was rediscovering that dimension in empirical terms which gave the lie to the modernists by reinvoking ancient truths whose old formulation had ceased to be convincing. With Kierkegaard, therefore, he was one of a small number of men who helped us forge the weapons with which to fend off the onrush of a naturalism bent on stripping us of our essentially human, our metaphysical, reality.

The reason that Dostoevsky is able to make these discoveries is not hard to find. It is well known that he started as a liberal and in "the house of the dead" gave up his youthful faith and turned toward orthodoxy. In Siberia he seems to have found, as many had found earlier and others have found since under adversity, that certain radical crises of the human spirit are neither intelligible nor manageable by means of any form of naturalistic philosophy. Dostoevsky's shift has frequently puzzled his readers. How was it possible for him, they have asked, to come out of prison with a heart free of resentment at the cruel mockery of the execution and the horror of the four years of prison? But no one can claim to be a serious reader of Dostoevsky who does not know the answer to this question. His books are the answer—if we remember that below their psychological is to be found a metaphysical level. Dostoevsky exhibits a fact that to the average Christian seems ridiculous: that the guilt of one man is the guilt of all. We see in his pages how concern with iniquity expresses itself in a liberal and in a Christian way. The former repudiates self-guilt, and this leads to cannibalism; the latter accepts it and seeks to dissolve evil in selflessness and love. This is one insight which is clear and at which Dostoevsky arrived because he was a religious man and not a naturalist.

Dostoevsky's turn toward political conservatism and religious orthodoxy has been taken by many of his critics as evidence that he was wrong about social and religious questions in spite of his great powers as an artist and his psychological acuity. One of his critics, Simmons, dismisses his philosophy because it implies the denial of progress. His critics pretend to admire his art but deplore the content of his philosophy, obviously blind to the organic connection between his skill as artist, his perspicacity as psychologist, and his metaphysical insight. But one has not begun to understand him until one has grasped how, as Dostoevsky deepened his insight into human nature, he came more and more clearly to see that man's plight, his unhappiness, his divided soul, his need for self-laceration, his viciousness, his pride and his shame, his ills in short, flow from the same fountain-head: his unbelief. But unbelief is lack of love which in turn is hell. Dostoevsky progressively gains a firmer grasp of this insight through his creative work and in his last novel he is finally able successfully to bring into a comprehensive dramatic synthesis all his views of man and of his relations to his fellows and to the universe. At the heart of all questions, he comes to see, is the question of God, which is the question of love. Early in *The Brothers* he tells us that if Alyosha decided that:

God and immortality did not exist he would at once have become an atheist and a socialist. For socialism is not merely the labor question, it is before all things the atheistic question, the question of the form taken by atheism today, the question of the tower of Babel built without God, not to mount to Heaven from earth but to set up Heaven on earth.

This is to say that the labor question as it has been formulated since his day is the critical mode through which contemporary secularism manifests itself. For what socialism seeks is the recognition and institutionalization—achieved in Russia with the revolution—of a historical process already fully manifest in bourgeois society since the seventeenth century, but which the bourgeoisie has resisted acknowledging explicitly: Socialism would have man define his destiny exclusively in historical terms and denies the validity or necessity of metaphysical agencies. This process, which Dewey has called "the conclusion of natural science," would uproot as obstructive vestiges all religious institutions and beliefs and would substitute for them a conception of human destiny defined in terms of secular meliorism.

This problem poses itself in Dostoevsky's mind in terms of a comprehensive metaphor possessing two conflicting terms, "Russia *versus* Europe." "Europe" promised happiness, but Dostoevsky saw that the price of an exclusively secular happiness was freedom. On this side one had only the choice between the Grand Inquisitor and the nihilism of Shigalov and Pyotr Stepanovich (in *The Possessed*), for whom is substituted the even more vicious and convincing figure of that "Bernard," Rakitin (in *The Brothers*). On the other side one had "Russia," and the term, Dostoevsky believed passionately, had to be accepted, so to speak, "as was" and without bargaining. The pictures of Shigalov and Rakitin need not give us pause, however, even if we find that we cannot accept them as probable, since for these elements of the metaphor we can substitute at discretion the more up-to-date picture of the commissar with his automatic always at the back of the head of anyone who challenges his will. The truth of the insight is what matters; and at this moment history threatens to give us a complete and irrefutable demonstration of it. Confronted with such an either/or Dostoevsky chose "Russia" in the belief that the Russian people would never accept atheistic socialism because they were too deeply and genuinely Christian. If we take the metaphor as intended we cannot fairly maintain that Dostoevsky was wrong. Indeed he came very close to the truth. But we must add in the same breath that one element of the metaphor's tenor, "Russia," was not in his day to be found and never will be either in history or in geography.

The other element of the tenor, "Europe," includes "the state" which is force, with its instruments, mysticism, miracle, and authority; justice without love, which involves blood; equality in things; and the multiplication of desires. Those at the controls of such a society are condemned to isolation and spiritual suicide and the ruled are sentenced to envy or murder. In contrast "Russia," which in justice to Dostoevsky we should remember he conceived as an ideal not yet adequately actualized, includes the church after it has absorbed the state, the denial of desires, the brotherhood of all living beings, spiritual dignity, justice in Christ and instead of pride and envy, humility and recognition of one's own sinfulness, and hence one's responsibility for the sins of all other men. The first term, "Europe," is of course exaggerated, and the second an improbable idealization. And if the reader should inquire by what means did Dostoevsky identify church bureaucracy and worldliness with Europe-Rome and what permitted him to clear the Russian hierarchy of all charges, so as to make it the potential kingdom of heaven on earth, the answer, unsatisfactory to us who do not love Russia and do not hate Europe as he did, runs something like this: Dostoevsky knew that the City of God is not of this world, but the route to it must be through "Russia" and not through "Europe," since the latter has been corrupted beyond redemption by the Grand Inquisitor, the Bernards and the socialists—who are three peas from the same pod. That a man who finds the ethical essence of Christianity in love could so inordinately hate Rome-Europe, or indeed could without shame exhibit the sores of his anti-Semitism, is something which no admirer of his ought to conceal or should try to apologize for. There is wisdom enough in him to make up for his ugly defects.

The question of God, however, is not a question that Dostoevsky settles easily by falling back on simple faith. Dostoevsky, who can easily be convicted of blindness to the evils of his own state and church, refuses flatly to compromise with the facts of individual experience, untoward as he knows them to be to his religious beliefs. Referring to *The Brothers* he is quoted as having said:

> Even in Europe there have never been atheistic expressions of such power. Consequently, I do not believe in Christ and His confession as a child, but my hosanna has come through a great furnace of doubt.

In his notebook, and referring to criticisms of *The Brothers*, he writes

> The villains teased me for my ignorance and a retrograde faith in God. These thickheads did not dream of such a powerful negation of God as that put in "The (Grand) Inquisitor" and in the preceding chapter. . . . I do not believe in God like a fool (a fanatic). And they wished to teach me, and laughed over my backwardness! But their stupid natures did not dream of such a powerful negation as I have lived through. It is for them to teach me!

But we do not need this statement in order to discover how prolonged and anguished was his struggle with the religious question. All we need in order to make the discovery is a hasty reading of *The Brothers*. It has often been said of Milton that he did better by his Satan than by his God; and similarly it has been argued that Dostoevsky's good and saintly characters, Prince Myshkin in *The Idiot*, Father Tikhon in *The Possessed*, and Father Zosima, are far more tenuous than the human devils that abound in his books. There is, I believe, some truth in this observation. But the statement is partly false if it is forgotten that Dostoevsky believed that genuine goodness can only be reached by those who plunge down to the bottom and there in their darkest hour, somehow find God. This was his own personal experience and it was borne out by observation. If this is true, it is Zosima, and not Prince Myshkin (in *The Idiot*), who is the truly good man. But it cannot be denied that none of his good or saintly characters—Sonya in *Crime and Punishment*, Myshkin, and even Zosima—is endowed with as dense and authentic a humanity as his evil characters. Dostoevsky was aware of this criticism, which is not difficult to answer. The reason why they are not, is that genuine goodness and saintliness are harmonious, unassertive and hence undramatic, dull, affairs. But this is not a comment on them or on Dostoevsky but on us, his readers.

Be that as it may, in the portraits of his great sinners and criminals Dostoevsky did not merely study the effects of vice but the effects of disbelief. He traces the effect of vice, pride, and hatred on the disintegration of the personality and he is most successful in drawing men in whom vice is connected with their repudiation of their condition as creatures and with their consequent effort to set themselves up wittingly or unwittingly as gods. And he shows how men who do not believe in God end up by believing in their own omnipotence. At the root of this transposition we find pride, which would not have welled up and flooded one's consciousness had he been able to grasp clearly the fact that he is a creature, which is to say, finite and dependent. But this kind of pride is in turn traced by Dostoevsky to the misuse of reason, the belief that science and the intelligence are enough for the development of human life. In the early *Notes from the Underground* he stated fully what for lack of a more adequate term we must refer to as his anti-intellectualism. From that book on, the worst evil of his characters is in one way or another connected with the belief in the self-sufficiency of the intellect. There is of course evil in the sensual animalism of Fyodor Karamazov, but there is greater evil in Rakitin. And the greatest responsibility for the crime must be assumed by Ivan, the source of whose corruption we have already looked at.

But Dostoevsky is not a propagandist and much less a dogmatist. He is, in the most important sense of that word of many meanings, a genuine philosopher, for he really inquired, questioned, sought the truth, instead of seeking bad reasons for what he already believed on faith (if I may be allowed to spoil Bradley's famous epigram). It would not be inexact to say that Dostoevsky was forced against his will by the facts that his experience disclosed to him into the conviction that atheism is fatal practically and false theoretically. But he would never allow any argument or any fact to involve him in the denial of an aspect of experience which presented itself to him as authentic.

But then, how can one believe in God?—How, that is, if one is not a peasant woman of simple faith but has the brains, the education, and the range of experience of an Ivan? One cannot, is Ivan's answer, so long as the evil of the world remains to give the lie to God. It is known that Dostoevsky called Chapters 4 and 5 of Book V of *The Brothers*— to which we have already referred—"the culminating point of the novel." The first of these chapters contains Ivan's case against God. I call it "Ivan's dossier," because he introduced his case by saying to Alyosha that he is "fond of collecting certain facts and anecdotes copied from newspapers." This is data one cannot neglect, if one is going to attempt an explanation of the ways of God to man. There is the case of Richard, the Swiss savage, burnt at the stake in Geneva; the case of the Russian peasant who beats the horse in the eyes, and then the cases of the children, culminating in the story of the child thrown to the savage dogs in front of his mother.

> The General orders the child to be undressed; the child is stripped naked. He shivers numb with terror, not daring to cry. . . . "Make him run" commands the General. "Run, run!" shout the dog-boys. The boy runs. "At him!" yells the General, and he sets the whole pack of hounds on the child. The hounds catch him and tear him to pieces before his mother's eyes.

One sentence completes the story, and it is superbly ironic in its bathos: "I believe the General was afterwards declared incapable of administering his estates." How, in view of such things, can you believe in Providence?

Dostoevsky knew perfectly well that in his own terms Ivan could not be answered. The furnace of doubt through which Dostoevsky said he had passed before he was able to arrive at his faith, consisted of at least two flames: the devastating knowledge he had of the criminal and depraved tendencies to be found at the bottom of the human soul and of which he gives us in *The Brothers* three superb examples, Fyodor, Rakitin, and Smerdyakov; and the knowledge he has that injustice is inherent in the structure of human living and cannot be dislodged from it. These two flames, as I may continue to call them, cannot be smothered with social reforms or mechanical improvements. This is the hope of the rationalistic liberal, a hope that springs from his shallow grasp of human nature, and which, when it is not a mere pretense, as it is with Miüsov, is a diabolical lie, as it is with Rakitin. In "The Grand Inquisitor" he finally brought to full expression the implication of the conflict between God and freedom on the one hand and the atheistic effort to bring heaven to earth by dispensing with God on the other. The point of the conflict cannot be stated abstractly without vulgarizing it, but since the long marginal commentary which would be required to do it justice is not possible here we must risk a brief statement. The conflict is between The Grand Inquisitor and Father Zosima. The alternatives are clear and exhaustive, since compromises are unstable and futile for they reproduce the undesirable features of both terms and none of the virtues of either. The villain of Ivan's poem is Jesus, who rejected the prizes offered him by The Great Spirit, Satan, and wittingly loaded man with a burden he cannot carry, freedom. It is not freedom that man wants, but miracle, mystery, and authority. He "is tormented by no greater anxiety than to find someone quickly to whom he can hand over that gift of freedom with which the ill-fated creature is born." The Roman Catholic Church has managed to correct the harm that Jesus attempted to do, and socialism but carries on from where Rome leaves off. In order to give man happiness it has been necessary for the Church to take the sword of Caesar and in taking it of course it rejected Jesus and chose Satan. For this reason Dostoevsky believes that socialism and Catholicism are identical as to ends: both seek to relieve man of the burden of freedom. But happiness without God is a delusion that leads men to devour one another or leads a strong man to gain power over his fellows for their own good, and gives them happiness at the price of keeping them from realizing their full humanity.

The alternative then to the ideal of The Grand Inquisitor is to accept God, freedom, and immortality. But this alternative has somehow to dispose of Ivan's dossier. To give man freedom is not only to open to him the door of eternal salvation, it is also to open the other door, whose threshold hope cannot cross. You cannot have Heaven without Hell; Heaven entails the General and his dogs. It is a terrible choice and no one knew more clearly than Dostoevsky how terrible it was: *happiness without freedom, or freedom and hell.* Ivan's dossier cannot be exorcised into thin air. What is the answer? It is found in Father Zosima, and that means in our acceptance of our condition as creatures. This calls for love at the heart of human existence; but not the abstract and self-deceived love of your rationalistic liberal, your Miüsov, but the personal love of Father Zosima. The answer resolves the conflict because it reveals that hell is life without love. And it also reveals that Ivan's dossier is possible only through a lie. For Ivan forgets that he is a creature, that he therefore has no right to challenge God, nor to demand that God answer his question in a manner satisfactory to him or he will refuse to accept His world and "return His ticket." This is, of course, to fall back on the inscrutable designs of the Deity which Spinoza called the refuge of ignorance. But Dostoevsky is not frightened by this retort, since he is faced clearly with an either/or: either God and love or the world which the Rakitins, the Miüsovs, and the Smerdyakovs would create, the world of the Grand Inquisitor. It will be retorted that what I have said makes no sense, for freedom rejects mystery and it is mystery Dostoevsky invokes when he invokes God. The answer is simple: what the Grand Inquisitor wants is mystification, superstition, and that is totally different from the mystery entailed by belief in a God of love.

It should not be overlooked, besides, that what Alyosha calls Ivan's rebellion is the challenge launched against God by a man who claims to be concerned with human tears:

> "I took the case of children only to make my case clearer. Of the other tears of humanity with which the earth is soaked from the crust to its center, I will say nothing."

But it is simply not true that Ivan loves man as he says he does. If he did, he would follow in the steps of Father Zosima. That, and that only, is the way of true love. The man who loves his fellows has neither time nor energy for rebellion. He realizes that he himself is guilty, for even if his own hands are not stained with blood, he is responsible for the blood shed by his fellows. And instinct with love and active about the misery of others he no longer hugs with bravado his little dossier against God. But this Ivan was not capable of doing at this point in the novel. He first had to be an accomplice in the murder of his father, had to be brought by his complement, Smerdyakov, to see his complicity, and had to peer into the depths of his soul in the form of the devil, before there could be any hope that he might be reborn. As the novel closes we are left with the clear indication that that hope is a possibility. But we are also left with the insight that so long as a man remains in the world that possibility cannot be fully realized. Ultimately Dostoevsky's vision of secular life is supremely tragic.

## 4

The psychological and the metaphysical make up the concrete reality of Dostoevsky's human world. But the structure of that world and the values it embodies have only been referred to in passing, and the reader is entitled to ask what the critic takes them to be. Unfortunately a complete answer would require a study at least as long as the present; in the last few pages of this essay only a hasty sketch can be attempted.

By way of introduction let us note that Dostoevsky's great novels mirror comprehensively the bourgeois world of the nineteenth century, which is to say, a world in the first stages of an illness, which we today have the melancholy opportunity of seeing in a more advanced phase. Dostoevsky had a ground for optimism on which we cannot fall back: his faith that Zosima's "Russia" marked the direction toward which civilization would turn. But Rakitin and the other "Bernards" whom Dostoevsky dreaded have won, and the process by which man will destroy himself is already well under way. Thus the utopia of The Grand Inquisitor turns out to be a relatively pleasant morning dream as compared with the brave new world which our twentieth-century Bernards and Rakitins have begun to build. We are not going back to Zosima's "Russia," but to the world of Marx and Dewey. Shigalov was a poet whose prophecy fell too short. Dostoevsky feared Fourier and Claude Bernard; we face the realities of Dewey and Marx.

What Dostoevsky achieves is a definition of the destiny of Western man: he defines the alternatives and the corresponding values of each. Against the background of nineteenth-century humanity move the heroes of his books. In his inclusive world there is only one specimen lacking, the militant industrial proletariat, and the reason is that he did not have models of this type in his industrially backward native land. Saints, murderers, debauchees, intellectuals mad with pride, virginal whores and depraved ladies are the heroes. The mediocre, who lack the energy to become heroes, are pathetic rather than tragic, self-deceived rather than hypocritical, and unhappy, although ignorant of the malaise from which they suffer. Out of this mass emerge two groups of men who are in opposition: the saintly on the one side and those I have called "liberals" and the sensualists on the other. Zosima is Dostoevsky's outstanding religious character, but Dostoevsky "studies" the religious type as objectively as he studies the other, and unsparingly exhibits the pathological perversions to which it can lead. This group is not exclusively made up of monks or priests, but includes also self-deceived "ladies of little faith" and "peasant women who have faith." Alyosha, who is called the hero of the book, belongs to this group of course, but his portrait is not fully enough developed for us to be able to say whether in the two volumes that were never written, his role was to mediate between the world of Zosima and the secular world. Is it possible to live according to the teachings of Zosima outside the monastery? Could a Karamazov do it? Perhaps Alyosha can, although Prince Myshkin could not. We shall never know.

Between sensualists and liberals there is a formal identity of ends, since the sensualist uses his body as instrument of pleasure and the intellectual his mind. As between these two types of men it may be hard to choose; but Dostoevsky seems to reveal in a man like Rakitin a greater depth of villainy than in Fyodor, since he is the source of far-spreading corruption, while the power of evil of a man like Fyodor Karamazov is limited to himself and those he uses for his pleasure. The sensualist is consumed with self-hatred and shame, and his end is to destroy himself, but the intellectual, consumed with pride, seeks either to challenge God or to become God, and succeeds in wreaking havoc among men. Above the adult world is the world of the children, whom Dostoevsky could depict with inward fidelity, without sentimentality or condescension. Most of his children are lovable but some, like Kolya, have already begun to be corrupted, and some are full-blown little demons: Lise knows clearly that she loves evil and wants to destroy herself.

From Dostoevsky's novels, as I have insisted, one can neither abstract an ethical imperative nor a systematic philosophy capable of doing justice to the dramatic tensions to be found in life as he grasped it. A Marxist or a Deweyean will find that the picture of Zosima expresses the failure of nerve which he thinks characterizes our society. But there is no question that the picture painted by Dostoevsky, for all its dramatic irony, reveals a vision of the world in which the answer to Ivan is found in the love of Zosima. In other words, Dostoevsky views human destiny from the standpoint of an antirationalism which is more radical than that of Kierkegaard or Schopenhauer or Nietzsche. His rejection of "reason,"—"the stone wall constituted of the laws of nature, of the deductions of learning, and of the science of mathematics"—is clearly stated very early in his *Notes from the Underground*. But the full implications of "reason," and of his rejection of it, awaited the explorations which are to be found in his subsequent work, and particularly in the four major novels. It is his antirationalism which is the "source and head" of all his insights and attitudes, theological, psychological and political, and which therefore furnishes the ground on which he is often disposed of as a reactionary. That he should be dismissed in this way is intelligible; what is difficult to understand is how any serious reader can accept his psychological insights and simply ignore the matrix whence they rise and the theoretical and practical implications to which they lead. At a time when the conflict between "life" and "reason"—the reason of the stone wall—was not yet resolved, Dostoevsky, with full awareness of what he was doing, threw his lot on the side of life and against the stone wall. Old Karamazov is a depraved buffoon, shameless and corrupt; but there is a tremendous energy in him and love of life— the energy of the Karamazovs—and there is passion; there is something elemental in his sinfulness which flows whence all life, whether good or evil, flows, and which therefore draws our admiration since it is true, as Lise says, that in our secret hearts we all love evil. By contrast Rakitin is a thoroughly depraved and contemptible reptile with nothing to his favor. Thus the meaning of human destiny which Dostoevsky reveals is not difficult to formulate: a life not built on love is not human, and a world without God is a world in which a triumphant cannibal frees the mass from the burden of their freedom in exchange for happiness. What Dostoevsky could not admit to himself is that the Bernards in the not too long run will win. One may sympathize with the writer of the *Notes from the Underground* when he says, "I am not going to accept that wall merely because I have to run up against it, and have no means to knock it down." But one should not forget that the tragic alternative is ineluctable: either accept it or smash your head against it.

# Preface to Dostoevsky's
## *The Grand Inquisitor*

## *by D. H. Lawrence*

It is a strange experience, to examine one's reaction to a book over a period of years. I remember when I first read *The Brothers Karamazov,* in 1913, how fascinated yet unconvinced it left me. And I remember Middleton Murry[1] saying to me: "Of course the whole clue to Dostoevsky is in that Grand Inquisitor story." And I remember saying: "Why? It seems to me just rubbish."

And it was true. The story seemed to me just a piece of showing off: a display of cynical-satanical pose which was simply irritating. The cynical-satanical pose always irritated me, and I could see nothing else in that black-a-vised Grand Inquisitor talking at Jesus at such length. I just felt it was all pose; he didn't really mean what he said; he was just showing off in blasphemy.

Since then I have read *The Brothers Karamazov* twice, and each time found it more depressing because, alas, more drearily true to life. At first it had been lurid romance. Now I read *The Grand Inquisitor* once more, and my heart sinks right through my shoes. I still see a trifle of cynical-satanical showing off. But under that I hear the final and unanswerable criticism of Christ. And it is a deadly, devastating summing up, unanswerable because borne out by the long experience of humanity. It is reality versus illusion, and the illusion was Jesus', while time itself retorts with the reality.

If there is any question: Who is the Grand Inquisitor?—then surely we must say it is Ivan himself. And Ivan is the thinking mind of the human being in rebellion, thinking the whole thing out to the bitter end. As such he is, of course, identical with the Russian revolutionary of the thinking type. He is also, of course, Dostoevsky himself, in his thoughtful,

"Preface to Dostoevsky's *The Grand Inquisitor*." From *Selected Literary Criticism,* edited by Anthony Beal (New York: The Viking Press, Inc., 1961), pp. 233-241. Copyright © 1936 by Frieda Lawrence. Reprinted by permission of the Viking Press, Inc.
[1] Before this preface was published in *The Grand Inquisitor* the name of Katherine Mansfield was substituted for that of Middleton Murry.

as apart from his passional and inspirational self. Dostoevsky half hated Ivan. Yet, after all, Ivan is the greatest of the three brothers, pivotal. The passionate Dmitri and the inspired Alyosha are, at last, only offsets to Ivan.

And we cannot doubt that the Inquisitor speaks Dostoevsky's own final opinion about Jesus. The opinion is, baldly, this: Jesus, you are inadequate. Men must correct you. And Jesus in the end gives the kiss of acquiescence to the Inquisitor, as Alyosha does to Ivan. The two inspired ones recognize the inadequacy of their inspiration: the thoughtful one has to accept the responsibility of a complete adjustment.

We may agree with Dostoevsky or not, but we have to admit that his criticism of Jesus is the final criticism, based on the experience of two thousand years (he says fifteen hundred) and on a profound insight into the nature of mankind. Man can but be true to his own nature. No inspiration whatsoever will ever get him permanently beyond his limits.

And what are the limits? It is Dostoevsky's first profound question. What are the limits to the nature, not of Man in the abstract, but of men, mere men, everyday men?

The limits are, says the Grand Inquisitor, three. Mankind in the bulk can never be "free," because man on the whole makes three grand demands on life, and cannot endure unless these demands are satisfied.

1. He demands bread, and not merely as foodstuff, but as a miracle, given from the hand of God.
2. He demands mystery, the sense of the miraculous in life.
3. He demands somebody to bow down to, and somebody before whom all men shall bow down.

These three demands, for miracle, mystery and authority, prevent men from being "free." They are man's "weakness." Only a few men, the elect, are capable of abstaining from the absolute demand for bread, for miracle, mystery, and authority. These are the strong, and they must be as gods, to be able to be Christians fulfilling all the Christ-demand. The rest, the millions and millions of men throughout time, they are as babes or children or geese, they are too weak, "impotent, vicious, worthless, and rebellious" even to be able to share out the earthly bread, if it is left to them.

This, then, is the Grand Inquisitor's summing up of the nature of mankind. The inadequacy of Jesus lies in the fact that Christianity is too difficult for men, the vast mass of men. It could only be realized by the few "saints" or heroes. For the rest, man is like a horse harnessed to a load he cannot possibly pull. "Hadst Thou respected him less, Thou wouldst have demanded less of him, and that would be nearer to love, for his burden would be lighter."

Christianity, then, is the ideal, but it is impossible. It is impossible because it makes demands greater than the nature of man can bear. And therefore, to get a livable, working scheme, some of the elect, such as the Grand Inquisitor himself, have turned round to "him," that other great Spirit, Satan, and have established Church and State on "him." For the Grand Inquisitor finds that to be able to live at all, mankind must be loved more tolerantly and more contemptuously than Jesus loved it, loved, for all that, more truly, since it is loved for itself, for what it is, and not for what it ought to be. Jesus loved mankind for what it ought to be, free and limitless. The Grand Inquisitor loves it for what it is, with all its limitations. And he contends his is the kinder love. And yet he says it is Satan. And Satan, he says at the beginning, means annihilation, and not-being.

As always in Dostoevsky, the amazing perspicacity is mixed with ugly perversity. Nothing is pure. His wild love for Jesus is mixed with perverse and poisonous hate of Jesus: his moral hostility to the devil is mixed with secret worship of the devil. Dostoevsky is always perverse, always impure, always an evil thinker and a marvellous seer.

Is it true that mankind demands, and will always demand, miracle, mystery, and authority? Surely it is true. Today, man gets his sense of the miraculous from science and machinery, radio, airplanes, vast ships, zeppeline, poison gas, artificial silk: these things nourish man's sense of the miraculous as magic did in the past. But now, man is master of the mystery, there are no occult powers. The same with mystery: Medicine, biological experiment, strange feats of the psychic people, spiritualists, Christian scientists—it is all mystery. And as for authority, Russia destroyed the Tsar to have Lenin and the present mechanical despotism, Italy has the rationalized despotism of Mussolini, and England is longing for a despot.

Dostoevsky's diagnosis of human nature is simple and unanswerable. We have to submit, and agree that men are like that. Even over the question of sharing the bread, we have to agree that man is too weak, or vicious, or something, to be able to do it. He has to hand the common bread over to some absolute authority, Tsar or Lenin, to be shared out. And yet the mass of men are *incapable* of looking on bread as a mere means of sustenance, by which man sustains himself for the purpose of true living, true life being the "heavenly bread." It seems a strange thing that men, the mass of men, cannot understand that *life* is the great reality, that true living fills us with vivid life, "the heavenly bread," and earthly bread merely supports this. No, men cannot understand, never have understood that simple fact. They cannot see the distinction between bread, or property, money, and vivid life. They think that property and money are the same thing as vivid life. Only the few, the potential heroes or the "elect," can see the simple distinction. The mass *cannot* see it, and will never see it.

Dostoevsky was perhaps the first to realize this devastating truth, which Christ had not seen. A truth it is, none the less, and once recognized it will change the course of history. All that remains is for the elect to take charge of the bread—the property, the money—and then give it back to the masses as if it were really the gift of life. In this way, mankind might live happily, as the Inquisitor suggests. Otherwise, with the masses making the terrible mad mistake that money is life, and that therefore no one shall control the money, men shall be "free" to get what they can, we are brought to a condition of competitive insanity and ultimate suicide.

So far, well and good, Dostoevsky's diagnosis stands. But is it then to betray Christ and turn over to Satan if the elect should at last realize that instead of refusing Satan's three offers, the heroic Christian must now accept them? Jesus refused the three offers out of pride and fear: he wanted to be greater than these, and "above" them. But we now realize, no man, not even Jesus, is really "above" miracle, mystery, and authority. The one thing that Jesus is truly above, is the confusion between money and life. Money is not life, says Jesus, therefore you can ignore it and leave it to the devil.

Money is not life, it is true. But ignoring money and leaving it to the devil means handing over the great mass of men to the devil, for the mass of men *cannot* distinguish between money and life. It is hard to believe: certainly Jesus didn't believe it: and yet, as Dostoevsky and the Inquisitor point out, it is so.

Well, and what then? Must we therefore go over to the devil? After all, the whole of Christianity is not contained in the rejection of the three temptations. The essence of Christianity is a love of mankind. If a love of mankind entails accepting the bitter limitation of the mass of men, their inability to distinguish between money and life, then accept the limitation, and have done with it. Then take over from the devil the money (or bread), the miracle, and the sword of Caesar, and, for the love of mankind, give back to men the bread, with its wonder, and give them the miracle, the marvellous, and give them, in a hierarchy, someone, some men, in higher and higher degrees, to bow down to. Let them bow down, let them bow down *en masse,* for the mass, who do not understand the difference between money and life, should always bow down to the elect, who do.

And is that serving the devil? It is certainly not serving the spirit of annihilation and not-being. It is serving the great wholeness of mankind, and in that respect, it is Christianity. Anyhow, it is the service of Almighty God, who made men what they are, limited and unlimited.

Where Dostoevsky is perverse is in his making the old, old, wise governor of men a Grand Inquisitor. The recognition of the weakness of man has been a common trait in all great, wise rulers of people, from the Pharaohs and Darius through the great patient Popes of the early Church right down to the present day. They have known the weakness of men, and felt a certain tenderness. This is the spirit of all great government.

But it was not the spirit of the Spanish Inquisition. The Spanish Inquisition in 1500 was a newfangled thing, peculiar to Spain, with her curious death-lust and her bullying, and, strictly, a Spanish-political instrument, not Catholic at all, but rabidly national. The Spanish Inquisition was diabolic. It could not have produced a Grand Inquisitor who put Dostoevsky's sad question to Jesus. And the man who put those sad questions to Jesus could not possibly have been a Spanish Inquisitor. He could not possibly have burnt a hundred people in an *auto-da-fé*. He would have been too wise and far-seeing.

So that, in this respect, Dostoevsky showed his epileptic and slightly criminal perversity. The man who feels a certain tenderness for mankind in its weakness or limitation is not therefore diabolic. The man who realizes that Jesus asked too much of the mass of men, in asking them to choose between earthly and heavenly bread, and to judge between good and evil, is not therefore satanic. Think how difficult it is to know the difference between good and evil! Why, sometimes it is evil to be good. And how is the ordinary man to understand that? He can't. The extraordinary men have to understand it for him. And is that going over to the devil? Or think of the difficulty in choosing between the earthly and heavenly bread. Lenin, surely a pure soul, rose to great power simply to give men—what? The earthly bread. And what was the result? Not only did they lose the heavenly bread, but even the earthly bread disappeared out of wheat-producing Russia. It is most strange. And all the socialists and the generous thinkers of today, what are they striving for? The same: to share out more evenly the earthly bread. Even *they,* who are practicing Christianity *par excellence,* cannot properly choose between the heavenly and earthly bread. For the poor, they choose the earthly bread, and once more the heavenly bread is lost: and once more, as soon as it is really chosen, the earthly bread begins to disappear. It is a great mystery. But today, the most passionate believers in Christ believe that all you have to do is to struggle to give earthly bread (good houses, good sanitation, etc.) to the poor, and that is in itself the heavenly bread. But it isn't. Especially for the poor, it isn't. It is for them the loss of heavenly bread. And the poor are the vast majority. Poor things, how everybody hates them today! For benevolence is a form of hate.

What then is the heavenly bread? Every generation must answer for itself. But the heavenly bread is life, is living. Whatever makes life vivid and delightful is the heavenly bread. And the earthly bread must come as a by-product of the heavenly bread. The vast mass will never understand this. Yet it is the essential truth of Christianity, and of life itself. The few will understand. Let them take the responsibility.

Again, the Inquisitor says that it is a weakness in men, that they must have miracle, mystery, and authority. But is it? Are they not bound up in our emotions, always and for ever, these three demands of miracle, mystery, and authority? If Jesus cast aside miracle in the Temptation, still there is miracle again in the Gospels. And if Jesus refused the earthly bread, still he said: "In my Father's house are many mansions." And for authority: "Why call ye me Lord, Lord, and do not the things which I say?"

The thing Jesus was trying to do was to supplant physical emotion by moral emotion. So that earthly bread becomes, in a sense, immoral, as it is to many refined people today. The Inquisitor sees that this is the mistake. The earthly bread must in itself be the miracle, and be bound up with the miracle.

And here, surely, he is right. Since man began to think and to feel vividly, seed-time and harvest have been the two great sacred periods of miracle, rebirth, and rejoicing. Easter and harvest-home are festivals of the earthly bread, and they are festivals which go to the roots of the soul. For it is the earthly bread as a miracle, a yearly miracle. All the old religions saw it: the Catholic still sees it, by the Mediterranean. And this is not weakness. This is *truth*. The rapture of the Easter kiss, in old Russia, is intimately bound up with the springing of the seed and the first footstep of the new earthly bread. It is the rapture of the Easter kiss which makes the bread worth eating. It is the absence of the Easter kiss which makes the Bolshevist bread barren, dead. They eat dead bread, now.

The earthly bread is leavened with the heavenly bread. The heavenly bread is life, is contact, and is consciousness. In sowing the seed man has his contact with earth, with sun and rain: and he *must not* break the contact. In the awareness of the springing of the corn he has his ever-renewed consciousness of miracle, wonder, and mystery: the wonder of creation, procreation, and re-creation, following the mystery of death and the cold grave. It is the grief of Holy Week and the delight of Easter Sunday. And man must not, must not lose this supreme state of consciousness out of himself, or he has lost the best part of him. Again, the reaping and the harvest are another contact, with earth and sun, a rich touch of the cosmos, a living stream of activity, and then the contact with harvesters, and the joy of harvest-home. All this is life, life, it is the heavenly bread which we eat in the course of getting the earthly bread. Work is, or should be, our heavenly bread of activity, contact and consciousness. All work that it not this, is anathema. True, the work is hard; there is the sweat of the brow. But what of it? In decent proportion, this is life. The sweat of the brow is the heavenly butter.

I think the older Egyptians understood this, in the course of their long and marvellous history. I think that probably, for thousands of years, the masses of the Egyptians were happy, in the hierarchy of the State.

Miracle and mystery run together, they merge. Then there is the third thing, authority. The word is bad: a policeman has authority, and no one bows down to him. The Inquisitor means: "that which men bow down to." Well, they bowed down to Caesar, and they bowed down to

Jesus. They will bow down, first, as the Inquisitor saw, to the one who has the power to control the bread.

The bread, the earthly bread, while it is being reaped and grown, it is life. But once it is harvested and stored, it becomes a commodity, it becomes riches. And then it becomes a danger. For men think, if they only possessed the hoard, they need not work; which means, really, they need not live. And that is the real blasphemy. For while we live we must live, we must not wither or rot inert.

So that ultimately men bow down to the man, or group of men, who can and dare take over the hoard, the store of bread, the riches, to distribute it among the people again. The lords, the givers of bread. How profound Dostoevsky is when he says that the people will forget that it is their own bread which is being given back to them. While they keep their own bread, it is not much better than stone to them—inert possessions. But given back to them from the great Giver, it is divine once more, it has the quality of miracle to make it taste well in the mouth and in the belly.

Men bow down to the lord of bread, first and foremost. For, by knowing the difference between earthly and heavenly bread, he is able calmly to distribute the earthly bread, and to give it, for the commonalty, the heavenly taste which they can never give it. That is why, in a democracy, the earthly bread loses its taste, the salt loses its savor, and there is no one to bow down to.

It is not man's weakness that he needs someone to bow down to. It is his nature, and his strength, for it puts him into touch with far, far greater life than if he stood alone. All life bows to the sun. But the sun is very far away to the common man. It needs someone to bring it to him. It needs a lord: what the Christians call one of the elect, to bring the sun to the common man, and put the sun in his heart. The sight of a true lord, a noble, a nature-hero puts the sun into the heart of the ordinary man, who is no hero, and therefore cannot know the sun direct.

This is one of the real mysteries. As the Inquisitor says, the mystery of the elect is one of the inexplicable mysteries of Christianity, just as the lord, the natural lord among men, is one of the inexplicable mysteries of humanity throughout time. We must accept the mystery, that's all.

But to do so is not diabolic.

And Ivan need not have been so tragic and satanic. He had made a discovery about men, which was due to be made. It was the rediscovery of a fact which was known universally almost till the end of the eighteenth century, when the illusion of the perfectibility of men, of all men, took hold of the imagination of the civilized nations. It was an illusion. And Ivan has to make a restatement of the old truth, that most men *cannot* choose between good and evil, because it is so extremely difficult to know which is which, especially in crucial cases: and that most men *cannot* see the difference between life-values and money-values: they can only see money-values; even nice simple people who *live* by the life-values, kind and natural, yet can only estimate value in terms of money. So let the specially gifted few make the decision between good and evil, and establish the life-values against the money-values. And let the many accept the decision, with gratitude, and bow down to the few, in the hierarchy. What is there diabolical or satanic in that? Jesus kisses the Inquisitor: Thank you, you are right, wise old man! Alyosha kisses Ivan: Thank you, brother, you are right, you take a burden off me! So why should Dostoevsky drag in Inquisitors and *autos-da-fé,* and Ivan wind up so morbidly suicidal? Let them be glad they've found the truth again.

# Dostoevsky and Parricide

## by Sigmund Freud

Four facets may be distinguished in the rich personality of Dostoevsky: the creative artist, the neurotic, the moralist and the sinner. How is one to find one's way in this bewildering complexity?

The creative artist is the least doubtful: Dostoevsky's place is not far behind Shakespeare. *The Brothers Karamazov* is the most magnificent novel ever written; the episode of the Grand Inquisitor, one of the peaks in the literature of the world, can hardly be valued too highly. Before the problem of the creative artist analysis must, alas, lay down its arms.

The moralist in Dostoevsky is the most readily assailable. If we seek to rank him high as a moralist on the plea that only a man who has gone through the depths of sin can reach the highest summit of morality, we are neglecting a doubt that arises. A moral man is one who reacts to temptation as soon as he feels it in his heart, without yielding to it. A man who alternately sins and then in his remorse erects high moral standards lays himself open to the reproach that he has made things too easy for himself. He has not achieved the essence of morality, renunciation, for the moral conduct of life is a practical human interest. He reminds one of the barbarians of the great migrations, who murdered and did penance for it, till penance became an actual technique for enabling murder to be done. Ivan the Terrible behaved in exactly this way; indeed this compromise with morality is a characteristic Russian trait. Nor was the final outcome of Dostoevsky's moral strivings anything very glorious. After the most violent struggles to reconcile the instinctual demands of the individual with the claims of the community, he landed in the retrograde position of submission both to temporal and spiritual authority, of veneration both for the Tsar and for the God of the Christians, and of a narrow Russian nationalism—a position which lesser minds have reached with smaller effort. This is the weak point in that great personality. Dostoevsky threw away the chance of becoming a

"Dostoevsky and Parricide." From the *Standard Edition of the Collected Psychological Works* edited by James Strachey (London: Hogarth Press, 1961), Vol. XXI, pp. 177-94. Translated by D. F. Tait, revised by J. Strachey. Reprinted by permission of the Hogarth Press and Basic Books, Inc.

teacher and liberator of humanity and made himself one with their gaolers. The future of human civilization will have little to thank him for. It seems probable that he was condemned to this failure by his neurosis. The greatness of his intelligence and the strength of his love for humanity might have opened to him another, an apostolic, way of life.

To consider Dostoevsky as a sinner or a criminal rouses violent opposition, which need not be based upon a philistine assessment of criminals. The real motive for this opposition soon becomes apparent. Two traits are essential in a criminal: boundless egoism and a strong destructive urge. Common to both of these, and a necessary condition for their expression, is absence of love, lack of an emotional appreciation of (human) objects. One at once recalls the contrast to this presented by Dostoevsky —his great need of love and his enormous capacity for love, which is to be seen in manifestations of exaggerated kindness and caused him to love and to help where he had a right to hate and to be revengeful, as, for example, in his relations with his first wife and her lover. That being so, it must be asked why there is any temptation to reckon Dostoevsky among the criminals. The answer is that it comes from his choice of material, which singles out from all others violent, murderous and egoistic characters, thus pointing to the existence of similar tendencies within himself, and also from certain facts in his life, like his passion for gambling and his possible confession to a sexual assault upon a young girl.[1] The contradiction is resolved by the realization that Dostoevsky's very strong destructive instinct, which might easily have made him a criminal, was in his actual life directed mainly against his own person (inward instead of outward) and thus found expression as masochism and a sense of guilt. Nevertheless, his personality retained sadistic traits in plenty, which show themselves in his irritability, his love of tormenting and his intolerance even towards people he loved, and which appear also in the way in which, as an author, he treats his readers. Thus in little things he was a sadist towards others, and in bigger things a sadist towards himself, in fact a masochist—that is to say the mildest, kindliest, most helpful person possible.

We have selected three factors from Dostoevsky's complex personality, one quantitative and two qualitative: the extraordinary intensity of his emotional life, his perverse innate instinctual disposition, which inevitably marked him out to be a sado-masochist or a criminal, and his unanalyzable artistic gift. This combination might very well exist without

[1] See the discussion of this in Fülöp-Miller and Eckstein (1926). Stefan Zweig (1920) writes: "He was not halted by the barriers of bourgeois morality; and no one can say exactly how far he transgressed the bounds of law in his own life or how much of the criminal instincts of his heroes was realized in himself." For the intimate connection between Dostoevsky's characters and his own experiences, see René Fülöp-Miller's remarks in the introductory section of Fülöp-Miller and Eckstein (1925), which are based upon N. Strakhov [1921].

neurosis; there are people who are complete masochists without being neurotic. Nevertheless, the balance of forces between his instinctual demands and the inhibitions opposing them (plus the available methods of sublimation) would even so make it necessary to classify Dostoevsky as what is known as an "instinctual character." But the position is obscured by the simultaneous presence of neurosis, which, as we have said, was not in the circumstances inevitable, but which comes into being the more readily, the richer the complication which has to be mastered by the ego. For neurosis is after all only a sign that the ego has not succeeded in making a synthesis, that in attempting to do so it has forfeited its unity.

How then, strictly speaking, does his neurosis show itself? Dostoevsky called himself an epileptic, and was regarded as such by other people, on account of his severe attacks, which were accompanied by loss of consciousness, muscular convulsions, and subsequent depressions. Now it is highly probable that this so-called epilepsy was only a symptom of his neurosis and must accordingly be classified as hystero-epilepsy—that is, as severe hysteria. We cannot be completely certain on this point for two reasons—firstly, because the anamnestic data on Dostoevsky's alleged epilepsy are defective and untrustworthy, and secondly, because our understanding of pathological states combined with epileptiform attacks is imperfect.

To take the second point first. It is unnecessary here to reproduce the whole pathology of epilepsy, for it would throw no decisive light on the problem. But this may be said. The old *morbus sacer* is still in evidence as an ostensible clinical entity, the uncanny disease with its incalculable, apparently unprovoked convulsive attacks, its changing of the character into irritability and aggressiveness, and its progressive lowering of all the mental faculties. But the outlines of this picture are quite lacking in precision. The attacks, so savage in their onset, accompanied by biting of the tongue and incontinence of urine and working up to the dangerout *status epilepticus* with its risk of severe self-injuries, may, nevertheless, be reduced to brief periods of *absence,* or rapidly passing fits of vertigo or may be replaced by short spaces of time during which the patient does something out of character, as though he were under the control of his unconscious. These attacks, though as a rule determined, in a way we do not understand, by purely physical causes, may nevertheless owe their first appearance to some purely mental cause (a fright, for instance) or may react in other respects to mental excitations. However characteristic intellectual impairment may be in the overwhelming majority of cases, at least *one* case is known to us (that of Helmholtz) in which the affliction did not interfere with the highest intellectual achievement. (Other cases of which the same assertion has been made are either disputable or open to the same doubts as the case of Dostoevsky himself.) People who are victims of epilepsy may give an impression of dullness and arrested development just as the disease often accompanies the most palpable idiocy and the grossest cerebral defects, even though not as a necessary component of the clinical picture. But these attacks, with all their variations, also occur in other people who display complete mental development and, if anything, an excessive and as a rule insufficiently controlled emotional life. It is no wonder in these circumstances that it has been found impossible to maintain that "epilepsy" is a single clinical entity. The similarity that we find in the manifest symptoms seems to call for a functional view of them. It is as though a mechanism for abnormal instinctual discharge had been laid down organically, which could be made use of in quite different circumstances—both in the case of disturbances of cerebral activity due to severe histolytic or toxic affections, and also in the case of inadequate control over the mental economy and at times when the activity of the energy operating in the mind reaches crisis-pitch. Behind this dichotomy we have a glimpse of the identity of the underlying mechanism of instinctual discharge. Nor can that mechanism stand remote from the sexual processes, which are fundamentally of toxic origin: the earliest physicians described coition as a minor epilepsy, and thus recognized in the sexual act a mitigation and adaptation of the epileptic method of discharging stimuli.

The "epileptic reaction," as this common element may be called, is also undoubtedly at the disposal of the neurosis whose essence it is to get rid by somatic means of amounts of excitation which it cannot deal with psychically. Thus the epileptic attack becomes a symptom of hysteria and is adapted and modified by it just as it is by the normal sexual process of discharge. It is therefore quite right to distinguish between an organic and an "affective" epilepsy. The practical significance of this is that a person who suffers from the first kind has a disease of the brain, while a person who suffers from the second kind is a neurotic. In the first case his mental life is subjected to an alien disturbance from without, in the second case the disturbance is an expression of his mental life itself.

It is extremely probable that Dostoevsky's epilepsy was of the second kind. This cannot, strictly speaking, be proved. To do so we should have to be in a position to insert the first appearance of the attacks and their subsequent fluctuations into the thread of his mental life; and for that we know too little. The descriptions of the attacks themselves teach us nothing and our information about the relations between them and Dostoevsky's experiences is defective and often contradictory. The most probable assumption is that the attacks went back far into his childhood, that their place was taken to begin with by milder symptoms and that they did not assume an epileptic form until after the shattering experience of his eighteenth year—the murder of his father.[2] It would be very

---

[2] See René Fülöp-Miller (1924). Of especial interest is the information that in the novelist's childhood "something terrible, unforgettable and agonizing" happened, to

much to the point if it could be established that they ceased completely during his exile in Siberia, but other accounts contradict this.[3]

The unmistakable connection between the murder of the father in *The Brothers Karamazov* and the fate of Dostoevsky's own father has struck more than one of his biographers, and has led them to refer to "a certain modern school of psychology." From the standpoint of psychoanalysis (for that is what is meant), we are tempted to see in that event the severest trauma and to regard Dostoevsky's reaction to it as the turning point of his neurosis. But if I undertake to substantiate this view psychoanalytically, I shall have to risk the danger of being unintelligible to all those readers who are unfamiliar with the language and theories of psychoanalysis.

We have one certain starting point. We know the meaning of the first attacks from which Dostoevsky suffered in his early years, long before the incidence of the "epilepsy." These attacks had the significance of death: they were heralded by a fear of death and consisted of lethargic, somnolent states. The illness first came over him while he was still a boy, in the form of a sudden, groundless melancholy, a feeling, as he later told his friend Solovyov, as though he were going to die on the spot. And there in fact followed a state exactly similar to real death. His brother Andrey tells us that even when he was quite young Fyodor used to leave little notes about before he went to sleep, saying that he was afraid he might fall into this death-like sleep during the night and therefore begged that his burial should be postponed for five days. (Fülöp-Miller and Eckstein, 1925, lx).

We know the meaning and intention of such deathlike attacks. They signify an identification with a dead person, either with someone who is really dead or with someone who is still alive and whom the subject wishes dead. The latter case is the more significant. The attack then has the value of a punishment. One has wished another person dead, and

---

which the first signs of his illness were to be traced (from an article by Suvorin in the newspaper *Novoe Vremya*, 1881, quoted in the introduction to Fülöp-Miller and Eckstein, 1925, xlv). See also Orest Miller (1921, 140): "There is, however, another special piece of evidence about Fyodor Mikhailovich's illness, which relates to his earliest youth and brings the illness into connection with a tragic event in the family life of his parents. But, although this piece of evidence was given to me orally by one who was a close friend of Fyodor Mikhailovich, I cannot bring myself to reproduce it fully and precisely since I have had no confirmation of this rumor from any other quarter." Biographers and scientific research workers cannot feel grateful for this discretion.

[3] Most of the accounts, including Dostoevsky's own, assert on the contrary that the illness only assumed its final, epileptic character during the Siberian exile. Unfortunately there is reason to distrust the autobiographical statements of neurotics. Experience shows that their memories introduce falsifications which are designed to interrupt disagreeable causal connections. Nevertheless, it appears certain that Dostoevsky's detention in the Siberian prison markedy altered his pathological condition. Cf. Fülöp-Miller (1924, 1186).

now one *is* this other person and is dead oneself. At this point psycho-analytical theory brings in the assertion that for a boy this other person is usually his father and that the attack (which is termed hysterical) is thus a self-punishment for a death-wish against a hated father.

Parricide, according to a well-known view, is the principal and primal crime of humanity as well as of the individual. (See my *Totem and Taboo*, 1912-13). It is in any case the main source of the sense of guilt, though we do not know if it is the only one: researches have not yet been able to establish with certainty the mental origin of guilt and the need for expiation. But it is not necessary for it to be the only one. The psychological situation is complicated and requires elucidation. The rela-tion of a boy to his father is, as we say, an "ambivalent" one. In addition to the hate which seeks to get rid of the father as a rival, a measure of tenderness for him is also habitually present. The two attitudes of mind combine to produce identification with the father; the boy wants to be in his father's place because he admires him and wants to be like him, and also because he wants to put him out of the way. This whole devel-opment now comes up against a powerful obstacle. At a certain moment the child comes to understand that an attempt to remove his father as a rival would be punished by him with castration. So from fear of castra-tion—that is, in the interests of preserving his masculinity—he gives up his wish to possess his mother and get rid of his father. In so far as this wish remains in the unconscious it forms the basis of the sense of guilt. We believe that what we have here been describing are normal proc-esses, the normal fate of the so-called "Oedipus complex"; nevertheless it requires an important amplification.

A further complication arises when the constitutional factor we call bisexuality is comparatively strongly developed in a child. For then, under the threat to the boy's masculinity by castration, his inclination becomes strengthened to diverge in the direction of femininity, to put himself instead in his mother's place and take over her role as object of his father's love. But the fear of castration makes *this* solution impos-sible as well. The boy understands that he must also submit to castration if he wants to be loved by his father as a woman. Thus both impulses, hatred of the father and being in love with the father, undergo repres-sion. There is a certain psychological distinction in the fact that the hatred of the father is given up on account of fear of an *external* danger (castration), while the being in love with the father is treated as an *internal* instinctual danger, though fundamentally it goes back to the same external danger.

What makes hatred of the father unacceptable is *fear* of the father; castration is terrible, whether as a punishment or as the price of love. Of the two factors which repress hatred of the father, the first, the direct fear of punishment and castration, may be called the normal one; its pathogenic intensification seems to come only with the addition of the second factor, the fear of the feminine attitude. Thus a strong innate bisexual disposition becomes one of the preconditions or reinforcements of neurosis. Such a disposition must certainly be assumed in Dostoevsky, and it shows itself in a viable form (as latent homosexuality) in the important part played by male friendships in his life, in his strangely tender attitude towards rivals in love and in his remarkable understanding of situations which are explicable only by repressed homosexuality, as many examples from his novels show.

I am sorry, though I cannot alter the facts, if this exposition of the attitudes of hatred and love towards the father and their transformations under the influence of the threat of castration seems to readers unfamiliar with psychoanalysis unsavory and incredible. I should myself expect that it is precisely the castration complex that would be bound to arouse the most general repudiation. But I can only insist that psychoanalytic experience has put these matters in particular beyond the reach of doubt and has taught us to recognize in them the key to every neurosis. This key, then, we must apply to our author's so-called epilepsy. So alien to our consciousness are the things by which our unconscious mental life is governed!

But what has been said so far does not exhaust the consequences of the repression of the hatred of the father in the Oedipus complex. There is something fresh to be added: namely that in spite of everything the identification with the father finally makes a permanent place for itself in the ego. It is received into the ego, but establishes itself there as a separate agency in contrast to the rest of the content of the ego. We then give it the name of *super-ego* and ascribe to it, the inheritor of the parental influence, the most important functions. If the father was hard, violent, and cruel, the super-ego takes over those attributes from him and, in the relations between the ego and it, the passivity which was supposed to have been repressed is re-established. The super-ego has become sadistic, and the ego becomes masochistic—that is to say, at bottom passive in a feminine way. A great need for punishment develops in the ego, which in part offers itself as a victim to Fate, and in part finds satisfaction in ill-treatment by the super-ego (that is, in the sense of guilt). For every punishment is ultimately castration and, as such, a fulfilment of the old passive attitude towards the father. Even Fate is, in the last resort, only a later projection of the father.

The normal processes in the formation of conscience must be similar to the abnormal ones described here. We have not yet succeeded in fixing the boundary line between them. It will be observed that here the largest share in the outcome is ascribed to the passive component of repressed femininity. In addition, it must be of importance as an accidental factor whether the father, who is feared in any case, is also especially violent in reality. This was true in Dostoevsky's case, and we can trace back the fact of his extraordinary sense of guilt and of his masochistic conduct of life to a specially strong feminine component. Thus the formula for Dostoevsky is as follows: a person with a specially strong innate bisexual disposition, who can defend himself with special intensity against dependence on a specially severe father. This characteristic of bisexuality comes as an addition to the components of his nature that we have already recognized. His early symptoms of deathlike attacks can thus be understood as a father-identification on the part of his ego, which is permitted by his super-ego as a punishment. "You wanted to kill your father in order to be your father yourself. Now you *are* your father, but a dead father"—the regular mechanism of hysterical symptoms. And further: "Now your father is killing *you*." For the ego the death symptom is a satisfaction in phantasy of the masculine wish and at the same time a masochistic satisfaction; for the super-ego it is a punitive satisfaction—that is, a sadistic satisfaction. Both of them, the ego and the super-ego, carry on the role of father.

To sum up, the relation between the subject and his father-object, while retaining its content, has been transformed into a relation between the ego and the super-ego—a new setting on a fresh stage. Infantile reactions from the Oedipus complex such as these may disappear if reality gives them no further nourishment. But the father's character remained the same, or rather, it deteriorated with the years, and thus Dostoevsky's hatred for his father and his death-wish against that wicked father were maintained. Now it is a dangerous thing if reality fulfills such repressed wishes. The phantasy has become reality and all defensive measures are thereupon reinforced. Dostoevsky's attacks now assumed an epileptic character; they still undoubtedly signified an identification with his father as a punishment, but they had become terrible, like his father's frightful death itself. What further content they had absorbed, particularly what sexual content, escapes conjecture.

One thing is remarkable: in the aura of the epileptic attack, one moment of supreme bliss is experienced. This may very well be a record of the triumph and sense of liberation felt on hearing the news of the death, to be followed immediately by an all the more cruel punishment. We have divined just such a sequence of triumph and mourning, of festive joy and mourning, in the brothers of the primal horde who murdered their father, and we find it repeated in the ceremony of the totem meal.[4] If it proved to be the case that Dostoevsky was free from his attacks in Siberia, that would merely substantiate the view that they were his punishment. He did not need them any longer when he was being punished in another way. But that cannot be proved. Rather does this necessity for punishment on the part of Dostoevsky's mental economy explain the fact that he passed unbroken through these years of misery and humiliation. Dostoevsky's condemnation as a political prisoner

[4] See *Totem and Taboo* [(1912-13), Section 5 of Essay IV, Standard Ed., 13, 140].

was unjust and he must have known it, but he accepted the undeserved punishment at the hands of the Little Father, the Tsar, as a substitute for the punishment he deserved for his sin against his real father. Instead of punishing himself, he got himself punished by his father's deputy. Here we have a glimpse of the psychological justification of the punishments inflicted by society. It is a fact that large groups of criminals want to be punished. Their super-ego demands it and so saves itself the necessity for inflicting the punishment itself.

Everyone who is familiar with the complicated transformation of meaning undergone by hysterical symptoms will understand that no attempt can be made here to follow out the meaning of Dostoevsky's attacks beyond this beginning.[5] It is enough that we may assume that their original meaning remained unchanged behind all later accretions. We can safely say that Dostoevsky never got free from the feelings of guilt arising from his intention of murdering his father. They also determined his attitude in the two other spheres in which the father-relation is the decisive factor, his attitude towards the authority of the State and towards belief in God. In the first of these he ended up with complete submission to his Little Father, the Tsar, who had once performed with him in *reality* the comedy of killing which his attacks had so often represented in *play*. Here penitence gained the upper hand. In the religious sphere he retained more freedom: according to apparently trustworthy reports he wavered, up to the last moment of his life, between faith and atheism. His great intellect made it impossible for him to overlook any of the intellectual difficulties to which faith leads. By an individual recapitulation of a development in world-history he hoped to find a way out and a liberation from guilt in the Christ ideal, and even to make use of his sufferings as a claim to be playing a Christ-like role. If on the whole he did not achieve freedom and became a reactionary, that was because the filial guilt, which is present in human beings generally and on which religious feeling is built, had in him attained a super-individual intensity and remained insurmountable even to his great intelligence. In writing this we are laying ourselves open to the charge of having abandoned the impartiality of analysis and of subjecting Dostoevsky to judgements that can only be justified from the partisan standpoint of a particular *Weltanschauung*. A conservative would take the side of the Grand Inquisitor and would judge Dostoevsky differently. The objection is just; and one can only say in extenuation that Dostoevsky's decision has every

[5] The best account of the meaning and content of his attacks was given by Dostoevsky himself, when he told his friend Strakhov that his irritability and depression after an epileptic attack were due to the fact that he seemed to himself a criminal and could not get rid of the feeling that he had a burden of unknown guilt upon him, that he had committed some great misdeed, which oppressed him. (Fülöp-Miller, 1924, 1188.) In self-accusations like these psychoanalysis sees signs of a recognition of "psychical reality," and it endeavors to make the unknown guilt known to consciousness.

appearance of having been determined by an intellectual inhibition due to his neurosis.

It can scarcely be owing to chance that three of the masterpieces of the literature of all time—the *Oedipus Rex* of Sophocles, Shakespeare's *Hamlet* and Dostoevsky's *The Brothers Karamazov*—should all deal with the same subject: parricide. In all three, moreover, the motive for the deed, sexual rivalry for a woman, is laid bare.

The most straightforward is certainly the representation in the drama derived from the Greek legend. In this it is still the hero himself who commits the crime. But poetic treatment is impossible without softening and disguise. The naked admission of an intention to commit parricide, as we arrive at it in analysis, seems intolerable without analytic preparation. The Greek drama, while retaining the crime, introduces the indispensable toning-down in a masterly fashion by projecting the hero's unconscious motive into reality in the form of a compulsion by a destiny which is alien to him. The hero commits the deed unintentionally and apparently uninfluenced by the woman; this latter element is however taken into account in the circumstance that the hero can only obtain possession of the queen mother after he has repeated his deed upon the monster who symbolizes the father. After his guilt has been revealed and made conscious, the hero makes no attempt to exculpate himself by appealing to the artificial expedient of the compulsion of destiny. His crime is acknowledged and punished as though it were a full and conscious one—which is bound to appear unjust to our reason, but which psychologically is perfectly correct.

In the English play the presentation is more indirect; the hero does not commit the crime himself; it is carried out by someone else, for whom it is not parricide. The forbidden motive of sexual rivalry for the woman does not need, therefore, to be disguised. Moreover, we see the hero's Oedipus complex, as it were, in a reflected light, by learning the effect upon him of the other's crime. He ought to avenge the crime, but finds himself, strangely enough, incapable of doing so. We know that it is his sense of guilt that is paralyzing him; but, in a manner entirely in keeping with neurotic processes, the sense of guilt is displaced on to the perception of his inadequacy for fulfilling his task. There are signs that the hero feels this guilt as a super-individual one. He despises others no less than himself: "Use every man after his desert, and who should 'scape whipping?"

The Russian novel goes a step further in the same direction. There also the murder is committed by someone else. This other person, however, stands to the murdered man in the same filial relation as the hero, Dmitri; in whose case the motive of sexual rivalry is openly admitted: the murderer is a brother of the hero's, and it is a remarkable fact that Dostoevsky has attributed to him his own illness, the alleged epilepsy, as though he were seeking to confess that the epileptic, the neurotic, in himself was a parricide. Then, again, in the speech for the defence at the trial, there is the famous mockery of psychology—it is a "knife that cuts both ways":[6] a splendid piece of disguise, for we have only to reverse it in order to discover the deepest meaning of Dostoevsky's view of things. It is not psychology that deserves the mockery, but the procedure of judicial enquiry. It is a matter of indifference who actually committed the crime; psychology is only concerned to know who desired it emotionally and who welcomed it when it was done. And for that reason all of the brothers, except the contrasted figure of Alyosha, are equally guilty— the impulsive sensualist, the sceptical cynic and the epileptic criminal. In *The Brothers Karamazov* there is one particularly revealing scene. In the course of his talk with Dmitri, Father Zosima recognizes that Dmitri is prepared to commit parricide, and he bows down at his feet. It is impossible that this can be meant as an expression of admiration; it must mean that the holy man is rejecting the temptation to despise or detest the murderer and for that reason humbles himself before him. Dostoevsky's sympathy for the criminal is, in fact, boundless; it goes far beyond the pity which the unhappy wretch has a right to, and reminds us of the "holy awe" with which epileptics and lunatics were regarded in the past. A criminal is to him almost a Redeemer, who has taken on himself the guilt which must else have been borne by others. There is no longer any need for one to murder, since *he* has already murdered; and one must be grateful to him, for, except for him, one would have been obliged oneself to murder. That is not kindly pity alone, it is identification on the basis of similar murderous impulses— in fact, a slightly displaced narcissism. (In saying this, we are not disputing the ethical value of this kindliness.) This may perhaps be quite generally the mechanism of kindly sympathy with other people, a mechanism which one can discern with especial ease in this extreme case of a guilt-ridden novelist. There is no doubt that this sympathy by identification was a decisive factor in determining Dostoevsky's choice of material. He dealt first with the common criminal (whose motives are egotistical) and the political and religious criminal; and not until the end of his life did he come back to the primal criminal, the parricide, and use him, in a work of art, for making his confession.

The publication of Dostoevsky's posthumous papers and of his wife's diaries has thrown a glaring light on one episode in his life, namely the period in Germany when he was obsessed with a mania for gambling (cf. Fülöp-Miller and Eckstein, 1925), which no one could regard as anything but an unmistakable fit of pathological passion. There was no lack of rationalizations for this remarkable and unworthy behavior. As

---

[6] In the German (and in the original Russian) the simile is "a stick with two ends." The "knife that cuts both ways" is derived from Constance Garnett's English translation. The phrase occurs in Book XII, Chapter X, of the novel.

often happens with neurotics, Dostoevsky's sense of guilt had taken a tangible shape as a burden of debt, and he was able to take refuge behind the pretext that he was trying by his winnings at the tables to make it possible for him to return to Russia without being arrested by his creditors. But this was no more than a pretext and Dostoevsky was acute enough to recognize the fact and honest enough to admit it. He knew that the chief thing was gambling for its own sake—*le jeu pour le jeu*.[7] All the details of his impulsively irrational conduct show this and something more besides. He never rested until he had lost everything. For him gambling was a method of self-punishment as well. Time after time he gave his young wife his promise or his word of honor not to play any more or not to play any more on that particular day; and, as she says, he almost always broke it. When his losses had reduced himself and her to the direst need, he derived a second pathological satisfaction from that. He could then scold and humiliate himself before her, invite her to despise him and to feel sorry that she had married such an old sinner; and when he had thus unburdened his conscience, the whole business would begin again next day. His young wife accustomed herself to this cycle, for she had noticed that the one thing which offered any real hope of salvation—his literary production—never went better than when they had lost everything and pawned their last possessions. Naturally she did not understand the connection. When his sense of guilt was satisfied by the punishments he had inflicted on himself, the inhibition upon his work became less severe and he allowed himself to take a few steps along the road to success.[8]

What part of a gambler's long-buried childhood is it that forces its way to repetition in his obsession for play? The answer may be divined without difficulty from a story by one of our younger writers. Stefan Zweig, who has incidentally devoted a study to Dostoevsky himself (1920), has included in his collection of three stories *Die Verwirrung der Gefühle* [*Confusion of Feelings*] (1927) one which he calls *"Vierundzwanzig Stunden aus dem Leben einer Frau"* ["Four-and-Twenty Hours in a Woman's Life"]. This little masterpiece ostensibly sets out only to show what an irresponsible creature woman is, and to what excesses, surprising even to herself, an unexpected experience may drive her. But the story tells far more than this. If it is subjected to an analytical interpretation, it will be found to represent (without any apologetic intent) something quite different, something universally human, or rather something mas-

[7] "The main thing is the play itself," he writes in one of his letters, "I swear that greed for money has nothing to do with it, although Heaven knows I am sorely in need of money."

[8] "He always remained at the gaming tables till he had lost everything and was totally ruined. It was only when the damage was quite complete that the demon at last retired from his soul and made way for the creative genius." (Fülöp-Miller and Eckstein, 1925, lxxxvi.)

culine. And such an interpretation is so extremely obvious that it cannot be resisted. It is characteristic of the nature of artistic creation that the author, who is a personal friend of mine, was able to assure me, when I asked him, that the interpretation which I put to him had been completely strange to his knowledge and intention, although some of the details woven into the narrative seemed expressly designed to give a clue to the hidden secret.

In this story, an elderly lady of distinction tells the author about an experience she has had more than twenty years earlier. She has been left a widow when still young and is the mother of two sons, who no longer need her. In her forty-second year, expecting nothing further of life, she happens, on one of her aimless journeyings, to visit the Rooms at Monte Carlo. There, among all the remarkable impressions which the place produces, she is soon fascinated by the sight of a pair of hands which seem to betray all the feelings of the unlucky gambler with terrifying sincerity and intensity. These hands belong to a handsome young man— the author, as though unintentionally, makes him of the same age as the narrator's elder son—who, after losing everything, leaves the Rooms in the depth of despair, with the evident intention of ending his hopeless life in the Casino gardens. An inexplicable feeling of sympathy compels her to follow him and make every effort to save him. He takes her for one of the importunate women so common there and tries to shake her off; but she stays with him and finds herself obliged, in the most natural way possible, to join him in his apartment at the hotel, and finally to share his bed. After this improvised night of love, she exacts a most solemn vow from the young man, who has now apparently calmed down, that he will never play again, provides him with money for his journey home and promises to meet him at the station before the departure of his train. Now, however, she begins to feel a great tenderness for him, is ready to sacrifice all she has in order to keep him and makes up her mind to go with him instead of saying goodbye. Various mischances delay her, so that she misses the train. In her longing for the lost one she returns once more to the Rooms and there, to her horror, sees once more the hands which had first excited her sympathy: the faithless youth had gone back to his play. She reminds him of his promise, but, obsessed by his passion, he calls her a spoil-sport, tells her to go, and flings back the money with which she has tried to rescue him. She hurries away in deep mortification and learns later that she has not succeeded in saving him from suicide.

The brilliantly told, faultlessly motivated story is of course complete in itself and is certain to make a deep effect upon the reader. But analysis shows us that its invention is based fundamentally upon a wishful phantasy belonging to the period of puberty, which a number of people actually remember consciously. The phantasy embodies a boy's wish that his mother should herself initiate him into sexual life in order to save him from the dreaded injuries caused by masturbation. (The numerous creative works that deal with the theme of redemption have the same origin.) The "vice" of masturbation is replaced by the addiction to gambling;[9] and the emphasis laid upon the passionate activity of the hands betrays this derivation. Indeed, the passion for play is an equivalent of the old compulsion to masturbate; "playing" is the actual word used in the nursery to describe the activity of the hands upon the genitals. The irresistible nature of the temptation, the solemn resolutions, which are nevertheless invariably broken, never to do it again, the stupefying pleasure and the bad conscience which tells the subject that he is ruining himself (committing suicide)—all these elements remain unaltered in the process of substitution. It is true that Zweig's story is told by the mother, not by the son. It must flatter the son to think: "If my mother only knew what dangers masturbation involves me in, she would certainly save me from them by allowing me to lavish all my tenderness on her own body." The equation of the mother with a prostitute, which is made by the young man in the story, is linked up with the same phantasy. It brings the unattainable woman within easy reach. The bad conscience which accompanies the phantasy brings about the unhappy ending of the story. It is also interesting to notice how the façade given to the story by its author seeks to disguise its analytic meaning. For it is extremely questionable whether the erotic life of women is dominated by sudden and mysterious impulses. On the contrary, analysis reveals an adequate motivation for the surprising behavior of this woman who had hitherto turned away from love. Faithful to the memory of her dead husband, she had armed herself against all similar attractions; but—and here the son's phantasy is right—she did not, as a mother, escape her quite unconscious transference of love on to her son, and Fate was able to catch her at this undefended spot.

If the addiction to gambling, with the unsuccessful struggles to break the habit and the opportunities it affords for self-punishment, is a repetition of the compulsion to masturbate, we shall not be surprised to find that it occupied such a large space in Dostoevsky's life. After all, we find no cases of severe neurosis in which the auto-erotic satisfaction of early childhood and of puberty has not played a part; and the relation between efforts to suppress it and fear of the father are too well known to need more than a mention.[10]

[9] [In a letter to Fliess of December 22, 1897, Freud suggested that masturbation is the "primal addiction," for which all later addictions are substitutes (Freud, 1950a, Letter 79).]

[10] Most of the views which are here expressed are also contained in an excellent book by Jolan Neufeld (1923).

# The Theme of the
# Double in Dostoevsky

## by Dmitri Chizhevsky

### I

The double is one of Dostoevsky's most characteristic themes. It is almost a fixed idea—it recurs in his work many times and in several versions. Little, however, has been written about its deep meaning. The first version of the theme, *The Double* (1846) received rather unfavorable criticism, and until recently was considered an unoriginal work, influenced either by Gogol's *Overcoat* or his *Nose* or by Western European models.

Dostoevsky himself had a very different opinion of *The Double*. While working on the story, he wrote to his brother Michael (November 16, 1845): "This will be my *chef d'œuvre.*" On the day of publication (February 1, 1846) he wrote to him: "*Golyadkin* [the name of the hero of *The Double*] is ten times better than *The Poor People*. My friends say that there is nothing comparable since *The Dead Souls,* that it is a work of genius." Dostoevsky did not think such praise exaggerated. "Really *Golyadkin* turned out exceedingly well," he adds, "you will like it even more than *The Dead Souls.*" Still, the disappointment of his friends (Belinsky in particular) after the publication of the story affected Dostoevsky. "I am tired of *Golyadkin,*" he confessed to his brother (April 1, 1846). But Dostoevsky was persuaded only that the artistic *form* was not a success. He had not the slightest doubt that the *idea* of his "Petersburg poem" was important: "I have disappointed expectations and bungled the work which could have been a great achievement." A year later Dostoevsky wavered again and was ready to agree with those who

"The Theme of the Double in Dostoevsky." From *O Dostoevskom. Sbornik statei.* edited by A. L. Bem (Prague, 1929). Translated from the Russian by René Wellek. Reprinted by permission of the author. A somewhat different, fuller, version appears in *Dostojevskij-Studien,* edited by D. Chizhevsky. Reichenberg, 1931, pp. 19-50.

spoke enthusiastically of *The Double*. "I hear about *Golyadkin* indirectly (and from many sources) wonderful things," he wrote to his brother (December 1, 1847). "Some people say openly that this work is a miracle and has not yet been properly appreciated. It will play an enormous role in the future, it is enough for me to have written only *Golyadkin* . . . it does one good to know that one is understood."

Even after the years of penal servitude Dostoevsky did not lose interest in the theme of *The Double*. In the very first letter (Omsk, February 22, 1854) to his brother Michael after his release from the camp Dostoevsky asked: "Who is Chernov who published a *Double* in 1850?" When he was planning a new edition of his writings, Dostoevsky did not want to include *The Double*—not because he did not think it worthy of inclusion, but because he wanted to publish it separately (May 9, 1859): "*The Double* could be published last—revised, or rather rewritten to perfection." He hoped that the new version would bring out what his contemporaries had misunderstood: "Believe me, brother, that this revision, with a preface, will be worth as much as a new novel. They will see at last what *The Double* is. I hope that it will arouse great interest. In a word I'll challenge them all." Also at that time Dostoevsky considered the *idea* of *The Double* most important (October 1, 1859): "Why should I abandon an excellent idea, a type of great social importance, which I was the first to discover and of which I was the first prophet?"

Even thirty years after the publication of *The Double*, when Dostoevsky surveyed his career, he held a high opinion of the idea of the story. He admits in *The Diary of a Writer* (November 1877) that *The Double* was "a complete failure," that "the story did not come off." But Dostoevsky wanted to draw attention to the idea of *The Double*: "The idea was very clever and I have never propounded anything more serious in literature." He considered the idea topical and urgent even for that time: "If I were today to take up this idea and propound it again, it would assume a very different form; but in 1846 I had not found the form and had not mastered the story."

But did Dostoevsky never return to the idea after *The Double*? Did he never attempt to give it "a very different form"? The idea which in Dostoevsky's own words was "more serious than anything he had propounded in literature," by which he would "challenge all," was not forgotten. It recurs throughout his writing in various metamorphoses. We can even say that this idea is an answer to the deepest spiritual problems of the nineteenth century and that it is still alive in the philosophy of our own time. It is really one of the main ideas for Dostoevsky: it leads us into the very center of his religious and ethical views. It will be our task to trace the role of the idea of the double in Dostoevsky's work and to uncover its philosophical meaning.

## II

The starting point of our analysis is the fact that Dostoevsky's style is based on an interpenetration of "naturalistic" and "unrealistic" elements. The ordinariness of everyday life is strangely shot through with the fantastic, naturalistic portrayal alternates with the pathos of an abstract idea, the sober striving for reality with ecstatic visions of the world beyond the confines of reality. Dostoevsky's power as an artist lies precisely in his ability to avoid mixing or confusing these sharply contradictory elements, and to succeed in weaving them together, fusing them into an organic unity. No doubt this style is closely linked with literary tradition (E. T. A. Hoffmann, Gogol, Dickens, Balzac) and with the deepest personal experiences of Dostoevsky. The important thing for us is to recognize that Dostoevsky's "realistically psychological" analysis is at the same time also "transcendentally psychological," "existential," and that all events and the whole pattern of his theme are always an ideological construct as well. This duality, where the plot develops on two planes of meaning, is particularly important for our analysis.

From the very first pages of *The Double* Dostoevsky insists that the meaning of the younger Golyadkin's appearance lies exclusively in the peculiar psychic "situation" of the elder Golyadkin, even though the strange event might well be explained on the plane of reality. Just as in *The Landlady* the fantastic scenes appear always on the background of the almost delirious state of Ordynov, so also Golyadkin's double appears to him first while he is in an abnormal state of mind:

> Mr. Golyadkin halted in exhaustion . . . and began looking intently at the black and troubled waters of the canal. There is no knowing what length of time he spent like this. . . . At that instant Mr. Golyadkin reached such a pitch of despair, was so harassed, so tortured, so exhausted, and so weakened in what feeble faculties were left him that he forgot everything . . . All at once . . . he started and involuntarily skipped a couple of paces aside. With unaccountable uneasiness he began gazing about him . . . he fancied that just now, that every minute, some one was standing near him, beside him, also leaning on the railing . . . a new sensation took possession of Mr. Golyadkin's whole being: agony upon agony, terror upon terror. . . . a feverish tremor ran through his veins.

At this moment Mr. Golyadkin's double—his "double in every respect" —appears out of the snow storm. Later, the double also appears side by side with him in the coffeehouse, and at his Excellency's "he made his appearance through a door which our hero had taken for a looking-glass." The double again appears next to Mr. Golyadkin "as if he had stepped out of his reflection in the shop windows of the Nevsky Prospekt" and, after his visit to Golyadkin Senior, he disappears so mysteriously—without leaving a trace—that one could doubt his reality altogether.

Mr. Golyadkin's double—whatever may be the status of his physical reality—is conditioned psychologically: it rises from the depths of Golyadkin's soul. Even if one could show from the point of view of psychopathology that there is a causal necessity for this appearance, it matters only that Golyadkin's psychic situation, depicted at the beginning, must inevitably lead to a tragic end. At the beginning of the story the delusion has not yet entered Golyadkin's soul. But even then his whole behavior testifies to the pathological character of his split personality. Dostoevsky has us meet his hero at the moment when he has to make a decision, when he is getting ready for an action that is to change his whole life. He behaves "as if" he had such a plan. But only—"as if." His very first steps show that he is by nature incapable of making a decision. Fear, anxiety, the feeling of being menaced from all sides, prepare the appearance of the double. Mr. Golyadkin goes so far as to deny his own existence not only in the momentary intention to "shoot himself, one way or another, that night," but also by his vain attempts to quiet himself by asking: "Should I pretend that I am not myself, but somebody else, strikingly like me?" Mr. Golyadkin tries to find a way out by asserting his "independence," if only in the sphere of his "private life." But the double—and it does not matter how far he is real—leaves neither Golyadkin's "official relations" nor his "private life" undisturbed as soon as he enters his life.

In the second part of *The Double*, after the appearance of the double, Dostoevsky gives at last—through Golyadkin—a formula containing the idea of his work. Against the background of the same constant vacillation between decisiveness and passive withdrawal, between "humility" and pathological retreat from imaginary or real dangers, a new and much deeper tone is sounded. Mr. Golyadkin's double crowds him out of all spheres of his life; he replaces, "impersonates," him in the office and with his fellow clerks, and in his "private life" in the family of Olsufy Ivanovich; or, as Golyadkin phrases it: "he forcibly enters the circle of my existence and of all my relations in practical life." The double has "the strange pretension and dishonorable and fantastic desire to squeeze others out of the position which those others occupy, by their very existence in this world, and to take their place." The title of a chapter in the first edition of the novel was "The Depraved Man Takes the Place of Mr. Golyadkin in Practical Life." "Imposture and shamelessness do not pay nowadays . . . Grishka Otrepyev[1] was the only one who gained by imposture," says Golyadkin several times. "Otrepyevs are not possible in our time." "My views in regard to keeping one's own place are purely moral," he remarks.

[1] Supposedly the actual name of the so-called false Demetrius (of 1606). [Translator's note.]

In order to make it perfectly clear that what matters is not the behavior of a real younger Golyadkin, but rather the feelings and introspection of the older Golyadkin, Dostoevsky expounds the same situation in a (consciously unreal) dream of the older Golyadkin. In this dream the younger Golyadkin "takes his place in the service and in society" and succeeds in proving that "Golyadkin Senior was not the genuine one at all, but the sham, and that he—Golyadkin Junior—was the real one." Finally the Golyadkins multiply indefinitely.

> Beside himself with shame and despair, the utterly ruined though perfectly innocent Mr. Golyadkin dashed headlong away, wherever fate might lead him; but with every step he took, with every thud of his foot on the granite of the pavement, there leapt up as though out of the earth a Mr. Golyadkin precisely the same, perfectly alike and of a revolting depravity of heart. And all these precisely alike Golyadkins set to running after one another as soon as they appeared, and stretched in a long chain like a file of geese, hobbling after the real Mr. Golyadkin, so there was nowhere to escape from these duplicates; so that Mr. Golyadkin, who was in every way deserving of compassion, was breathless with terror; so that the whole town was obstructed at last by duplicate Golyadkins.

This weird dream is the center of the work. The answer to the question of "one's own place" is clear. Golyadkin (and here lies his typical—or, as Dostoevsky says, "social"—significance) has no place of his own, he has never achieved one in his life, he has no "sphere" of his own in life except possibly the corner behind the cupboard or the stove where he hides from the imaginary persecutions of his enemies. In this respect Golyadkin is very similar to other characters in Dostoevsky: the "dreamer" in *The White Nights,* and *The Petersburg Chronicle,* the heroes of *The Faint Heart,* and *Mr. Prokharchin* (in part, at least), and Marmeladov in *Crime and Punishment.* There is something inhuman, thing-like in this lack of a place of one's own. (Golyadkin feels that he is being treated like a "rag.") The appearance of the double and his success in squeezing out Golyadkin from his place only shows that Golyadkin's place was completely illusory to begin with. For even the double can keep all his "places"—from the office to his Excellency's cabinet—only through the purely external traits of his character: by the flattery and servility which the older Golyadkin would have liked to master himself but which are no less superficial, unessential, and inhuman and incapable of ensuring him a "place" in life. Here Dostoevsky raises the ethical and ontological problems of the fixity, reality, and security of individual existence—surely one of the most genuine problems of ethics. The reality of human personality cannot be secured simply on the empirical plane of existence but needs also other (non-empirical) conditions and presuppositions.

## III

We do not know why, exactly, Dostoevsky was dissatisfied with the form of his "Petersburg poem." If we judge from the vicissitudes of the idea of the double in Dostoevsky's later writings, we have to conclude that one of the defects in the development of the theme of the double was the fact that a weak character in a dependent social position—in short, a petty official—was made the hero of the story. The ontological instability of a personality, however, is not necessarily connected with psychological instability ("weakness of character") or social instability ("dependence"). Dostoevsky links the further development of the theme of the double with characters of a very different type. The double occurs again in *The Possessed* (1872-73), *A Raw Youth* (1875), and *The Brothers Karamazov* (1879-80).

The theme of the double is handled in the simplest—even schematic— manner in *A Raw Youth*. There only one motif of the complex theme is used: the instability of the self, which is expressed by the ambiguity of Versilov's individual actions and general behavior. Versilov's instability is not explained by any psychological "weakness": his personality is in its way brilliant and sharply defined. Dostoevsky gives us no clue to understanding the division in Versilov. He merely describes it: "I feel as though I were split in two. . . . Yes, I am really split in two mentally, and I'm horribly afraid of it. It's just as though one's double were standing beside one." The description of this period in Versilov's life is concluded by a theoretical reflection: "What is the double, exactly? The double, according to a medical book written by an expert that I purposely read afterward, is nothing else than the first stage of serious mental derangement which may take a fatal turn." It is "a duality of will and feelings." An explanation of this loss of self, of its unity, is only hinted at, *e.g.*, when Makar Ivanovich alludes to "infidels" who "let themselves go and give up taking notice of themselves." But other traits, characteristic of Versilov's inner division, are clarified in *The Possessed* and *The Brothers Karamazov*.

A great deal of light is thrown on the figure of Stavrogin by the scenes which Dostoevsky dropped when the novel appeared in book form. In these scenes Stavrogin talks to Dasha about the appearance of a double, of a "demon":

> "I saw him again . . . at first here in the corner, there near the stove and then he sat next to me, all night, and stayed there even after I left the house . . . Now begins a series of his visitations. Yesterday he was stupid and impudent . . . I got angry that my own demon could appear in such a miserable mask . . . . I was silent all the time, on purpose: and not only

silent, I did not move. He got furious at that and I was glad that he got furious. I don't believe in him. I don't believe in him as yet. I know that it is I myself divided in different ways and that I speak with myself. Still, anyhow, he got very angry: he terribly wanted to be an independent demon and that I would believe in him as a reality."

Stavrogin also tells Tikhon about him, how he suffered, especially at night, from certain strange hallucinations; how he sometimes saw or felt close beside him an evil being, derisive and rational: "It shows different faces and assumes different characters, and yet is always the same and always infuriates me. . . . It's myself in various forms and nothing else."

But the devil of Stavrogin does not remain a mere hallucination. Fedka the Convict—an incarnation of the same devil—tells Stavrogin in a deleted passage: "There were terribly many devils here yesterday— terribly many. They crept out of all the swamps. One of them suggested to me yesterday on the bridge that I should cut the throat of Lebyadkin and Marya Timofeevna." In reality, both Kirilov and Shatov are simply two emanations of the spirit of Stavrogin—each of whom accepts him from his own point of view—while Fedka the Convict only does what he thinks Stavrogin wants from him and Pyotr Verkhovensky is acknowledged by Stavrogin as his "ape." In Stavrogin there is great spiritual treasure, but it is somehow "spilt," "scattered," "wasted." Stavrogin (like Versilov but unlike Golyadkin) has a great enough spiritual force to become the ideologist of religious Slavophilism (Shatov), of the revolt against God (Kirilov), and of the revolution (Pyotr Verkhovensky). Shatov's whole ideology comes from Stavrogin. "It was a teacher uttering weighty words, and a pupil who was raised from the dead. I was that pupil and you were the teacher," confesses Shatov to Stavrogin. "You were sowing the seed of God and the Fatherland in my heart." Shatov feels "condemned to believe" in Stavrogin "through all eternity" for only he "could raise that flag"—*i.e.*, the flag of his particular brand of Slavophilism. Even though his ideology is too shallow to need the help of Stavrogin's spiritual midwifery, Pyotr Verkhovensky nevertheless feels that the fate of his plans is completely dependent on Stavrogin's "raising the flag": "I love an idol. You are my idol. . . . It's just such a man as you that I need. You are the leader, you are the sun and I am your worm." He expounds a half-crazy though grandiose plan for a revolution which Stavrogin the Pretender would head as Ivan the Tsarevich. Such a plan could have arisen in Pyotr Verkhovensky's shallow and petty mind only as a response to the great personality of Stavrogin. Finally, the mad genius of Kirilov too could rise only from the depths of Stavrogin's soul. "He is your creation," Shatov reproaches Stavrogin, "You were infecting the heart of that hapless creature with poison . . . you confirmed false malignant ideas in him, and brought him to the verge of insanity."

Kirilov is the only one of the "emanations" of Stavrogin who never ceases to have a "warm and kindly" relation with his master though, also, he expected from Stavrogin that he "would undertake burdens nobody else can bear." Fedka the Convict too is—to a lesser degree—an "emanation" of the spirit of Stavrogin. But Stavrogin is right, after all, when he calls Fedka his "little devil." Fedka's last crime is a response to Stavrogin's perhaps unconscious wishes, though they are distorted and strained by the soul of Pyotr Verkhovensky.

Thus Stavrogin lives among the "emanations" of his spirit, in a world of phantoms, of "demons." Or more exactly: others live for him (especially the women of the novel) and "of him" but he himself does not really live; he is only a Pretender, in reality and in possibility, an "Ivan the Tsarevich," a "Grishka Otrepyev." Real people follow him, but they take him for something totally different from what he really is. For in reality he is "split," he is "split into two," he has no face, or many faces, or even all faces. Others see in him "faces" which he does not have. But in any case, two contradictory faces are clearly visible: one bright, the other dark. Some (Shatov, Kirilov, Dasha) expect a "great deed" from him, the "undertaking of burdens," and others (Pyotr Verkhovensky and his gang) see in him an "extraordinary aptitude for crime." He actually sees "no distinction between some brutal obscene action and any great exploit, even the sacrifice of life for humanity": "I am still capable of desiring to do something good, and I get a feeling of pleasure from it; at the same time I desire evil and feel pleasure from that too." It is not surprising that people consider him capable "of any mad action even when in full possession of his faculties." In other words Stavrogin is "neither cold nor hot" not because he does not know the difference between good and evil (like *e.g.* Pyotr Verkhovensky or Fyodor Karamazov). He knows what is good. He tries to "rise from the dead." He tries—more than once—to waken to the good: by revealing his marriage to Marya Timofeevna and by the publication of the "Confession" which he gave to Tikhon to read. But in order to "wake to the good" it is not enough to know what is good—it is not enough to know it theoretically or aesthetically. Stavrogin knows only this "theoretical" awakening. And even then Stavrogin with all his beauty, elegance, gentlemanliness, education, wit, courage, and self-reliance remains outwardly and inwardly passive in the face of life and concrete reality. He is torn off, isolated from all the world, absolutely alone; he has no point of support in the concrete world. He understands much, but he does not love anything. We are struck by Stavrogin's power—his enormous spiritual power— "illimitable, great power." But this power of Stavrogin's (in the original sketches of the novel called "Prince") is "immediate, it does not know on what to rely." This is the source of his indifference, boredom, absent-mindedness, even his laziness. He does not have a human face; he wears some kind of mask. The cause of Stavrogin's loneliness is in himself: he is divided from living reality by his pride, his limitless presumption, his scornful relation to life, his contempt for his concrete neighbors.

Kirilov, we are told, was "consumed" by his idea. Possibly Stavrogin is partly right when he writes to Dasha that he can "never believe in an idea to such a degree as he [Kirilov] did. I cannot even be interested in an idea to such a degree." Still, Kirilov is right when he says that "the idea has also consumed" Stavrogin. Stavrogin is right—though these ideas may be contradictory—that "one may argue about everything endlessly, but for me nothing has come but negation, with no greatness of soul, no force." "Only negation"—that means that assertion needs not only knowledge, but also love, not only the "abstract reason" of Stavrogin but the *nous erōn* of Kirilov. Yes, even Kirilov, who perishes tragically, aims at something definite: the "Man-God," "self-will." But there is no "tension" in Stavrogin, no "magnetic meridian" of the soul, no "magnetic pole" to which, according to Dostoevsky, every living soul is drawn. He knows no God. A living, concrete human evistence—a "place" in the world—is possible only through the living link of man with the Divine Being. The anecdote of Pyotr Stefanovich is certainly a central point of the novel:

> "I was drinking with the officers . . . They were discussing atheism and I need hardly say they made short work of God. They were squealing with delight . . . One grizzled old captain sat mum, not saying a word. All at once he stands up in the middle of the room and says aloud, as though speaking to himself: 'If there's no God, how can I be a captain then?' "

Just as one cannot be an army captain without God, so Stravrogin cannot without God be a Slavophile, or a revolutionary, or even a militant atheist (like Kirilov). For his unlimited but godless power there remains then only one "place" in the world, similar to the "places" where Golyadkin was hiding. This "one place" is "in the mountains of Switzerland," "a gloomy place" to which he calls Marya Timofeevna. There he wants to hide again with Dasha: "a very dull place, a narrow valley, the mountains restrict both vision and thought. It's very gloomy. I don't want to go anywhere else ever." But even this "place" is not granted to him. We know the end: "The citizen of the canton Uri was hanging behind the door."

But one cannot deny that for Stavrogin there was a way open to concreteness. He does not take it, of course. It is the way of shame and disgrace. This sense of shame is possibly Stavrogin's last remaining link with other people and with human society. While he is completely indifferent to success, fame, and danger, he is deeply disturbed by the possibility of disgrace: "If one did something wicked, or worse still, something shameful, that is disgraceful, only very shameful and . . . ridiculous, such as people would remember for a thousand years and hold in scorn for a thousand years!" Liza has "a strong feeling" that Stavrogin "had something awful, loathsome, some bloodshed on his conscience . . . and yet something that would make him look very ridiculous. Beware of telling me, if it's true: I shall laugh you to scorn. I shall laugh at you for the rest of your life." Tikhon fears that he won't "endure the laughter of people . . . "The ugliness of the crime will kill it. It is truly an unbeautiful crime . . . there are truly shameful, disgraceful crimes which are not redeemed by horror." Tikhon advises him "sincerely to accept the blows and the spittle . . . It is always thus that the most degrading cross becomes a great glory and a great power, if only the humility of the act is sincere." Stavrogin's way to life could have led through "shame and disgrace." But, unable to endure the "blows and the spittle," he chose the way to death. Possibly the motive for his suicide was not only his own crime but the crimes—the "unbeautiful"—crimes of his "doubles." For the crimes of Pyotr Verkhovensky and of Fedka the Convict "are too unbeautiful." And all the "doubles," all the "emanations" of Stavrogin (with the exception of Pyotr Verkhovensky) die symbolically before he himself commits suicide.

Stavrogin's "devil" was dropped by Dostoevsky in the book-form edition of the novel: possibly because the depiction of the devil seemed to him too bold at that time or because it might simply have changed the tragedy of Stavrogin into a psychic illness. Still, there is another devil in Dostoevsky's works: the devil of Ivan Karamazov.

Ivan Karamazov is not mentally ill, he has not committed any crime, and he is not at all indifferent to life as Stavrogin is. But, like Stavrogin, he is divided from the people, from his neighbors, by pride. Ivan is conceited: he exalts himself over other people and considers himself their judge. Dmitri and his father are, in his opinion, "serpents"; his father deserves death: he does not doubt that Dmitri was the murderer. The source of Ivan's pride is his rationalism; his pride is "the pride of reason." His way to ethical insight is not—like Alyosha's—the way of faith nor—like Dmitri's—the way of suffering, but the way of madness and breakdown, the way of a division of personality. This division of personality is shown in the scenes with Smerdyakov and with the devil. Smerdyakov is also in a certain sense a "double" of Ivan. Not only have they in common basic character traits— "enlightened" rationalism, conceit, contempt for other people, loneliness, and complacency—but they also share an interest in common "themes." Smerdyakov tries to prove the right of man to mortal sin, Ivan argues that "everything is permitted." Both have a low opinion of Russia and Europe, and both recognize that there are people who have a different relation to God: Smerdyakov tells of "two pilgrims," Ivan recognizes the limits of "Euclidean" reason. Ivan himself admits his agreement with Smerdyakov on this point. That is why Smerdyakov worships Ivan—a point which Dosto-

evsky emphasizes several times. This inner link between Ivan and Smerdyakov is revealed particularly in the conversation at the gate in which
Ivan seems to make himself—unwittingly—an accomplice in the murder
of his father. After the murder a consciousness awakes in Ivan's soul that
he is—not empirically, but in some other sense—guilty with Smerdyakov,
guilty because of their similarity and because "the lackey Smerdyakov
sat in his soul." Ivan is ashamed of Smerdyakov and thus a recognition
of his own guilt penetrates into Ivan's mind in accord with the main
theme of the novel: "everybody is guilty for everything and everybody."
Shame is the key to the moral awakening of the rationalist Ivan. Ivan's
moral crisis is displayed in his "nightmare," in the appearance of his
double—the devil—who is, as Ivan says:

> "the incarnation of myself, but only of one side of me—of my thoughts
> and feelings, but only the nastiest and stupidest of them. . . . You are
> myself, myself only with a different face. . . . You choose only my worst
> thoughts, and what's more, the stupid ones. . . . All my stupid ideas—out-
> grown, thrashed out long ago, and flung aside like a dead carcass—you
> present me as something new. . . . I was never such a flunkey. How then
> could my soul beget a flunkey like you? . . . He is myself. All that's base in
> me, all that's mean and contemptible."

Thus Smerdyakov is not simply similar to Ivan but is in him. Ivan
came to this recognition through shame. Dostoevsky has not shown us
Ivan's moral rebirth. But in *The Brothers Karamazov* he has, in any
case, revealed new and deep aspects of the problem of the double.


# IV


We have asserted that the philosophical problem of the double in
Dostoevsky points to essential and central problems of nineteenth-century
philosophy. To uncover this link (without stopping to enquire how far
this answer to nineteenth-century philosophy lay in Dostoevsky's intentions) will be our further task.

The appearance of the double raises a question about the concreteness
of man's real existence. It shows that simply "to exist"—"to be"—is not a
sufficient condition for man's existence as an ethical individual. The
problem of "stability," of the ontological "fixity" of an ethical being
is the real problem of the nineteenth century; or, more accurately, the
problem of the distinction of human existence from any other kind of
existence, which could be defined generally and abstractly as anything
specific in space and time. The problem was put very clearly by Kierkegaard, but not by him only. It is one of the central problems in the
whole development of Hegelianism; it was stated expressly by Feuerbach,
Bruno Bauer, Stirner; and in some respects it determined the develop-

ment of Marx. The problem of individual existence also plays a central role in the philosophy of Nietzsche. Nietzsche's "new tables of values" are tables of ontological values that are to guarantee the concrete existence of the individual. I can only allude to the new formulations of the problem of concrete individual existence in recent philosophy, in Tillich and Heidegger, and in the tradition of the Hegelian Left and Nietzscheanism in Russian philosophy (*e.g.*, in Rozanov).

One could point out that though there is an indubitable similarity in the problem of the existence of the individual self as it confronts these thinkers and Dostoevsky, there is still a very great difference between their points of view. Kierkegaard and Nietzsche see the reasons for the loss of the ontological "fixity" of the self in abstract, theoretical, "pure," "immaculate" thought. But is the way Dostoevsky puts the problem really so different? We noted in Stavrogin his intellectual power combined with a complete absence of any living relation to concreteness, and Ivan is a typical intellectual. Stavrogin and Ivan are possible only on the soil of Russian "Enlightenment" and Dostoevsky expressly connects them with it. The Russian Enlightenment of the nineteenth century, with its universal rationalism, its conviction that reason is able to grasp all of reality and also to create a new and better reality, was the main thing in Russian life against which Dostoevsky fought all his life. The rationalization of the aesthetic sphere—the reduction of beauty to utility (see Dostoevsky's articles directed against Dobrolyubov); the rationalization of the ethical sphere—the substitution of rational arguments for immediate feeling (cf. *The Diary of a Writer*, 1876, II, 2; *The Grand Inquisitor*, the whole moral personality of Ivan); the rationalization of social life—the ideal of the "anthill" (cf. the theories of Shigalev in *The Possessed* and *The Grand Inquisitor*)—these are the central ideas of Russian "Enlightenment" which Dostoevsky fought incessantly. Dostoevsky's rejection of the Enlighteners was expressed possibly with the greatest clarity in the "Fragment of a Novel Shchedrodarov" where he puts into the mouth of the editors of the *Contemporary* the whole program of the Enlightenment:

"Every writer's and poet's highest goal is to popularize natural science. . . . A real apple is better than a painted apple. . . . shoes are in any case better than Pushkin. . . . The enlightened Kurochkin who destroys prejudices in any case stands incomparably higher than the unenlightened Homer. . . . For the happiness of all mankind, and equally for the happiness of every separate individual, first and most important of all, is the belly, or in other words, the stomach. . . . The anthill is the highest ideal of social organization one can imagine. . . . People are stupid, because they cannot figure out where their real advantage lies, because they rush after some childish toy, called art, after the useless, because they are steeped in prejudice, live separately and haphazardly, according to their will, rather, than according to rational books."

Dostoevsky answers this through the mouth of Shchedrodarov:

> "You are going against life. We are not supposed to prescribe laws for
> life and extract laws from life for ourselves. You are theoreticians . . . How
> can one stand on air, without feeling the soil under one . . . Before you
> can do anything you have to make yourselves into something, to assume
> your own shape, to become yourselves . . . But you are abstractions, you
> are shadows, you are nothing. And nothing can come from nothing. You
> are foreign ideas. You are a mirage. You do not stand on soil but on air.
> The light shines right under you. . . ." [2]

Here the same problem is put very clearly, as in Kierkegaard and
Nietzsche—with the difference that Kierkegaard and Nietzsche fought
the "professors," the "abstract thinkers," and the ideologists "of pure
reason" while in the Russia of the 1860's and 1870's every mediocre
liberal and every revolutionary member of the intelligentsia was a
theorist.

Golyadkin belongs to this group of problems. Of course, he is not
a "theorist" or a "thinker," but in Russia the "Enlightenment" in-
fected not only society but also the government. The society of the period of Emperor Nicholas I was also an attempt to build a thoroughly
organized "anthill." Pyotr Verkhovensky dreamt of it: "Nothing has
more influence than a uniform. I invent ranks and duties on purpose;
I have secretaries, secret spies, treasurers, presidents, registrars, their as-
sistants—they like it awfully, it's taken capitally." Gogol had fought
the government "anthill," and had confronted its rational organization
with the ideal of "a religious organization" of society. Golyadkin is,
so to say, the passive bearer of the rational principle—and its victim.
He, like the other clerks depicted by Dostoevsky, is devastated, exploited
by the rational principle, embodied in the government apparatus of
the period of Emperor Nicholas I. Rationalism devours Stavrogin and
Ivan from inside, not from outside.

## V

Dostoevsky does not remain on the surface of the question. He moves
from the social and psychological problem (*The Double*) to the ethical
and religious (*The Possessed* and *The Brothers Karamazov*). He is not
satisfied with an easy battle against Pyotr Verkhovensky, Shigalev and
Smerdyakov. In the figures of Stavrogin and Ivan loom the two basic
aspects of ethical rationalism. In Stavrogin we see primarily the "cold-

---

[2] Translated by Ralph E. Matlaw. From Appendix to his edition of *Notes from
Underground and The Grand Inquisitor* (New York: E. P. Dutton and Co., 1960), pp.
217-228.

ness," in Ivan "the abstractness," of ethical rationalism. These two sides are closely linked and arise from a common source.

The ethical action of man has three aspects. *Someone, somewhere,* and *somehow* are necessarily involved in any ethical action. The first two elements are thoroughly concrete and individual. The third, however, can be taken abstractly, in logical terms. The abstract is the most primitive, the simplest form of mind. (See Hegel, *"Wer denkt abstrakt?"*) This is why we note in the history of moral philosophy the tendency either to ignore the first two elements of ethical action or to schematize them in the manner of abstract thinking. This tendency expresses itself in the attempt to fix ethical laws or norms, devised on the model of natural laws or laws of logic, or on the model of norms of convention or of law. In other words the "how" of the ethical act is established by completely abstracting it from the "who" and the "where." The living subject of ethical action becomes an unnecessary adjunct to a system of ethical world-order—unnecessary because it can be replaced by any other ethical subject.

It is remarkable that even in thinkers who were not consciously ethical rationalists we find such lack of emphasis on the ethical subject. Even Kant's "categorical imperative" ignores the individual concreteness of the ethical subject. In Kant "moral prescriptions are to be conceived as general laws of nature" (*Grundlegung zu einer Metaphysik der Sitten*). The "ethical realm of ends," we are told, can be conceived "only on the analogy of the realm of nature." In other words the morality of man consists in his acting as if he would submit to mechanical causality, and thus the characteristic ethical act is one divorced from the concrete. The main trait of the ethical world is its uniformity and monotony. In such an ethical world live and act impersonal ethical subjects—the multitude of the "supremely similar ones," "the many too many," as Nietzsche called them.

One would think that Nietzsche, the apostle of free individuality, who—like Dostoevsky—poses the question of the reality of the ethical subject, could not be accused of ignoring the role of the ethical subject in the ethical act. But Nietzsche also was unwittingly subdued by the spirit of ethical rationalism. As Georg Simmel has clearly shown, his teaching about the "eternal recurrence" gives only another form to Kant's conception of the uniformity and monotony of the moral world. The "eternal recurrence" is a criterion of value. For the ethical subject can recognize as ethically valuable only something in relation to which he can ask for repetition "not once but innumerable times." Thus Nietzsche sees the criterion of morality in the same acceptance of action as something infinitely repeatable, which Kant demanded with his law of nature, and, even more sharply, Fichte, when he formulated the imperative: "Act in such a manner that you could conceive the law of your will as the eternal law of your action." In all three thinkers, in Kant,

Fichte and Nietzsche, the ethical subject loses the main trait of individual concreteness: it cannot be repeated, cannot be duplicated.

It is no chance that the devil of Ivan Karamazov appears as the defender of the theory of "eternal recurrence": "Our present earth may have been repeated a billion times . . . the same sequence may have been repeated endlessly and exactly the same to every detail, most unseemly and insufferably tedious." In the theory of "eternal recurrence"—at which (in one way or another) ethical rationalism must inevitably arrive—was concentrated the whole fierceness with which the meaning of the individual concrete being was rejected.

The feverish search for a "place" of one's own conducted by Dostoevsky's heroes appears as an expression of their insatiable desire for concreteness, for realization in a living "here" and "now." In the philosophy of the nineteenth century the problem of "one's own place" has been put by, among others, Fichte, who thinks it indispensable for an ethical subject to have its own special "sphere of freedom" (*Werke*. ed. Medicus II, 614ff, 623, II, 128) and puts this conception into the center of his legal and social schemes. A paradoxical sharpening of this idea occurs in the teachings of Max Stirner. Stirner could not save the individuality of the ethical subject but asserted the concreteness, the "uniqueness" of the sphere of freedom of the "unique" subject, and thus arrived at an original kind of "ethical solipsism." But after all, the concreteness of a "sphere of freedom" cannot replace the concreteness of the ethical subject itself. Kierkegaard and Nietzsche struggled with that difficulty.

Dostoevsky construes "his place" ("the sphere of freedom") differently; he starts from the Christian concept of the "neighbor," *i.e.*, by accepting as the basic ethical datum the concretely individual existence of a multitude of ethical subjects. Ethical rationalism understands only love for man in general, while the "neighbor" is strange and distant. It is, however, precisely the concrete individuality of the "neighbor" that should be the object of our ethical action. The ethical rationalist is incapable of loving a concrete man, *i.e.*, the idea of man hides the living man for him. Thus the Enlightener Nekrasov, according to Dostoevsky, "loved, on the Volga, man in general in the bargeman and suffered, strictly speaking, not for the bargeman himself but for the bargeman in general. You see, to love man in general necessarily means to despise and, at times, to hate the real man standing at your side." Also Versilov reflects:

> "To love one's neighbor and not to despise him . . . is impossible. I believe that man has been created physically incapable of loving his neighbor. . . . Love for humanity must be understood as love for that humanity which you have created in your soul. . . . To love people as

they are is impossible. And yet we must. And therefore do them good, overcoming your feelings, holding your nose and shutting your eyes (the latter's essential)."

Ivan Karamazov says the same: "I could never understand how one can love one's neighbors. It's just one's neighbors, to my mind, that one can't love, though one might love those at a distance." The elder Zosima tells of a doctor who said: "The more I love humanity in general, the less I love man in particular . . . the more I detest men individually the more ardent becomes my love for humanity."

In Dostoevsky's opinion, "not to judge" is the main condition of the specific relation to people through which they become our "neighbors." For Alyosha Karamazov "not judging" is the inescapable norm of ethics. "He did not care to be a judge of others—he would never take upon himself to judge and would never condemn anyone for anything." Alyosha asks Ivan: "Has any man a right to look at other men and decide which is worthy to live?" Such an attitude "restored the heart" to Grushenka—for Alyosha "did not speak as a judge but as the lowest of the judged." Alyosha "pierced the heart" of his father "living with him, seeing everything and blaming nothing." Fyodor says to him: "You are the only creature in the world who has not condemned me." Father Zosima says many times: "Remember particularly that you cannot be a judge of anyone." Precisely because of this unwillingness to judge, Alyosha gets to know his father, his brothers whom he had not known before, Grushenka, the boys, and the captain. In fact, he appears everywhere loving, near, and familiar; for him everybody is a neighbor in the genuine Christian sense of the world. His place—his "sphere of freedom" —is the whole moral world. Every special sphere, every "place," every "here and now" becomes "concrete" for him, and is filled with tasks which he does not flee but seeks out for himself. The whole world becomes to him ethically "transparent," becomes his own self through the active love which grows on the soil of "not judging."

Finally, the basis of Alyosha's active love and "not judging" lies in the sphere of religion; the ontological stability of his personality is due to his closeness to God. The religious and philosophical solution given by Dostoevsky is more essential than the "ethical and ontological" problem.

We can ask still another question: why does the specific ontological weakness and instability of the ethical subject that constructs itself according to rationalistic schemes express itself in a "splitting" of the personality which in pathological cases appears as an actual "doubling" and finally leads to madness?

First of all, rationalistic ethics carries a schism into the psychic life of man, setting abstract duty against concrete inclination. It sees the ethical aim of the individual as a sacrifice of the concrete to the abstract.

The schism and the struggle in the soul of the ethical subject are declared to be his "dignity," the essence of his ethical being. It is not by chance that after the establishment of the radically abstract ethical system of Kant this principle of the inner split became the object of bitter attacks by Schiller, Fichte, Hegel, the Hegelians (Feuerbach, Stirner), and later, Nietzsche. Nietzsche sees the meaning of Kant's moral philosophy in the struggle of a "higher" with a "lower" self and sees that the concrete man "is completely divorced from his higher self and becomes often an actor of his self." Still, none of these philosophers succeeded in overcoming ethical dualism. But this schism makes the concrete nonexistent, and the abstract powerless.

The schism brought into the life of an ethical subject by rationalistic ethics, can be even more clearly demonstrated by the fact that the only living, *i.e.*, nonabstract, ethical motive remaining is shame. Ethical rationalism requires a quantitative comparison of the ethical subjects, a distribution over steps on a ladder, an evaluation of the "higher" and "lower"—in short, "judging." Actually, however, ethical subjects are essentially incomparable—or, rather, they must not be compared—for everyone has his own individual scale of ethical values, incommensurable with the other scales of other subjects. In the abstract principle of duty all men are identical. Hence comes the shame man feels for his concreteness insofar as it appears identical with the concreteness of the "least man," of the "many, all too many." Stavrogin is ashamed at the naïve enthusiasm of Shatov, at Fedka the Convict, at Pyotr Verkhovensky, at his "demon." Shame is also the only key to Ivan Karamazov's ethical self-knowledge—shame for Smerdyakov, for the "devil." Dostoevsky sees the weakness of Stavrogin and Ivan in sense of shame. But in Nietzsche contempt, revulsion, scorn, "the great satiety" are identical with shame for the "last man," "the many all too many," the petty man—man insofar as he is "an ape and a torturing shame" of the superman: this is the main ethical stimulus. Although Nietzsche reflects that shame is a great ethical power, in Dostoevsky shame—the inability to overcome shame—leads to the impasses of both Stavrogin and Ivan and their divorce from concreteness. For the shame at concreteness (one's own and that of others) weakens and reduces power and the life of concreteness and reaffirms the split in the soul of the ethical subject that was caused in him by ethical rationalism.

This splitting in two prepares the appearance of the double. For concreteness—living and ontologically stable concreteness—is rejected and repulsed by the abstract principle. Still, it cannot take on ontological power and firmness. The existential sphere of the ethical subject is weakened. Fear, *Angst,* the feeling of being threatened on all sides arises. This can become the living source of religious insight (Paul Tillich's argument), but it can also bring about a total psychological disbelief of the ethical subject in its ontological stability, and can create an unstable situation in the soul. The soul craves the blow which would throw it out of this torturing situation. And this blow falls, naturally, on the weakest, unprotected point of the ethical subject. The subject, having lost the source and base of its ethical concreteness—the concreteness of the "I," its "who"—also loses that sphere of concreteness which it had still preserved: its "place," its concrete "sphere of freedom," its "here." In extreme cases, such a blow must on the strength of the psychological cause we have described (the split in the soul of the ethical rationalist) result in the appearance of a double, whether imaginary or real. The ethical function of the appearance of the double is obviously the same as the ethical function of death, *i.e.*, the loss of existence of the subject. Or shall we say that the loss of concreteness brings about a depersonalization of the subject: it becomes a "thing," it loses existence as a subject. Thus the double puts with extreme power the question: will the individual discover a new stability and a new life in absolute being or will he perish in Nothingness?

Thus Dostoevsky's raising of the problem of the double appears as one of the most significant milestones in the nineteenth-century philosophical struggle against ethical rationalism, a struggle which has not by any means been concluded and which may even have barely begun.

# Dostoevsky's Religious and
# Philosophical Views

## *by V. V. Zenkovsky*

### I: DOSTOEVSKY'S RELIGIOUS WORLD

Dostoevsky's *religious* searchings provided the foundation for his intellectual life and theoretical constructions. His was always a religious nature; throughout his life he was "tormented," to use his own expression, by the idea of God. In Dostoevsky, more than in anyone else, we see philosophic creativity *growing out of* the womb of the religious consciousness. But the extraordinary significance of his intellectual creativity consists precisely in the fact that he exhibited the complex of *religious* problems in anthropology, ethics, aesthetics, and historiosophy, with immense force and unsurpassed profundity. He was referring to his perception of these problems in the light of religion when he said that "God tormented him." "Even in Europe," we read in Dostoevsky's notebook, "there is not and never was such power of atheistic expression. It is not as a child that I believe in Christ and profess His teaching; my hosanna has burst through a purging flame of doubts." [1] But these doubts were generated in the depths of the *religious consciousness itself;* they were all clustered about a single theme: the mutual relationship of God and the world. Dostoevsky never doubted God's *existence,* but he was always troubled by the problem (which he solved differently in different periods) of what God's existence *entails* for the world—for man and man's historical activity. Is a religious (and Christian) conception of, and participation in, culture possible? Can man *as he is in reality,* with all his activities and searchings, be justified and made intelligible in religious

"Dostoevsky's Religious and Philosophical Views." From *A History of Russian Philosophy,* translated by George L. Kline (London: Routledge and Kegan Paul; New York: Columbia University Press, 1953), Vol. I, pp. 415-32. Reprinted by permission of the translator and the publishers. The original Russian version was published in Paris in 1948.

[1] Strakhov, *Biografiya* . . . Part II, p. 375.

terms? Can human evil, the evil in history, universal suffering, be religiously justified and accepted? These are, in a sense, different expressions of the *problem of theodicy*. Not only did "God torment" Dostoevsky all his life; he *struggled against God* all his life—and this intimate religious process underlay the dialectic of his whole spiritual development.

Dostoevsky bore, not as an outsider, but from within, all the *problems of culture*—its dreams and ideals, its inspirations and joys, its justices and its injustices. He did not assert that Christianity and culture were internally heterogeneous; on the contrary, he was profoundly confident that they could be truly and harmoniously combined. We never find in him the kind of hostility toward culture which we find in Tolstoy. But Dostoevsky rejected secularism—the disunion of Church and culture, radical individualism ("isolation," as he liked to call it), and the "atheistic" culture of the contemporary world—with even greater force. Secularism for him was a concealed or, more often, overt atheism.

During Dostoevsky's enthusiasm for socialism, he accepted its doctrines "passionately," [2] but even then he did not separate his "passionate" faith in the establishing of justice on earth from his faith in Christ. He very soon parted company with Belinsky—whom he first followed "passionately," by his own admission—because Belinsky "reviled" Christ. It is no exaggeration to say that Dostoevsky's enthusiasm for socialism was related to his *religious* searchings. To be sure, in subsequent years his thought moved wholly in a framework of antinomies: his positive views were matched by sharp and decisive negations; but the *strength* and *loftiness* of his thought were such as to make this inevitable. Very few Russian writers have felt the dialectical zigzag in the movement of ideas as keenly as he did. But Dostoevsky's antinomism was rooted in his religious consciousness, and apart from this consciousness it cannot be properly evaluated.

In any case, Dostoevsky's early enthusiasm for socialism brought his religious consciousness directly to the basic problems of culture. Here is the key to what I have called his "Christian naturalism"—his faith in the goodness of man and human "nature." During his last years Dostoevsky wrote (in the *Diary* of 1877): "Man's greatest beauty . . . and greatest purity are turned to no account, are of no use to mankind . . . solely because there has not been genius enough to direct the wealth of these gifts." These words clearly express one pole of Dostoevsky's basic historiosophical antinomy—a faith in "nature" and its hidden "sanctity," but also a recognition that there is not enough "ability" to "direct" this hidden wealth into fruitful action. We shall return to this theme in our systematic analysis of Dostoevsky's philosophic ideas. For the moment, let us point out that his thought did not hold to the position of Christian naturalism, but came close, with extraordinary profundity, to the op-

[2] See *The Diary of a Writer*, 1873, § II.

posing thesis of the inner *ambiguity* of human nature, and the ambiguity of beauty—approaching a doctrine of the tragic quality of the "natural" freedom which leads man to crime. It is wrong to assert, as Shestov, for example, does, that after Dostoevsky's penal servitude his former views degenerated completely, that "not a trace remained in Dostoevsky of his former convictions." [3] On the contrary, his thought moved in antinomies to the end of his days; specifically, a Christian naturalism, on the one hand, and a lack of confidence in "nature" on the other, continued to coexist in him without reaching a culminating or integral synthesis. A "cult of primitive immediacy"—as one of the manifestations of Christian naturalism—and at the same time the high ideal of a universal Christianity which transcends the boundaries of nationality; a passionate defense of the individual—ethical personalism in its highest and most intense expression—and at the same time an unmasking of the "man from the underground"; a faith that "beauty will save the world," and a bitter realization that "beauty is a dreadful and frightening thing"— these antinomies were not softened but, on the contrary, were heightened toward the end of Dostoevsky's life. This was the dialectic of his religious consciousness. Dostoevsky's philosophic significance, the influence of his ideas on the history of Russian thought, consists in his having exhibited the problems of a religious approach to culture with a wonderful force and profundity. In this sense, an historiosophical orientation dominates all of Dostoevsky's thought; his profound insights in anthropology, ethics, and aesthetics are all internally related to his historiosophical reflections.

Let us turn to a systematic analysis of Dostoevsky's ideas.[4]


## II: DOSTOEVSKY'S ANTHROPOLOGY

Dostoevsky's philosophic creativity has not *one* but *several* initial points; however the most important and decisive is the theme of man. Like all Russian thinkers he is anthropocentric, and his philosophic worldview is primarily a personalism—with a purely ethical coloring, to be sure, but at the same time achieving extraordinary force and profundity in this coloring. For Dostoevsky nothing is more precious or important

---

[3] L. Shestov, *Dostojewski und Nietzsche* [translated by R. von Walter], Cologne, 1924, p. 7.

[4] The philosophic literature on Dostoevsky is very extensive; however, the heritage of his ideas has not yet been completely assimilated. See N. A. Berdyaev, *Dostoievsky, An Interpretation* [translated from the French edition by D. Attwater], New York, 1934; Merezhkovsky, *op. cit.;* Shestov, *op. cit.;* L. A. Zander, *Dostoevsky* [translated by N. Duddington], London, 1948; P. Evdokimoff, *Dostoievsky et le problème du mal,* Valence, 1942.

than man, although nothing, perhaps, is more dreadful.[5] Man is an enigma, woven of contradictions, but at the same time—in the person of even the most insignificant human being—an absolute value. Indeed, Dostoevsky was not tormented by God so much as by man—his reality and profundity, his fatal and criminal impulses, as well as his luminous impulses toward good. Dostoevsky is customarily praised—and justly, of course—for the unsurpassed force with which he exhibits the "dark" side of man, man's power of destruction and limitless egoism, the fearful amoralism which is hidden in the depths of his soul. It is true that Dostoevsky's anthropology is devoted primarily to man's "underground." However, it would be very one-sided not to draw attention to the profundity with which he reveals the luminous powers of the soul,[6] its dialectic of the *good*. In this respect, of course, he is close to ancient Christian (*i.e.*, patristic) anthropology. Berdyaev is wholly wrong in asserting that "Dostoevsky's anthropology differs from patristic anthropology." [7] Dostoevsky exhibits not only the sin, corruption, egoism, and, in general, the "demonic" element in man with unprecedented force; he exhibits *no less profoundly* the impulses toward justice and good in the human soul, the "angelic" principle in man. The force and significance of Dostoevsky's use of antinomies in philosophical anthropology derives from the fact that both of the opposites are presented in their highest form.

We have called Dostoevsky's personalism "ethical"; this means, above all, that the value, the unanalyzable quality of human nature, is found not only in its "flowering"—its highest creative attainments—but also inheres in the tiny infant which is still helpless, impotent, and wholly incapable of expressing itself.[8] Dostoevsky's personalism is concerned not with the psychology, but the ontology of man—not with his empirical reality, but with his essence. However, Dostoevsky's conception of man is internally pervaded by an *ethical* category. He not only describes the struggle of good and evil in man; he *seeks* it. Man, of course, is a part of the order of nature, and subject to its laws, but he can and should be

---

[5] In this antinomy, too, Dostoevsky is very close to Schiller. We need only recall the latter's words:

> *Aber das Schrecklichste der Schrecken*
> *Das ist der Mensch in seinem Wahn.*

[6] Dostoevsky's anthropology is represented very one-sidedly in Shestov's book. But Fritz Lieb's special study (*"Die Anthropologie Dostojewskis"* in the collection of articles by various Russian thinkers entitled *Kirche, Staat und Mensch. Russischorthodoxe Studien,* Geneva, 1937) bears the stamp of this same one-sidedness, although it is somewhat mitigated. The two principles of Dostoevsky's anthropology are more correctly noted by Berdyaev, *op. cit.*, pp. 57 ff. See also Zander, *op. cit.*

[7] Berdyaev, *op. cit.*, p. 62.

[8] This was expressed with extraordinary force by Dostoevsky in a letter written after the death of his first child. See also the mother's heart-rending confession to *Starets* Zosima of her inconsolable grief at the death of her son (in *The Brothers Karamazov*).

independent of nature. In *Notes from the Underground* the human spirit's independence from nature is expressed with wonderful power; Dostoevsky declares that man's true essence consists only in his freedom.[9] "The whole human enterprise," we read in *Notes from the Underground,* "consists exclusively in man's proving to himself every moment that he is a man and not a cog." This self-affirmation is an assertion of man's independence from nature; it is in this that man's whole dignity consists.

But for this reason, only man's ethical life is genuinely human; only in it is man essentially a new, higher and incomparable being. In this sense we find, even in *Notes from the Underground,* an *apotheosis* of man, which makes him, if not the center of the world, at least its most important and precious phenomenon. The "anthropologism" which we have seen in the Russian positivists and semipositivists (Chernyshevsky, Lavrov, Kavelin, and Mikhailovsky) was wholly alien and repugnant to Dostoevsky; he was closest to Herzen, with his passionate assertion of the human spirit's independence from nature. Dostoevsky ridicules anthropological naturalism relentlessly in *Notes from the Underground.* His whole doctrine of man is profoundly different from later doctrines which, while agreeing with Dostoevsky concerning man's amoralism, treat this amoralism in the spirit of a primitive naturalism. For Dostoevsky the amoralism which is concealed in man's depths is also man's *apotheosis;* it is a spiritual phenomenon, unconnected with his biological processes.

But the more categorical his ontological exaltation of man, the more relentless is Dostoevsky's disclosure of the fatal disorganization and the dark impulses of the human spirit. The fundamental mystery of man consists for Dostoevsky in his being an ethical creature, invariably and inevitably faced with the dilemma of good and evil, a dilemma *from which he can never retreat.* The man who fails to take the path of good necessarily places himself on the path of evil. Dostoevsky does not *assume* that man's nature is ethical, or that man exhibits a fundamental ethical tendency; he *infers* this from his observation of men.

But here we find paradoxes which reveal not only man's basic ethical nature, but also the whole complex of human problems. First, Dostoevsky caustically ridicules the superficial intellectualism in the conception of man which reached its shallowest expression in the theoretical constructions of utilitarianism. *Notes from the Underground* demonstrate, in immortal pages, that "man is an improvident creature" who acts least of all for his own advantage. "When has there ever been a case in all the millennia of his existence in which man has acted from simple advantage?" The idea of man as a rational, and hence prudent, creature is a pure fic-

---

[9] "Great Heavens, what are the laws of nature to me! . . . Obviously I cannot pierce this wall with my forehead . . . , but neither will I reconcile myself to it just because it is a stone wall." (*Notes from the Underground.*)

tion, "for human nature acts *as a whole*—unconsciously as well as consciously." "Desire may, of course, coincide with rationality . . . , but very often, and for the most part, it is completely and stubbornly at odds with rationality." "I wish to live," continues the man from the underground, "in order to satisfy my whole capacity to live, not merely to satisfy my rational capacity. Rationality satisfies only man's rational capacity, but desire is a manifestation of his whole life." The most precious thing for man is "his own free desire, his own caprice, even though it be absurd." The most precious and important thing for man is "to live by *his own* stupid will," and therefore "man always and everywhere, wherever he is, loves to act as he desires, and not as reason and conscience bid him."

In Dostoevsky, psychological voluntarism imperceptibly merges into irrationalism—a recognition that the key to the understanding of man lies deeper than consciousness, conscience, or reason—in the "underground" where he "himself" exists. Dostoevsky's ethical personalism is clothed in the living flesh of reality: "the nucleus" of man, his genuine essence, is given in his *freedom*, his thirst for individual self-assertion ("to live according to his own stupid will"). Man's ontology is defined by this thirst for freedom, this thirst to be "oneself." But, because Dostoevsky sees man's hidden essence in his freedom, no one has had deeper insight into the mystery of freedom; no one has revealed its whole complex of problems or its "disorganization" more clearly than he. Berdyaev *Free-* has justly observed that for Dostoevsky "the freedom of the underground *dom* man contains the seed of death." Freedom is man's most precious possession, comprising his ultimate "essence"; nevertheless, it is a burden which is too heavy to bear. On the other hand, man's underground—and the "genuine" man is precisely the "natural" man, who has freed himself from all tradition and convention—in Dostoevsky's words, harbors a stench, an internal chaos; it is full of evil, even criminal impulses, as well as impulses which are merely disreputable or petty. Consider Raskolnikov, for example: after rationally analyzing all the precepts of traditional morality he comes to the tempting delusion that "everything is permissible," and proceeds to an act of crime. Morality appears without foundations in the depths of his soul; freedom becomes amoralism. Even in penal servitude Raskolnikov for a long time *felt no repentance.* The turning point came later, when his love for Sonya burst into flower, but before that he found in his freedom no ground for moral hesitation. This reveals the enigma of man's soul: the *blindness of our freedom,* in so far as it is united only to naked reason. The path toward the good is not determined by *freedom alone.* It is irrational, of course, but only in the sense that it is not reason that moves us toward the good, but the will, the powers of the spirit. Hence freedom as such, isolated from the living impulses of love, contains the seed of death. Why death?—Because man cannot in fact evade the Good; and if, having yielded to the free

*Freedom = chaos*
*Freedom + God = Good.*

play of his passions, he turns his back on the good, a tormenting disease of the soul begins in him. Raskolnikov, Stavrogin, and Ivan Karamazov all suffered in different ways because they stifled the living sense of the Good (that is, of God) in themselves, remaining *with themselves alone.* Freedom, when it leaves us with ourselves alone, reveals only chaos in the soul, displaying our dark and ignoble impulses. It converts us into slaves of our passions, making us suffer torment. Man is an *ethical creature* and cannot cease to be one. Dostoevsky points out forcefully and painfully that crime does not indicate any natural amorality, but on the contrary testifies (negatively) to the fact that, in turning his back on the good, man loses something without which he cannot live. In *The House of the Dead* Dostoevsky wrote: "So many great energies have perished here in vain! For it must be said that these were unusual men, perhaps the most gifted and strongest of the nation." There is no doubt that these were men gifted not only with great strength but also with freedom; and this freedom tore them from the paths of "traditional" morality, impelling them toward crime. This is the seed of death! In *The Diary of a Writer* for 1877 Dostoevsky wrote: "Evil is hidden more deeply in man than is usually thought."[10] Shestov unjustly regards this as a "rehabilitation of the underground man";[11] on the contrary, in emphasizing the mysteriousness of evil in the human soul, Dostoevsky points out the disorganization, or rather disintegration, of the human spirit, and at the same time the impossibility of abandoning an ethical orientation. "The seed of death" which inheres in freedom shows that the disintegration of the spirit is not superficial but touches its ultimate depths, for nothing in man is deeper than his freedom.

The complex of problems of human freedom forms the summit of Dostoevsky's ideas in anthropology. Freedom is not the ultimate truth about man; this truth is defined by the ethical principle in man, by the fact that in his freedom he moves either toward evil or toward good. Therefore freedom may contain the "seed of death" and self-destruction, but it may also lift man to the height of transfiguration. Freedom gives ample scope to the demonic in man, but it may also exalt the angelic principle in him. The impulses of freedom comprise a dialectic of evil, but also a dialectic of good. Is this not the significance of the need for suffering which Dostoevsky liked to emphasize, saying that the dialectic of good is set in motion through suffering—and often through sin?

This aspect of Dostoevsky's anthropology is often neglected or undervalued; however, it affords a key to the explanation of the system of ideas which we have characterized as "Christian naturalism." The words which are quoted in passing (in *The Idiot*) that "beauty will save the world" reveal the specific quality of Dostoevsky's aesthetic utopia. All

---

[10] *The Diary of a Writer*, July-August 1877, Chapter II, § 3.
[11] *Op. cit.*, p. 91.

of his doubts concerning man, his disclosure of the chaos and the "seed of death" in him, are neutralized by his conviction that hidden in man is a great force, capable of saving man and the world. The only misfortune is that mankind does not know how to make use of this force. In *The Diary of a Writer* Dostoevsky once wrote (1877): "Man's greatest beauty . . . and greatest purity . . . are turned to no account, are of no use to mankind . . . solely because there has not been genius enough to *direct the wealth* of these gifts." Thus the key to man's transfiguration and harmony lies in man himself, but we do not know how to master this key. "We do not understand," says *Starets* Zosima, "that life is a paradise [at present], for we have only to wish to understand this and it will immediately appear before us in all its beauty." The remarkable words of Versilov (in *The Raw Youth*), concerning a painting by Lorrain, express this same idea: light and truth are already in the world, but they remain unnoticed by us. "A sense of *happiness,* such as I had never before experienced, pierced my heart to the point of pain." This sense of the sanctity in man is conveyed in marvellous form in the brilliant "Dream of a Ridiculous Man." In the materials for *The Possessed* we find the following passage:

> Christ walked on earth to show mankind that even in its earthly nature the human spirit can manifest itself in heavenly radiance, in the flesh, and not merely in a dream or ideal—and that this is both *natural* and *possible.*

It is clear from these words that Dostoevsky's basic doctrine of man is closer to Rousseau's anthropology, with its basic principle of man's radical goodness, than to that of Kant, with his doctrine of "man's radical evil."

However, the dialectic of a "natural and possible" good presupposes a religious life.[12] "The whole law of human existence," Stepan Trofimovich says in *The Possessed,* "is that man should worship something immeasurably great. The Immeasurable and the Infinite are just as necessary to man as is the tiny planet on which he lives." The misfortune of mankind is that "the aesthetic idea has become muddied" in man. Hence beauty has become a "dreadful and frightening thing," "something mysterious in which the devil wrestles with God—and the battlefield is the human heart" (*The Brothers Karamazov*). This "muddying of the aesthetic idea"—as a result of which the devil dominates the man who is aroused to aesthetic rapture—explains why men have lost the "ability" to master the sanctity which is revealed to the heart.

Dostoevsky's anthropology touches the ultimate depths of the human spirit, revealing the invincible power of the ethical principle in man, but also the muddying of the human heart as a result of which the direct

---

[12] See the doctrine of the "mystical root" of man's impulses toward good in *The Diary of a Writer,* 1880, Chapter III, § 4.

path to the good is closed. Freedom has sucked up the "seed of death"; there is a stench in the depths of the soul which is muddied by sin, but the force of good continues to live in man. Only through suffering, and often through crime, is man liberated from the temptations of evil, turning again to God. Hence Alyosha says of *Starets* Zosima: "His heart contains the mystery of renewal for all men, the power which, in the end will establish justice on earth. . . ." The socialist dream of Dostoevsky's earlier years, the romantic dream of "restoring" the good in men (a term taken from Victor Hugo), remained to the end of his life. His anthropology stands halfway between a purely ecclesiastical and a secular idea of man. Dostoevsky's views did not correspond completely to Church doctrine because he failed to give central importance to the Christian emphasis on the suffering and death of the Saviour as a necessary preliminary to His saving Resurrection. We have already said that, in Dostoevsky's Christian conception of the world, emphasis falls on what was revealed about the world and man in the Incarnation and Transfiguration; but he neglects what was given in Golgotha. Nevertheless, Dostoevsky's *faith in man* triumphs over his "disclosures" of the chaos and foul-smelling underground in man. And at this point his anthropology is pierced with the rays of the Easter experience, an experience essential to the basic tonality of Orthodoxy.[13] Dostoevsky retained the aesthetic humanism which was so characteristic of Russian thinkers, but he treated the nature of aesthetic experience in a new way (see below § IV).

It is often held that in *The Grand Inquisitor* Dostoevsky shows man's insignificance especially harshly and cruelly, portraying him as a creature unequal to the "burden" of Christian freedom. But it is forgotten that the words: Christ "judged men too highly"; "man was created weaker and lower than Christ thought"—are all spoken deliberately by the Grand Inquisitor to justify his conversion of churchgoing people into slaves. His mistrust of man is rejected by Dostoevsky, although *The Grand Inquisitor* contains many very profound thoughts concerning the problem of freedom. The fact that man cannot live without God and that the man who loses faith in God places himself on the path of Kirilov in *The Possessed* (although he may not go to the end of it), *i.e.*, enters the path of mangodhood—remains for Dostoevsky a basic truth about man. Whoever rejects Godmanhood as a revelation about man—a creature who finds his fullness in God—inevitably tends toward mangodhood.


## III: ETHICAL VIEWS

We have already emphasized that the ethical category occupies the foreground in Dostoevsky's anthropology and in his whole conception

[13] Concerning the Orthodox conception of man, see my book *Das Bild vom Menschen in der Ostkirche* [translated by H. Strauss], Stuttgart, 1951.

of man. In fact the ethical reflections which fill Dostoevsky's works are defined by the initial ethicism of his thought. His ethical maximalism and the passionate intensity of his ethical searchings, which give such a profound significance to his basic artistic images, follow from the predominance in his thinking of the complex of problems of the good, and of the paths to it. Dostoevsky was profoundly independent[14] in his ethical searchings, and it was in this field that his influence on Russian philosophic thought was especially great. Who among succeeding generations of Russian thinkers has not felt his profound influence?[15] Dostoevsky was filled to overflowing with ethical passion; indeed, the chief root of his philosophic reflections is in the sphere of ethics.

When Dostoevsky, upon returning from penal servitude, began to express himself on ethical problems—both in articles on social and political themes and in his literary works—he first took issue with the oversimplified and shallow conception of man's moral sphere which we have seen in Chernyshevsky, Kavelin, and other representatives of utilitarianism and semi-positivism. Dostoevsky himself was to some extent—but only to some extent—close to these tendencies during the period of his enthusiasm for socialism. We need only recall the passionate pages devoted to this period in his reminiscences of the influence of George Sand (*The Diary of a Writer*, June 1876, Chapter I). But the elements of naturalism, which he derived—through Fourier—from Rousseau, remained only in his *religious* views, in what we have called his "Christian naturalism." In his conception of ethical psychology these elements vanished completely after his penal servitude. In such an early work as *Notes from the Underground* we find an extraordinarily sharp and relentless critique of utilitarianism and moral rationalism. In *Crime and Punishment* the ethical theme appears with a profundity which was new not only for Russian but for European thought. We have already seen, in our analysis of Dostoevsky's anthropology, that he exhibits the decisive ineradicability of man's ethical orientation and the inner dialectic of good in the human soul.

Ethical maximalism attained exceptionally clear and strong expression in Dostoevsky. Ivan Karamazov's revolt against God is defined by an ethical maximalism which refuses to accept the world because its "future harmony" is based on suffering. Suffering, especially that of children—

---

[14] S. Hessen in his articles on Dostoevsky and Solovyov (*"Borba utopi i avtonomi dobra v mirovozreni Dostoyevskovo i V. Solovyova"* ["The Struggle for Utopia and the Autonomy of the Good in the World-View of Dostoevsky and V. Solovyov"], *Sovremennyie zapiski* (1931), 45 and 46), in pointing out the particular closeness of Dostoevsky and Solovyov after the beginning of 1877, admits Solovyov's influence only in the careful reworking of *The Brothers Karamazov* (in the dialectic of the idea of the good). On the other hand, he is inclined to admit a reverse influence of Dostoevsky on Solovyov.

[15] Berdyaev speaks of this most directly ("Dostoevsky has played a decisive part in my spiritual life," *op. cit.*, p. 7). See also V. Ivanov, *Rodnoye i vselenskoye* [*The Native and the Universal*], Moscow, 1917, p. 147.

a theme which greatly agitated Dostoevsky—is unacceptable to the moral consciousness. Was it not under the influence of Ivan Karamazov's passionate speeches that Vladimir Solovyov conceived his *Justification of the Good*? In any event, ethical maximalism reached its deepest and strongest expression in Dostoevsky, entering as an essential element into the ethical theories of subsequent thinkers.

The theme of freedom, as man's ultimate essence, attains equal acuteness and unsurpassed profundity of expression in Dostoevsky. The conception of freedom which is so vigorously repudiated by the Grand Inquisitor is in fact the deepest penetration into the mystery of freedom as revealed in Christ. Dostoevsky is unsurpassed in this respect. No one else has exhibited the full range of the problems of freedom with such force as he; we have already discussed this sufficiently in the preceding section. It may be said that no one—either before or after Dostoevsky—has equalled his profundity in the analysis of the impulses of good and evil, *i.e.*, man's moral psychology. Dostoevsky's faith in man rests not on a sentimental exaltation of man; on the contrary, it triumphs despite his immersion in the darkest impulses of the human soul.

We must admit that Hessen's interpretations of Dostoevsky's ethical views are greatly exaggerated.[16] But it is true that Dostoevsky repudiated not only the ethics of rationality, but also the ethics of *autonomism*, consciously defending a *mystical* ethics.[17] This means first of all that the moral impulses are not determined by feeling, rationality, or reason, but primarily by a living sense of God. Where this sense is lacking, the inevitable result is either an unlimited cynicism, leading to psychic disintegration, or mangodhood. On the other hand, Dostoevsky—and here he accepted the doctrine of the Slavophiles—felt very deeply the injustice and falseness of self-enclosed individualism ("isolation," in his favorite expression). The formula "all are guilty for all" is Dostoevsky's: all men are connected in a mysterious unity which contains the potentiality of genuine brotherhood. Dostoevsky warmly accepted the ideas of N. F. Fyodorov concerning the spirit of "nonbrotherhood" of contemporary life. We need only recall his merciless words in the *Winter Notes on Summer Impressions*: "Who but an abstract doctrinaire could accept the *comedy of bourgeois unity* which we see in Europe as the normal form of human unity on earth?" The idea of *genuine* brotherhood was at the basis of Dostoevsky's early socialism; and this idea remained strong in him throughout his life, determining the religious utopia with which his

---

[16] See his articles *"Tragediya dobra v Br. Karamazovykh"* ["The Tragedy of the Good in the Brothers Karamazov"] *Sovr. zapiski,* No. 36 (1928), and *"Tragediya zla"* ["The Tragedy of Evil"], *Put,* No. 36 (1932). See also the above-mentioned article on Dostoevsky and Solovyov.

[17] We have already quoted Dostoevsky's categorical opinion that the moral sphere in man draws its sustenance exclusively from a mystical root.

world-view was colored, the utopian idea of converting the state—*i.e.*, the whole earthly order—into a Church.

The mystical foundation of morality is expressed with great force and boldness in the words which *Starets* Zosima uttered before his death (*The Brothers Karamazov*):

> "God took seeds from other worlds and sowed them on this earth . . . and they germinated. . . . But that which grows lives and enjoys vitality only through its sense of contact with other mysterious worlds. . . . Much on earth is hidden from us, but in exchange we have been given a secret and hidden sense of our living bond with another world. . . ."

These words formulate Dostoevsky's mystical ethics: our vital and genuine relationship to life is measured only by a love which exceeds the boundaries of both rationality and reason. Love becomes super-reasonable, rising to a sense of inner connection with the whole world, even with the dead, and with inanimate objects. ("Brethren, love each thing. Love each thing and you will *comprehend the mystery of things*.") This universalism of love is wholly sustained by a living sense of God.

## IV: AESTHETIC VIEWS

In his early years Dostoevsky thought a great deal about the "function of Christianity in art." This preoccupation with problems of aesthetics shows the influence of Schiller, with his cult of the aesthetic principle in man and his deep faith in the unity of good and beauty. I think that the influence of A. Grigoryev, Dostoevsky's one-time collaborator on *Vremya* [*Time*], was also strong. Dostoevsky once wrote (*Vremya*, 1864):

> We believe that art has its own integral and organic life. . . . Art is just as much a human need as eating and drinking. The need for beauty and creation is inseparable from man. . . . Man thirsts for beauty, and accepts it without condition, simply because it is beauty.

"Beauty inheres in everything healthy. . . . It is harmony, and it contains a guarantee of tranquillity." "Beauty," Dostoevsky wrote in the same article, "already exists in eternity. . . ." Let us note one more idea, later developed by Dostoevsky in *The Possessed*: "If a nation preserves an ideal of beauty, this means that it has a need for health and a norm, and this very fact guarantees the higher development of such a nation." "Mankind can live without science," the elder Verkhovensky declares (in *The Possessed*), "and without bread; but he cannot live without *beauty*. The whole mystery is there, and the *whole of history*." The incarnation of the ideal, the possibility of its attainment in historical reality, is "guaranteed," according to Dostoevsky, by the fact that there is beauty in the world. "Nations are moved," we read in *The Possessed,* "by a force whose origin is unknown and inexplicable. This . . . is what philosophers call the aesthetic or moral principle; I call it simply the quest for God." Ethical experience appears as essentially mystical insofar as it impels our soul toward God. In the recently published materials we find this thought: "The Holy Spirit is a direct conception of beauty, a prophetic consciousness of harmony and hence a steadfast striving toward it."

The religious interpretation of aesthetic experience overcomes all the temptations of the world, mitigates its injustice, and gives the whole content of culture a higher religious meaning. This is not simply an *acceptance* of culture; it is a religious consecration of culture, the first step in its transfiguration. In Russia, only Archimandrite Bukharev expressed such views before Dostoevsky's time, but after Dostoevsky the problem of giving religious meaning to a culture which had grown out of the "blind" processes of history—the problem of the consecration of culture—became a central historiosophical theme. Dostoevsky himself exhibits a feature that is characteristic of these searchings—a recognition that the key to the transfiguration of culture is provided by *culture itself,* being contained in the depths of culture, and hidden from us only by sin. This is the "Christian naturalism" which was such a powerful temptation to Dostoevsky.

However, he began to doubt very early that "beauty would save the world." He himself wrote that "the aesthetic idea has been muddied in mankind." "I am a nihilist," said the young Verkhovensky, "but I love beauty." He thus emphasized the ambiguity of beauty. And Dmitri Karamazov expresses similar doubts as to the creative power of beauty with extraordinary force: "Beauty is a dreadful and frightening thing. . . . In it extremes meet and contradictions lie down together. . . . The dreadful thing is that what the mind [*i.e.,* moral consciousness] regards as shameful seems unalloyed beauty to the heart." The moral *ambiguity* of beauty, the internal discontinuity of beauty and the good, is at the same time a "mysterious" thing, for in beauty "the devil wrestles with God, and the battlefield is the human heart." This struggle proceeds under the cover of beauty. We may truly say: beauty will not save the world, but the beauty in the world must be saved.


## V: HISTORIOSOPHICAL VIEWS

Dostoevsky's thought has great dialectical power. He exhibits antinomies at points where other men appease themselves with the illicit extension of a one-sided premise. Only after elucidating and sharpening the antinomies which are present in reality does he rise above them. The higher sphere in which contradictions are "reconciled" is the "empyrean sphere," the realm of religion. This constant ascent to religious heights made Dostoevsky an inspiring force in Russian religious philosophy for subsequent generations (Berdyaev, Bulgakov, *et al.*). But Dostoevsky's own religious searchings reached their greatest acuteness in his historiosophy.

We have already quoted the passage from *The Possessed* concerning the "secret of history," the fact that nations are moved by an "aesthetic" or "moral" force, and that in the last analysis this movement is a "search for God." Every nation lives by this "search for God"—"its own" God. Dostoevsky's "cult of primitive immediacy" is, of course, a specific form of Populism, but it is even more closely connected with the ideas of Herder and Schelling (in their Russian interpretation) concerning the special "historical mission" of each nation. The secret of this mission is hidden in the depths of the national spirit; hence the motif of "independence and autonomy" which was so insistently put forward by the "young editorial board" of the *Moskvityanin,* and which Grigoryev brought home to Dostoevsky. But Dostoevsky's cult of primitive immediacy, as Berdyaev has justly emphasized,[18] goes much deeper: he is not bewitched by empirical history, but penetrates to the depths of the national spirit.

That Russia was destined for a special historical task was believed by Herzen and the Slavophiles, as well as by Dostoevsky. The high point in the development of Dostoevsky's ideas about Russia was his celebrated speech on Pushkin. But the idea of an all-embracing synthesis of the Western and Russian spirits, the idea that "we Russians have two homelands—Europe and our Russia," runs through all of his works. This did not preclude his regarding Europe, in the words of Ivan Karamazov, as a "precious cemetery." Criticism of Europe occupies a very large place in Dostoevsky's work; we need only recall Versilov's words on this theme. Russia's strength is in its Orthodoxy; hence, for Dostoevsky, historiosophical themes lead directly to a religious conception of history. He wrote extensively and profoundly on these themes in *The Diary of a Writer;* but without doubt the *The Grand Inquisitor* is the summit of his historiosophical reflections. This "legend" is an extraordinary attempt to exhibit the whole complex of historical problems from a Christian viewpoint. If Russian historiosophy, beginning with Herzen, shows a marked tendency toward alogism, it nevertheless acknowledges—as is most clearly expressed in Mikhailovsky—that meaning is introduced into history by man. Both Christian providentialism and Hegelian panlogism are here categorically rejected.

In Dostoevsky Russian historiosophical thought reverted to a religious conception of history: man's freedom, by divine intention, is the basis of the historical dialectic. The introduction of *human* meaning into history is represented in the grandiose project of the Grand Inquisitor.

---

[18] *Op. cit.,* p. 180.

Dostoevsky here emphasizes with great acuteness that to bring harmony into the historical process one must inevitably *suppress human freedom;* and he feels that this fact is profoundly related to all historiosophical rationalism. His insistence on the inadmissibility of such an approach to man, and his profound defense of the Christian gospel of freedom, do not throw Dostoevsky into the embraces of Christian irrationalism. He, like Vladimir Solovyov, sees the answer in a free movement of the nations toward "churchification" of the whole earthly order. Hessen justly criticizes Dostoevsky's scheme as a form of *utopianism,* but Dostoevsky (unlike the Marxists, and, to some extent, the proponents of Sophiological determinism[19]) does not assume that the ideal will *necessarily* be realized in history. On the contrary, he exhibits the dialectic of the idea of freedom with great profundity and acuteness: the figures of Stavrogin and Kirilov throw an ominous light on this dialectic. Dostoevsky is utopian, not in retaining elements of philosophic rationalism—as the above-mentioned theories do—but in failing to take the problem of redemption into account. His conception of "salvation," as we have frequently emphasized, neglects the mystery of Golgotha. Nevertheless, the grandiose and magnificent picture painted by the Grand Inquisitor is an attempt, unsurpassed in profundity to our day, to grasp the "mystery and secret of history." To be sure, Dostoevsky's indications of the positive paths of "Orthodox culture" are as vague as his critique of the "Catholic idea" and of historiosophical rationalism, generally, is powerful; but it must be admitted that the "metaphysics of history" is illuminated by Dostoevsky with a force of genius found in no one else.

## VI: GENERAL APPRAISAL

Let us sum up our brief analysis of Dostoevsky's ideas.

Dostoevsky's philosophic activity found its deepest inspiration in the "philosophy of the human spirit," but in this realm it achieved extraordinary significance. Anthropology, ethics, historiosophy, the problem of theodicy—all receive profound and acute treatment in Dostoevsky. His contribution to Russian (and not only Russian) thought is very large. It is with good reason that the great majority of Russian thinkers in subsequent generations linked their creative activity to that of Dostoevsky. Special importance attaches to the fact that Dostoevsky forcefully formulated the problem of culture *within the religious consciousness itself.* The prophetic expectation of an "Orthodox culture," which was first conceived by Gogol, and which marked out genuinely new paths of historical activity, became in Dostoevsky for the first time a central theme of historiosophical searchings and constructions. Secu-

---

[19] I have in mind the theories of S. Bulgakov.

larism, which the Slavophiles still conceived as the dialectically inevitable outcome of the religious process in the West, was viewed by Dostoevsky as a permanent, though one-sided, orientation of the human spirit, *a specific religious orientation.* Raskolnikov incarnates the radical break of the human spirit with the religious consciousness, and Kirilov exhibits the inevitable religious reformulation of this break with God in the ideology of mangodhood. The forces which in Western philosophy had long since made secularism a kind of religious immanentism, arise in Dostoevsky's heroes from the idea of reality—a reality dialectically inseparable from the religious principle. This reversion of thought from abstract radicalism to its primordial religious womb did not suppress or eliminate any of the profound problems of the human spirit; it merely placed the whole complex of problems on its basic foundation. Dostoevsky, in fact, opened a new period in the history of Russian thought. Although Russian thinkers had always recognized the fundamental importance of the religious orientation, Dostoevsky was the first to convert all the problems of the human spirit into religious problems. Of course, this immediately complicated the religious orientation, threatening a break with the classical formulations of the Church Fathers, but at the same time it formed the basis for an extraordinary and fruitful flowering of Russian religio-philosophic thought.

# Dostoevsky

## by Georg Lukács

*I go to prove my soul!*
Robert Browning

It is a strange, but often repeated fact that the literary embodiment
of a new human type with all its problems comes to the civilized world
from a young nation. Thus in the eighteenth century Werther came from
Germany and prevailed in England and France: thus in the second half
of the nineteenth century Raskolnikov came from far-off, unknown, almost legendary Russia to speak for the whole civilized West.

There is nothing unusual in the fact that a backward country produces
powerful works. The historical sense developed in the nineteenth century
has accustomed us to enjoy the literature and art of the whole globe and
the whole past. Works of art that have influenced the entire world origi-
nated in the remotest countries and ages: from Negro sculpture to Chinese
woodcuts, from the *Kalevala* to Rabindranath Tagore.

But the cases of Werther and Raskolnikov are very different. Their
effect is not touched in the slightest by a craving for the exotic. "Suddenly" there appeared from an underdeveloped country, where the troubles and conflicts of contemporary civilization could not yet have been
fully unfolded, works that stated—imaginatively—all the problems of
human culture at its highest point, stirred up ultimate depths, and presented a totality hitherto never achieved and never since surpassed, embracing the spiritual, moral, and philosophical questions of that age.

The word *question* must be underscored and must be supplemented
by the assertion that it is a poetic, creative question and not a question
put in philosophical terms. For this was and is the mission of poetry and
fiction: to put questions, to raise problems in the form of new men and
new fates of men. The concrete answers that naturally are given by
poetic works frequently have—seen from this distance—an arbitrary
character in bourgeois literature. They may even throw the actual poetic

"Dostoevsky." From *Der russische Realismus in der Weltliteratur*, by Georg Lukács
(Berlin, 1949), © 1953 by Georg Lukács. Translated from the German by René Wellek.
Reprinted by permission of the author. This essay dates from 1943.

problem into confusion. Goethe very soon saw this himself with Werther. Only a few years later he made Werther exhort the reader in a poem: "Be a man and don't follow me."

Ibsen quite deliberately considered questioning the task of the poet and declined, on principle, any obligation to answer his questions. Chekhov made a definitive statement about this whole matter when he drew a sharp distinction between "the solution of a question and the correct putting of the question. Only the last is required of the artist. In *Anna Karenina* and *Onegin* not a single question is solved yet these works satisfy us fully only because all questions are put in them correctly."[1]

This insight is particularly important for a judgment of Dostoevsky for many—even most—of his political and social answers are false, have nothing to do with present-day reality or with the strivings of the best today. They were obsolete, even reactionary, when they were pronounced.

Still, Dostoevsky is a writer of world eminence. For he knew how during a crisis of his country and the whole human race, to put questions in an imaginatively decisive sense. He created men whose destiny and inner life, whose conflicts and interrelations with other characters, whose attraction and rejection of men and ideas illuminated all the deepest questions of that age, sooner, more deeply, and more widely than in average life itself. This imaginative anticipation of the spiritual and moral development of the civilized world assured the powerful and lasting effect of Dostoevsky's works. These works have become even more topical and more fresh as time goes on.

## II

Raskolnikov is the Rastignac of the second half of the nineteenth century. Dostoevsky admired Balzac, had translated *Eugénie Grandet,* and surely quite consciously resumed the theme of his predecessor. The very nature of this connection shows his originality: his poetic grasp of the change of the times, of men, of their psychology and world-view.

Emerson saw the reason for the deep and general effect of Napoleon on the whole intellectual life of Europe in the fact that "the people whom he sways are little Napoleons." He put his finger on one side of this influence: Napoleon represented all the virtues and vices possessed by the great mass of men in his time and partly also in later times. Balzac and Stendhal turned the question round and made the necessary additions. Napoleon appeared to them as the great example for the saying that since the French Revolution every gifted man carries a marshall's baton in his knapsack, as the great example of the unimpeded rise of talents in a democratic society. Hence as the gage for the democratic character of a society: Is a Napoleon-like rise possible or not? From this question fol-

[1] A letter to A. Suvorin, October 27, 1888. (Translator's note.)

lowed the pessimistic criticism of Balzac and Stendhal: a recognition and admission that the heroic period of bourgeois society—and of the rise of individuals—was over and belonged to the past.

When Dostoevsky appeared, the heroic period had receded even further. The bourgeois society of Western Europe had consolidated itself. Against Napoleonic dreams had been erected inner and outer barriers different and more firm than those erected in the time of Balzac and Stendhal. The Russia of Dostoevsky was barely beginning a social transformation—that is why the Napoleonic dreams of Russian youth were more violent, more passionate than those of their Western European contemporaries. But the transformation encountered at first insuperable obstacles in the existing firm skeleton of the old society (however dead it may seem in the perspective of history). Russia was during this period a contemporary of the Europe after 1848, with its disillusionment with the ideals of the eighteenth century and its dreams of a renovation and reformation of bourgeois society. This contemporaneity with Europe arose, however, in a prerevolutionary period when the Russian *ancien-régime* still ruled unchecked, when the Russian 1789 was still in the distant future.

Even Rastignac saw Napoleon less as the concrete historical heir of the French Revolution than as a *"professeur d'énergie."* The fascinating figure of Napoleon set an example less by his ultimate aims than by his method, by the kinds and techniques of his action, by his way of overcoming obstacles. Still, in spite of all the psychological and moral attenuations and sublimations of the ideal, the peculiar aims of the generation of the Rastignacs remained clear and socially concrete.

The situation of Raskolnikov is even more decidedly reversed. The moral and psychological problem was for him almost exclusively concrete: the ability of Napoleon to step over men for the sake of great aims —an ability which Napoleon has, for instance, in common with Mohammed.

From such a psychological perspective the concrete action becomes fortuitous—an occasion rather than a real aim or means. The psychological and moral dialectic of the pro and con of the action becomes the crux of the matter: the test whether Raskolnikov has the moral capacity to become a Napoleon. Concrete action becomes a psychological experiment which, however, risks the whole physical and moral existence of the experimenter: an experiment whose "fortuitous occasion" and "fortuitous subject" is, after all, another human being.

In Balzac's *Père Goriot,* Rastignac and his friend Bianchon discuss briefly the moral problem whether one would have the right to press a button in order to kill an unknown Chinese mandarin if one received a million francs for it. In Balzac the conversations are episodes, witty byplay, moral illustrations for the concrete main problems of the novel. In Dostoevsky it becomes the central question: with great and deliberate art it is made the focus. The practical and concrete side of the act is pushed aside with equal deliberation. For example, Raskolnikov does not even know how much he has robbed from the pawnbroker, his murder is carefully planned but he forgets to shut the door, and so on. All these details emphasize the main point: can Raskolnikov morally endure the overstepping of the boundaries? And principally: what are the motives which work in him for and against the crime? what moral forces come into play? what psychological inhibitions affect his decision before and after the crime? what psychic forces is he able to mobilize for this decision and for his perseverance afterwards?

The mental experiment with himself assumes its own dynamism; it continues even when it has lost all practical significance. Thus the day after the murder Raskolnikov goes to the flat of the pawnbroker in order to listen again to the sound of the doorbell which had terrified and upset him so much after the killing and to test again its psychic effects on himself. The purer the experiment as such, the less can it give a concrete answer to concrete questions.

Raskolnikov's fundamental problem has become an event in world literature—precisely in connection and in contrast to his great predecessor. Just as the rise and effect of *Werther* would have been impossible without Richardson and Rousseau, so Raskolnikov is unthinkable without Balzac. But the putting of the central question in *Crime and Punishment* is just as original, stimulating, and prophetic as in *Werther*.

### III

The experiment with oneself, the execution of an action not so much for the sake of the contents and effects of the action, but in order to know oneself once for all, in depth, to the very bottom, is one of the main human problems of the bourgeois and intellectual world of the nineteenth and twentieth centuries.

Goethe took a very skeptical attitude toward the slogan "Know thyself," toward self-knowledge by self-analysis. For him action as a way to self-knowledge was still taken for granted. He possessed a stable system of ideals, though it may not have been expressly formulated. In striving for these ideals, actions which were significant for their contents, for their intimate relations to the ideals, were accomplished of necessity. Self-knowledge thus becomes a by-product of the actions. Man, by acting concretely in society, learns to know himself.

Even when these ideals change, even when—whether realized or not—they lose their weight and become relative, new ideals take the place of the lost ones. Faust, Wilhelm Meister (and of course Goethe himself) have their problems; but they have not become problems to themselves.

The same is true of the great egoists in Balzac. Looked at objectively, the turning inward, the making subjective of the ideals of individualism, appears very questionable when egoism—the exaltation at any price of the individual—becomes the central issue as it does so constantly in Balzac. But these objective problems lead only very rarely in Balzac to the self-dissolution of the subject. Individualism displays here its tragic (or comic) problems very early; but the individual itself has not yet become problematical.

Only when this individualism turns inward—when it fails to find an Archimedean point either in current social aims or in the spontaneous urge of an egotistical ambition—does the problem of Dostoevsky's experiments arise. Stavrogin, the hero of *The Possessed*, gives a summary of these problems in his farewell letter to Dasha Shatov immediately before his suicide:

> "I tried my strength everywhere. You advised me to do this so as to learn 'to know myself.' . . . But what to apply my strength to—that's what I have never seen and don't see now . . . I can still wish to do something good, as I always could, and that gives me a feeling of pleasure. At the same time I wish to do something evil and that gives me pleasure, too. . . . My desires are not strong enough, they cannot guide me. You can cross a river on a log but not on a chip of wood." [2]

Admittedly the case of Stavrogin is very special, very different from that of Raskolnikov and particularly different from these experiments in which the striving for self-knowledge appeals to the soul of other men: as, for instance, when the hero of *Notes from the Underground*, who lives almost exclusively by such experiments, speaks compassionately to the prostitute Liza in order to test his power over her feelings; or when, in *The Idiot*, Nastasya Filipovna throws the one hundred thousand rubles brought by Rogozhin into the fire in order fully to know and enjoy the meanness of Ganya Ivolgin, who would get the money if he could pull it from the fire, and so on.

All these cases, however diverse, have something important in common. First of all, they are without exception the actions of lonely men—men who are completely dependent on themselves as they understand life and their environment, who live so deeply and intensely in themselves that the soul of others remains to them forever an unknown country. The other man is to them only a strange and menacing power which either subjugates them or becomes subject to them. When young Dolgoruky in *A Raw Youth* expounds his "idea" of becoming a Rothschild and describes the experiments to realize his "idea," which are psychologically very similar to those of Raskolnikov, he defines their nature as "solitude" and "power." Isolation, separation, loneliness reduces the relations among

[2] From *The Possessed*. Modern Library ed., p. 685. Constance Garnett translation, modified.

men to a struggle for superiority or inferiority. The experiment is a sublimated spiritual form, a psychological turning inward of naked struggles for power.

But by this solitude, by this immersion of the subject in itself, the self becomes bottomless. There arises either the anarchy of Stavrogin, a loss of direction in all instincts, or the obsession of a Raskolnikov by an "idea." A feeling, an aim, an ideal acquires absolute sovereignty over the soul of a man: I, you, all men disappear, turn into shadows, exist only subsumed under the "idea." This monomania appears in a low form in Pyotr Verkhovensky (*The Possessed*), who takes men to be what he wishes them to be; in a higher form in the women who were hurt by life. Katerina Ivanovna (*The Brothers Karamazov*) loves only her own virtue, Nastasya Filipovna (*The Idiot*), her own humiliation: both imagine that they will find support and satisfaction in this love. We find the highest level of this psychic organization in the men of ideas such as Raskolnikov and Ivan Karamazov. A horrifying, caricaturing contrast to these is Smerdyakov (*The Brothers Karamazov*), the ideological and moral effect of the doctrine that "everything is permitted."

But precisely on the highest level does the overstrained subjectivity most obviously turn into its opposite: the rigid monomania of the "idea" becomes absolute emptiness. The "raw youth," Dolgoruky, very graphically describes the psychological consequences of his obsession by the "idea" of becoming a Rothschild:

> ". . . having something fixed, permanent, and overpowering in one's mind in which one is terribly absorbed, one is, as it were, removed by it from the whole world, and everything that happens (except the one great thing) slips by one. Even one's impressions are hardly formed correctly. . . . Oh, I have my 'idea,' nothing else matters, was what I said to myself. . . . The 'idea' comforted me in disgrace and insignificance. But all the nasty things I did took refuge, as it were, under the 'idea.' So to speak, it smoothed over everything, but also put a mist before my eyes." [3]

Hence comes the complete incongruity between action and soul in these people. Hence comes their panic fear of being ridiculous because they are constantly aware of this incongruity. The more extreme this individualism becomes, the more the self turns inward, the stronger it even becomes outwardly and the more it shuts itself off from objective reality with a Chinese wall, the more it loses itself in an inner void. The self which submerges itself in itself, cannot find any more firm ground; what seemed firm ground for a time turns out to be mere surface; everything that temporarily appeared with the claim of giving direction turns into its opposite. The ideal becomes completely subjective, an alluring but always deceptive *Fata Morgana*.

[3] *A Raw Youth.* Dial Press ed., pp. 100-101. Translated by Constance Garnett.

Thus the experiment is the desperate attempt to find firm ground within oneself, to know who one is—a desperate attempt to pull down the Chinese wall between the I and the You, between the self and the world—a desperate attempt and always a futile attempt. The tragedy—or the tragicomedy—of the lonely man finds its purest expression in the experiment.

## IV

A minor figure in Dostoevsky describes the atmosphere of these novels briefly and pointedly. She says of its characters: "They are all as if at a railroad station." And this is the essential point.

First of all, for these people every situation is provisional. One stands at a railroad station, waiting for the departure of the train. The railroad station naturally is not home, the train is necessarily a transition. This image expresses a pervasive feeling about life in Dostoevsky's world. In *The House of the Dead,* Dostoevsky remarks that even prisoners condemned to twenty years of penal servitude regard their life in prison as something transitory and consider it provisional. In a letter to the critic, Strakhov, Dostoevsky compares his story, *The Gambler,* which he was then planning, with *The House of the Dead.* He wanted to achieve an effect similar to the one he had achieved in *The House of the Dead.* The life of a gambler (also a symbolic figure for Dostoevsky and his world) is never life proper but rather only a preparation for the life to come, for real life. These men do not properly live in the present, but only in a constant tense expectation of the decisive turn in their fortune. But even when such a turn occurs—usually as a result of the experiment—nothing essential is changed in the organization of their inner world. One dream is punctured by the touch of reality: it collapses—and there arises a new dream of a new turn around the corner. One train has left the station, one waits for the next one—but a railroad station nevertheless remains a railroad station, a place of transit.

Dostoevsky is acutely aware that an adequate expression of such a world places him in complete opposition to the art of the past and the present. At the end of *A Raw Youth* he expresses this conviction in the form of a critical letter on the memoirs of the hero. He sees clearly that such a world could not possibly be dominated by the beauty of *Anna Karenina.* But then he justifies his own form, he does not do so by raising a question of pure aesthetics. On the contrary, he thinks that the beauty of Tolstoy's novels (Dostoevsky does not name them but the allusion is unmistakable) belongs really to the past and not to the present and that these works have, in their essence, already become historical novels. The social criticism concealed behind the aesthetic conflict is made concrete by describing the family whose fate is related in Dolgoruky's memoirs as not a normal but an "accidental family." According to the writer of the letter, the contrast of beauty and the new realism is due to a change in the structure of society. On the one hand, the "arbitrariness," the abnormality of the family appears in the minds of the individuals—the better people of the present age are almost all mentally ill, says a figure of that novel; and on the other hand, all the distortions within the family are only the most conspicuous expression of a deep crisis in the whole society.

In seeing and presenting this, Dostoevsky becomes the first and greatest poet of the modern capitalist metropolis. There were of course poetic treatments of city life long before Dostoevsky: as early as the eighteenth century Defoe's *Moll Flanders* emerged as a masterpiece of the city. Dickens, in particular, gave poetic expression to the peculiar solitude of the great city. (Dostoevsky loves and praises Dickens most enthusiastically for this very reason.) And Balzac had sketched the Dantesque circles of a new, contemporary Hell in his picture of Paris.

All this is true and one could add much more. But Dostoevsky was the first—and is still unsurpassed—in drawing the mental deformations that are brought about as a social necessity by life in a modern city. The genius of Dostoevsky consists precisely in his power of recognizing and representing the dynamics of a future social, moral, and psychological evolution from germs of something barely beginning.

We must add that Dostoevsky does not confine himself to description and analysis—to mere "morphology," to use a fashionable term of present-day agnosticism—but offers also a genesis, a dialectic, and a perspective.

The problem of genesis is decisive. Dostoevsky sees the starting point of the specific nature of his characters' psychological organization in the particular form of urban misery. Take the great novels and stories of Dostoevsky's mature period: *Notes from the Underground, The Insulted and the Injured, Crime and Punishment.* In each one of them we are shown how the problems that we discussed from the point of view of their psychic consequences, how the psychic organization of Dostoevsky's characters, how the deformations of their moral ideals grow out of the social misery of the modern metropolis. The insulting and injuring of men in the city is the basis of their morbid individualism, their morbid desire for power over themselves and their neighbors.

In general, Dostoevsky does not like descriptions of external reality: he is not a *paysagiste,* as Turgenev and Tolstoy are, each in his own manner. But because he grasps with the visionary power of a poet the unity of the inner and the outer—the social and the psychic—organization here in the misery of the city, unsurpassed pictures of Petersburg emerge, particularly in *Crime and Punishment,* pictures of the new metropolis—from the coffinlike furnished room of the hero through the stifling narrowness of the police station to the center of the slum district, the Haymarket, and the nocturnal streets and bridges.

Yet Dostoevsky is never a specialist in milieu. His work embraces the whole of society, from the "highest" to the "lowest," from Petersburg to a remote provincial village. But the "primary phenomenon"—and this artistic trait throws a strong light on the social genesis of the books—remains always the same: the misery of Petersburg. What is experienced in Petersburg is generalized by Dostoevsky as valid for the whole of society. Just as in the provincial tragedies, *The Possessed* and *The Brothers Karamazov*, Petersburg characters (Stavrogin and Ivan) set the tone, so in the depiction of the whole society the pattern is set by what has grown out from "down there" in misery.

Balzac recognized and represented the deep psychological parallelism between the "upper" and the "lower" and saw clearly that the forms of expression of the socially lower would have great advantages over those of the upper stratum.

But Dostoevsky is concerned with much more than a problem of artistic expression. The Petersburg misery, particularly that of intellectual youth, is for him the purest, classical symptom of his "primary phenomenon": the alienation of the individual from the broad stream of the life of the people, which to Dostoevsky is the last and decisive social reason for all the mental and moral deformations we have sketched above. One can observe the same deformations also in the upper strata. But here one sees rather the psychological results, while in the former the social and psychological process of their genesis comes out much more clearly. "Up there" the historical connection of this psychic organization with the past can be discerned. Gorky very acutely sees in Ivan Karamazov a psychic descendant of the passive nobleman Oblomov. "Down there," however, the rebellious element gains the upper hand and points to the future.

This divorce between the lonely individual and the life of the people is the prevailing theme of bourgeois literature in the second half of the nineteenth century. This type dominates the bourgeois literature of the West during this period—whether it is accepted or rejected, lyrically idealized, or satirically caricatured. But even in the greatest writers, in Flaubert and Ibsen, the psychological and moral consequences appear more prominently than their social basis. Only in Russia, in Tolstoy and Dostoevsky, is the problem raised in all its breadth and depth.

Tolstoy contrasts his heroes who have lost contact with the people—and hence have lost the objectivity of their ideals, their moral standards, and their psychological support—with the peasant class, which was then apparently quite immobile, but was actually going through a process of complete transformation. Its slow and often contradictory transition to social action became important for the fate of the democratic renewal of Russia only much later.

Dostoevsky investigates the same process of the dissolution of old Russia and the germs of its rebirth primarily in the misery of the cities among the "insulted and injured" of Petersburg. Their involuntary alienation from the old life of the people—which only later became an ideology, a will and activity, their—provisional—inability to "connect" with the popular movement which was still groping for an aim and direction, was Dostoevsky's "primary social phenomenon."

Only this point of view illuminates the alienation of the upper strata from the people in Dostoevsky. With a different emphasis, but essentially as in Tolstoy, it is idleness, life without work—the complete isolation of the soul which comes from idleness—which may be tragic or grotesque or, most frequently, tragicomic—but always deforming. Whether it is Svidrigailov, Stavrogin, Versilov, Liza Khokhlakov, Aglaya Yepanchin or Nastasya Filipovna: for Dostoevsky their idle or, at most, aimlessly active lives are always the foundation of their hopeless solitude.

## V

This plebeian trait sharply distinguishes Dostoevsky from parallel Western literary movements which, in part, arose simultaneously with him and, in part, arose at a later stage—under his influence—from the diverse trends of literary psychologism.

In the West this literary trend—which in France Edmond de Goncourt helped to prepare and Bourget, Huysmans, and others helped to realize —was primarily a reaction against the plebeian tendencies of naturalism, which were not particularly strong anyway. Goncourt considered the change an artistic conquest of the upper strata of society, while naturalism had concerned itself largely with the lower classes. In the later representatives of this tendency—up to Proust—the aristocratic and *mondain* trait of literary psychologism comes out even more forcefully.

The cult of the inner life appears as a privilege of the upper classes of society, in contrast to the brutal earthy conflicts of the lower classes that naturalism tried to comprehend artistically by heredity and environment. The cult therefore takes on a double aspect. On the one hand, it is coquettish, vain, highly self-conscious—even in cases where it led individually to tragic destinies. On the other hand, it is decidedly conservative, because most Western authors cannot oppose the mental and moral instability of lonely city individualists here described with anything more than the old spiritual forces—primarily the authority of the Roman Catholic Church, as something that might offer refuge to erring souls.

Dostoevsky's answers in his journalistic writings—and also in his novels —parallel these tendencies of bourgeois literature in his appeal to the Russian Orthodox Church. But the correctness and depth of his poetic questionings lead him far beyond his narrow horizon and push him into sharp opposition to parallel phenomena in the West.

In particular the world of Dostoevsky lacks any trace of worldly skep-

tical coquetry, of vain self-consciousness, or of toying with his own loneliness and despair. "We always play, and who knows this, is wise," says
Arthur Schnitzler and thereby expresses the most extreme contrast to the
world of Dostoevsky's characters. For their despair is not the spice of
life, which is otherwise bored and idle, but despair in the most genuine,
most literal sense. Their despair is an actual banging at closed doors, an
embittered, futile struggle for the meaning of life which is lost or in
danger of being lost.

Because this despair is genuine, it is a principle of excess, again in
sharp contrast to the worldly polished forms of most of the Western
skeptics. Dostoevsky shatters all forms—beautiful and ugly, genuine and
false—because the desperate man can no longer consider them an adequate expression for what he is seeking for his soul. All the barriers that
social convention has erected between men are pulled down in order that
nothing but spontaneous sincerity, to the most extreme limits, to the
utter lack of shame, may prevail among men. The horror at the loneliness of men erupts here with irresistible power precisely because all these
pitiless destructions are still unable to remove the solitude.

The journalist Dostoevsky could speak consolingly in a conservative
sense, but the human content, the poetic tempo and the poetic rhythm
of his speech, have a rebellious tone and thus find themselves constantly
in opposition to his highest political and social intentions.

The struggle of these two tendencies in Dostoevsky's mind yields very
diverse results. Sometimes, rather frequently, the political journalist wins
out over the poet: the natural dynamics of his characters, dictated by his
vision—independently of his conscious aims—and not by his will are
violated and distorted to fit his political opinions. The sharp criticism
made by Gorky that Dostoevsky slanders his own characters applies to
such cases.

But very frequently the result is rather the opposite. The characters
emancipate themselves and lead their own lives to the very end, to the
most extreme consequences of their inborn nature. The dialectics of their
evolution, their ideological struggle, takes a completely different direction
than the consciously envisaged goals of the journalist Dostoevsky. The
poetic question, correctly put, triumphs over the political intentions, the
social answer of the writer.

Only there does the depth and correctness of Dostoevsky's questioning
assert itself fully. It is a revolt against that moral and psychic deforma-
tion of man which is caused by the evolution of capitalism. Dostoevsky's
characters go to the end of the socially necessary self-distortion unafraid,
and their self-dissolution, their self-execution, is the most violent protest that could have been made against the organization of life in that
time. The experimentation of Dostoevsky's characters is thus put into a
new light: it is a desperate attempt to break through the barriers which
deform the soul and maim, distort, and dismember life. The creator

Dostoevsky does not know the correct direction of the breakthrough, and could not know it. The journalist and philosopher pointed in the wrong direction. But that this problem of the breakthrough occurs with every genuine upsurge of the mind points to the future and demonstrates the unbreakable power of humanity which will never be satisfied with half measures and false solutions.

Every genuine man in Dostoevsky breaks through this barrier, even though he perishes in the attempt. The fatal attraction of Raskolnikov and Sonya is only superficially one of extreme opposites. Quite rightly Raskolnikov tells Sonya that by her boundless spirit of self-sacrifice, by the selfless goodness which made her a prostitute in order to save her family, she herself had broken the barrier, and transcended the limits—just as he had done by murdering the pawnbroker. For Dostoevsky this transcendence was in Sonya more genuine, more human, more immediate, more plebeian than in Raskolnikov.

Here the light shines in the darkness and not where the journalist Dostoevsky fancied he saw it. Modern solitude is that darkness. "They say," says a desperate character in Dostoevsky, "that the well-fed cannot understand the hungry, but I would add that the hungry do not always understand the hungry." [4] There is apparently not a ray of light in this darkness. What Dostoevsky thought to be such a ray was only a will-o'-the-wisp.

The ways that Dostoevsky points out for his characters are impassable. As a creator he himself feels these problems deeply. He preaches faith, but in reality—as a creator of men—he does not himself believe that the man of his age can have faith in his sense. It is his atheists who have genuine depth of thought, a genuine fervor for the quest.

He preaches the way of Christian sacrifice. But his first positive hero, Prince Myshkin in *The Idiot,* is fundamentally atypical and pathological because he is unable, largely due to his illness, to overcome inwardly his egoism—even in love. The problem of victory over egoism, to which Prince Myshkin was supposed to find the answer creatively, cannot be put concretely, creatively, because of this pathological foundation. It may be said in passing that the limitless compassion of Myshkin causes at least as much tragic suffering as the darkly individualistic pathos of Raskolnikov.

When, at the end of his career, Dostoevsky wanted to create a healthy positive figure in Alyosha Karamazov, he vacillated constantly between two extremes. In the extant novel Alyosha actually seems to be a healthy counterpart of Prince Myshkin, a Dostoevskean saint. But the novel as we know it—just from the point of view of the main hero—is only a beginning, only the story of his youth. We also know something of Dostoevsky's plans for a continuation. In a letter to the poet Maikov he

---

[4] The old Ichmenyev in *The Insulted and the Injured.* Translated by Constance Garnett. New York, 1950, p. 262. (Translator's note.)

writes: "The hero in the course of his life is for a while an atheist, then a believer, then again a zealot and sectarian, and at the end he becomes again an atheist." This letter fully confirms what Suvorin reports of a conversation with Dostoevsky, which may sound startling at first. Suvorin tells us that "the hero is to commit a political crime at the proper moment and is to be executed; he is a man thirsting for truth who in his quest has quite naturally become a revolutionary." We cannot know of course whether and how far Dostoevsky would have carried the character of Alyosha in this direction. Still, it is more than characteristic that the inner dynamics of his favorite hero had to take this direction.

Thus the world of Dostoevsky's characters dissolves his political ideals into chaos. But this chaos itself is great in Dostoevsky: his powerful protest against everything false and distorting in modern bourgeois society. It is no chance that the memory of a picture by Claude Lorrain, *Acis and Galathea,* recurs several times in his novels. It is always called "The Golden Age" by his heroes and is described as the most powerful symbol of their deepest yearning.

The golden age: genuine and harmonious relations between genuine and harmonious men. Dostoevsky's characters know that this is a dream in the present age but they cannot and will not abandon the dream. They cannot abandon the dream even when most of their feelings sharply contradict it. This dream is the truly genuine core, the real gold of Dostoevsky's Utopias; a state of the world in which men may know and love each other, in which culture and civilization will not be an obstacle to the development of men.

The spontaneous, wild, and blind revolt of Dostoevsky's characters occurs in the name of the golden age, whatever the contents of the mental experiment may be. This revolt is poetically great and historically progressive in Dostoevsky: here really shines a light in the darkness of Petersburg misery, a light that illuminates the road to the future of mankind.

# Dostoevsky

## by D. A. Traversi

### I

The reading of a good deal of modern Christian thought prompts one to the reflection that it should be the first axiom of valid thinking that nothing can serve as a substitute for anything else. In particular, the less definable parts of metaphysics are not an alternative to literary criticism. So, when I read in Berdyaev's book on Dostoevsky that "This is not to be a book of literary criticism. My aim is to display Dostoevsky's spiritual side," I began to doubt whether what was to be displayed would turn out to be much more than Berdyaev's own preoccupations. In what way precisely is the "spiritual" side of a writer separable from the literary expression of his experience? How, except by the methods of the despised criticism, are we to get at that experience? And when, further on, I found that "Even the mind of Goethe, great among the greatest, had not the same keenness and dialectical profundity," I realized that my misgivings were at least in part justified. For a little concern with literary criticism would have told Berdyaev that Goethe was among the first of the irresponsible amateurs of thought, of those who tried to cover their spiritual poverty by an elaborate embroidery of unrelated words. Only literary criticism can differentiate infallibly between the artistic power of *The Idiot* or *The Brothers Karamazov* and the unctuous philosophizing of *Faust*. There is no substitute for the sincere and unimpeded action of sensibility in the appreciation of literature. The findings of criticism can help the metaphysician, but they cannot be short-circuited by him. A great writer like Dostoevsky concentrates in himself the qualities of his society, and serves, to those who can read him critically, as a mirror of its culture. This essay is a tentative effort to point to the kind of conclusions that a critical investigation would reach.

In accordance with sound principles, we begin, not with generalizations on "Man" or "Freedom" or any abstraction, but with the text of

"Dostoevsky." From *The Criterion*, XVI (1937), 585-602. © 1937 by Derek Traversi. Reprinted by permission of the author.

Dostoevsky. Anyone who has read the novels with any sympathy will find that the two following passages, one from *The Idiot* and one from *The Possessed,* contain something of the essential and peculiar quality of this author's work. The first deals with the feelings of a condemned criminal on the way to the guillotine:

> "And only think that it must be like that up to the last quarter of a second, when his head lies on the block and he waits and . . . knows, and suddenly hears above him the clang of the iron! He must hear that! If I were lying there, I should listen on purpose and hear. It may last only the tenth part of a second, but one would be sure to hear it. And only fancy, it's still disputed whether, when the head is cut off, it knows for a second after that it has been cut off! What an idea! And what if it knows it for five seconds?" [1]

The second passage discusses annihilation by the fall of a huge stone upon a man:

> "A stone as big as a house? Of course it would be fearful."
> "I speak not of the fear. Will it hurt?"
> "A stone as big as a mountain, weighing millions of tons? Of course it wouldn't hurt."
> "But really stand there and while it hangs you will fear very much that it will hurt. The most learned man, the greatest doctor, all, all, will be very frightened. Everyone will know that it won't hurt, and everyone will be afraid that it will hurt." [2]

Now these two passages have undeniably a common sensibility behind them. They are not concerned with the normal life of the senses at all, but with a desire to transcend experience and stretch the capacity of the mind beyond the limit of the conceivable: they seek, in fact, to comprehend what we call the infinite. They are, of course, connected with the senses, since it is through these that the artist gains any experience to work on. But the essential fact is that these senses, and in particular the feeling of pain, are only used in an effort to pass beyond them and to attain a state that is beyond imagination. This causes, indeed, a definite and peculiar strain on the feeling of the reader, perhaps best described by a chance phrase in *Crime and Punishment*: "He felt as if a nail were being driven into his skull." There is, in fact, in Dostoevsky's experience an odd and fundamental paradox; the senses are continually being put to work with an almost incredible intensity in an effort to transcend the sensible, until we can feel the stuff of experience being brutally torn apart between these two incompatible impulses.

[1] *The Idiot.*
[2] *The Possessed.*

We are conscious that our senses are continually being mobilized to the furthest limit of their intensity, only to be driven beyond the frontiers of the palpable, until we break down before the prospect of an infinite voyage into nonentity.

This continual craving to outstrip the senses is particularly interesting because it clashes with the practice of the great writers of western Europe. Of these, Shakespeare is the outstanding instance. In total opposition to Dostoevsky, Shakespeare was concerned above all with pressing the utmost out of sensible experience. Read, for example, *Troilus and Cressida,* and you will be left with a sense of life itching at the finger-tips and breaking into sores at the surface. The experiences of Troilus in his love are turned over and over on the palate until they become "thrice repured nectar." [3] The whole human body becomes a delicate instrument for recording experience, and over it the poetic judgment, if I may be permitted a convenient abstraction for a process largely intuitive, is set to select the relevant and refuse the superfluous. This appears to me to be the only possible course for the artist, who is a sounding-board for human experience, which he reflects in its most significant form, showing the life of the whole man in its richest interrelation and fullest function. Dostoevsky, on the other hand, tried to abandon the only possible foundation for human experience. He sought to use the sensible simply as an instrument to attain independence from everything distinctively human. He tried to transcend sensible experience without having first extracted its full value, and so he tended to a purely abstract universality, which we feel to be baseless and continually on the edge of collapse. This accounts for a strange vortex-like movement in his writing, as though we felt the life he was considering circling faster and faster until, at the crucial moment, it collapsed. The whole of *The Possessed* is an example of such movement. The plot which it describes gathers impetus at an amazing speed under the guidance of Pyotr Stepanovich: then comes the impact of Shatov's murder and the whole structure is resolved in a few pages into chaos. No doubt this is the cause of the book's success as a picture of the baselessness of Russian society, but it is also a faithful account of Dostoevsky's own experience. The novels are full of parallel cases on a smaller scale. I remember at random the wonderful chapter describing Myshkin's growing feverish thought and the sudden appearance of Rogozhin with his knife which causes him to fall into epilepsy;[4] also the ever-quickening sweep of events at the party which culminates in the Idiot's breaking of the vase. Dostoevsky's own preoccupations are represented in these incidents, and indeed his rejection (note that I do not write "transcendence") of sensible experience made them inevitable.

[3] See *e.g.* III.2. ls. 15-26.
[4] *The Idiot.*

These considerations justify us in describing the great novels as metaphysical in type. I do not use the word, of course, as it is used in describing the poetry of Donne and Marvell: indeed, that use involves a complete contrast with Dostoevsky's type of work. In the seventeenth century, the epithet "metaphysical" is applied to a subtle fusion of thought and feeling, effected through the medium of the conceit. In Dostoevsky, the word implies a preoccupation with the abstract, and a determination to use characters and situations as shadows of the impalpable and intangible. The novels, in fact, turn on the "mysticism" of their author, and this "mysticism" is conditioned by the peculiar texture of his experience. Once again, the key-passage is from *The Idiot*:

> He remembered among other things that he always had one minute just before the epileptic fit (if it came on while he was awake), when suddenly in the midst of sadness, spiritual darkness and oppression, there seemed at moments a flash of light in his brain, and with extraordinary impetus all his vital forces suddenly began working at their highest tension. The sense of life, the consciousness of self, were mutiplied ten times at these moments which passed like a flash of lightning. His mind and his heart were flooded with extraordinary light: all his uneasiness, all his doubts, all his anxieties were relieved at once: they were all merged in a lofty calm, full of serene, harmonious joy and hope. But these moments, these flashes, were only the prelude of that final second (it was never more than a second) with which the fit began. That second was, of course, unendurable. Thinking of that moment later, when he was all right again, he often said to himself that all these gleams and flashes of the highest sensation of life and self-consciousness, and therefore also of the highest form of existence, were nothing but disease, the interruption of the normal condition: and, if so, it was not at all the highest form of being, but on the contrary must be reckoned the lowest.

Here, surely, we have the crux of Dostoevsky, for Myshkin's "mystical" experience is simply the old vortex-like movement in its most acute form. His malady is in the realm of experience as much as in that of physical and mental health. The key to the whole is in that word "self-consciousness." Dostoevsky's mysticism is a frightening concentration on the self, a tremendous effort to apprehend that self apart from what he regarded as the distractions of experience. The nervous quality we sense in Myshkin's account is tremendously, terribly keen; but it is working in a void, reaching after an impossible abstraction of self-awareness, and so it collapses. The Prince's emotions climb to their utmost intensity, their greatest measure of freedom from human circumstance, and, at the very moment of attainment the whole structure falls into annihilation. The issue, as we shall see, is between divinity and delusion, and the nature of Dostoevsky's experience made any solution impossible. The point of interest, to those who wish to regard Dostoevsky as a religious prophet, is that this "mysticism" is baseless and false. It is a mysticism born of its author's peculiar desire to transcend normal feeling, and leads to anarchy. For it, experience is nothing but an unfortunate barrier separating man from infinity, a barrier which his nature prevents him from passing, but which he must none the less consume himself in trying to pass. The result is that the fragile compound of humanity is torn between two incompatible forces, and falls into epilepsy: the epilepsy was, of course, the contribution of its author's own disease, but it also fitted perfectly into the wider relevance of his experience. Compare this "mysticism" with that of St. John of the Cross, most severe and recollected of the Church's saints, and you will find an essential difference. In *The Spiritual Canticle* we see the flame of the soul transfiguring the more inert matter of the body in its ascent to God: but there is no suggestion of an inconceivable flame burning in a vacuum. That was the essential flaw in Dostoevsky, and the cause of Myshkin's collapse.

In the light of this central truth several outstanding points in the novels become clear. Among them is his fixed hatred for the Papacy, for the Roman Church, and for the Jesuits. Berdyaev is content to ascribe this to lack of knowledge, but the considerations I have advanced seem to suggest a deeper reason for the prejudice. In this connection, I was interested to find Berdyaev quoting a pregnant remark from Dostoevsky's *Diary*: "Nihilism has appeared among us because we are all nihilists." And it was precisely because he had no real use for human relationships and human experiences that Dostoevsky, although a Christian, could see no real reason for a visible Church. The Grand Inquisitor brings this out very well. His speech is the means by which Dostoevsky accuses the Church of having betrayed the ideal of Christian perfection to give happiness and satisfaction to the multitude. He postulates a dilemma between a Christian ideal based on freedom of conscience, than which "nothing is a greater cause of suffering," and the Grand Inquisitor's desire to give religion to all humanity at the expense of stamping out this heart-rending freedom. But surely the dilemma is, from a truly Christian point of view, unreal. For the Redemption is for all humanity, and the Church is, in Christian thought, a pledge that the love of God extends to the human and temporal society he created, and not only to a metaphysical abstraction. The Catholic can appreciate the genuine and continual sense of division between the goodness of God and the common unworthiness of man. But he cannot appreciate the division, to which Dostoevsky logically leads us, between the imperfect mass of humanity and a few "mystics" who aim at living in a state of complete abstraction from the kind of society which the body of human experience seems to postulate. Least of all can he accept the implication that perfection consists in the attempted renunciation of all experience whatever. The "lacerations" of Ivan in his great monologue (for it is significant that Alyosha, who might be expected to provide the religious philosophy of the book, scarcely opens his mouth) are simply the product

of Dostoevsky's intolerable dualism. It should be noted, too, that there is
no place for the Incarnation in Dostoevsky's theology, except, perhaps,
as an impalpable abstraction on some distant metaphysical plane. For,
in the light of the crux we have examined, the Incarnation must have
seemed to Dostoevsky an intolerable, almost a blasphemous compromise
between pure "mysticism" and the shameful weakness of normal humanity. Here he is with the great heresies of the East, the Gnostics and
the Manichaeans, who affirmed the duality and incompatibility of body
and soul. His "metaphysical" passion is in final opposition to the social
ideal of Western Christendom.

But we can go further, and explain by the results of our critical enquiry other traits of Dostoevsky's work. His love of humiliation has been
noted before. He describes it as a prominent feature of the Russian
character: he writes: "Russia was being put to shame publicly, before
everyone. Who could fail to roar with delight?" [5] It cannot be stressed too
much that we are here dealing, not with Christian humility, which consists in a reasonable estimate of one's value and position in the universe,
but with a passion for the depths of humiliation. This is constantly re-
curring in the lives of the heroes of the novels. We find Myshkin announcing in public: "Ha-ha! You know, I was a complete idiot! Ha-ha!"
Indeed, the very attempt to combine in Myshkin the qualities of saint
and idiot is Dostoevsky's most extreme example of this humiliation. We
meet it in the behavior of Stavrogin when struck by Shatov, and when
he announces his marriage to the mad cripple. And we find the key to
it in *The Idiot,* when Ippolit says:

> "Let me tell you, there is a limit of ignominy in the consciousness of
> one's own nothingness and impotence beyond which a man cannot go, and
> beyond which he begins to feel immense satisfaction in his degradation. . . .
> Oh, of course, humility is a great force in that sense, I admit that—though
> not in the sense in which religion accepts humility as a force."

This humiliation is, in fact, simply another aspect of Dostoevsky's un-
bounded "metaphysical" egoism. He sought to transcend experience and
to ignore the flesh: so the flesh took its revenge for this inversion by
changing his highest egoism into his lowest humiliation. Humiliation
in the novels, in fact, is simply sadism on a spiritual plane, and this
accounts for the positive pleasure which Dostoevsky derives from it. It
is part of the same obscure feeling which turns the flesh of Father
Zosima, the confessed protagonist of Christian virtue against the scepti-
cism of Ivan, into a ridiculous corruption. "His elder stinks," as the
divinity student Rakitin gloatingly puts it: and his comment represents
the putrefaction of proud and unnatural virtue seen through the eyes

[5] *The Possessed.*

of the creeping vice which is its natural corollary. There is no force more destructive of humanity than that of the egoist let loose in the "metaphysical" ecstasy of pride.

In this manner the critical analysis of Dostoevsky's sensibility and the contradiction implied in it brings us to a complementary metaphysical dualism. The central point of the novels is their attitude to God. Like Kirilov in *The Possessed,* Dostoevsky is haunted by an irreconcilable dilemma. On the one hand, "God is necessary, and so must exist"; on the other, "But I know he doesn't and can't." For his "mysticism," as we have seen, conceives of God as purely transcendent, purely infinite, and only to be approached by an absolute denial of the sensible. Such a God, if he exists, necessarily excludes all free will and personality in man: for he can have no contact with, or sympathy for, his limited and sensitive creation. The result is that all Dostoevsky's "mystics"—of whom Myshkin and Kirilov are typical—are driven by their thirst for the divine into straining the boundaries of human experience, so that their ecstasy inevitably coincides with the dissolution of the personality into epileptic idiocy. So much we have established. But the further point is that Dostoevsky's very "spirituality" is founded on a boundless egoism. His desire to transcend the limits of the palpable is based upon the craving of his own nature for an infinity of existence. In this, he merely represents the romantic hero or superman freed from all the purely sentimental relics of Christian humanism and reaching out to a complete and all-embracing selfishness. The result, obviously, is a clash between the infinite self and the infinite God. If God exists, according to Dostoevsky, the free, personal self is necessarily a delusion. If he does not exist, man's free will is indeed absolute, but works in a void. For, without God, the egoism of the human soul is inextricably bounded by death, from which only the divine guarantee of immortality can extricate it. This being so, its only possible activity lies in self-destruction, in which death may be forestalled by a personal act: so Kirilov says: "I am killing myself to prove my independence and my new terrible freedom." But this conclusion implies, of course, a breakdown, for the egoism which began in a lust for absolute life cannot be satisfied by a contrary absolute of death. The "metaphysical" circle is complete.

## II

It is time to return to the novels and to show how the contradictions outlined above are reflected in the human sphere which is their material. I shall make no attempt at an exhaustive criticism. In the space of a short essay one can only hope to indicate how the novels fill in the outline already established, and many of the lesser points which go to make up a novelist's greatness cannot even be mentioned. The only aim of this essay is to indicate in what way and to what extent Dostoevsky is valuable to us.

*Crime and Punishment* is the first of the significant novels. Dealing at first sight with a romantic and almost sentimental theme of murder and remorse in a squalid environment, it is soon clear that deeper issues insist on obtruding themselves. Raskolnikov kills a mere human "louse": he kills her, superficially, to extricate himself from difficulties, but actually, as he says: "I wanted to become a Napoleon: I wanted to have the daring . . . and I killed her." In this way, Dostoevsky transports a commonplace murder to the "metaphysical" plane, and his treatment of the remorse shows a similar ambiguity. On the surface, he is persuaded by Sonya and his conscience that no human being can be judged by another as a "louse" and so disposed of. But there was a deeper cause, and that was provided by his egoism:

> "I wanted to prove one thing only, that the devil led me on then, and he has shown me since that I had not the right to take that path, because I am just such a louse as all the rest."

What made him a louse in his own eyes was precisely his conscience. Not all the talk about "regeneration" at the end of the book can conceal that Dostoevsky's deepest, almost unconscious, interests were elsewhere. In fact, they were with Svidrigailov. This perplexing man foreshadows Stavrogin. When Raskolnikov is horrified by the prospects of vice opened before him, Svidrigailov replies: "Tell me, what should I restrain myself for? Why should I give up women, since I have a passion for them?" This is the egoism which fascinated Dostoevsky. And when Raskolnikov goes on to ask him: "And could you shoot yourself?" further subtleties appear. Svidrigailov turns away: "I admit it's an unpardonable weakness, but I can't help it: I am afraid of death and I dislike its being talked of." In these words, he shows fully developed the insoluble crux already explained. He has an absolute lust for life and is afraid of death, yet he demands death as the ultimate sign of the self's free mastery, the conquest of his last fear, and the vindication of his freedom. So he shoots himself, just as the Jewish soldier is saying: "You can't do it here, it's not the place," and, like Stavrogin, he left a note to say that he died in full possession of his faculties.

*The Idiot* is perhaps the best of the novels, the most closely-knit, the one that best reflects Dostoevsky's nature. *Karamazov* may have greater gifts of character and description, but *The Idiot* has less blurred outlines and less inconclusiveness. Dostoevsky's letters tell us that he set out to portray in Myshkin a really good man, and that he found it very hard. Like all the other characters, the idiot Prince is dominated by the familiar egoism, but in him it is a "mystical" passion to transcend experience: self-centred in its source, it aspires to a complete selfless universality. Against him is placed Rogozhin, also an egoist, but on the purely sensual plane, and several others, of whom the consumptive Ippolit is the chief. He too has the common nostalgia for infinite life, strengthened by the fact that he is dying. Like Rogozhin, he hates the Idiot, and his hatred is a protest on the part of egoistic life against the contrary craving for death and selflessness:

> "Then let me tell you, if I hate anyone here . . . it's you, Jesuitical, treacly soul, idiot, philanthropic millionaire: I hate you more than anyone and everything in the world! . . . I don't want your benevolence, I won't take anything—anything, do your hear?—from anyone!"

This denunciation is typical. Myshkin was a "good man," a picture of the spiritual man as he should be: but he was also an idiot, and his idiocy and spirituality are inevitably connected. For his selfless mysticism sought to impose itself upon experience in a pure egoistic passion for negation, until it provoked a revolt in the self which led to disruption. The root of Myshkin's collapse is seen in his clash with Rogozhin over Nastasya Filipovna, whom he intended to marry. His attitude to her is seen in his phrase—"I don't love her with love, but with pity." And yet he was proposing to make her his wife! The strange entanglement of body and soul in a mutual perversion is typical. By his own confession he could not marry anyone, because he was an invalid: by implication, he shrank from human passion because of the impotence of disease: and yet, in fact, he was always preoccupied with love and marriage, and sought to replace the physical element in love by a twisted and unnatural pity. It is not surprising, with such an outlook, that Dostoevsky wrote in *The Possessed*: "There's always something depraving in charity." To the Catholic, such charity must seem to be false, based on a human and spiritual perversion, so that natural virtue is turned into supernatural vice. Against Myshkin is set Rogozhin, who frankly recognizes the sensual basis of his every action: "There's no sort of pity for her in me." And Nastasya Filipovna left Myshkin for him at the church door, because in Rogozhin there was at least a possibility of love: as she said to him: "Anyway, you are not a flunkey." Rogozhin did love her; when she threw her money into the fire to show her mastery over Ganya, he repeated, "That's like a queen!" But, having loved and married her, he proceeded to show that in Dostoevsky the sensual ecstasy is an unbridled passion for destruction. In fact, he murdered her, exactly as he had said he would. Over her dead body, the two devouring egoisms, the "spiritual" and the sensual, meet to console one another for their common inhumanity. *The Idiot* is the greatest of the novels because it is the most honest, and shows without evasion where the rent in Dostoevsky's nature had to lead.

In *The Possessed* Dostoevsky's frustration is projected in the form of bitter satire. Any attempt at Christian spirituality is abandoned. It is a picture of Russian society seen in the light of Dostoevsky's nature, and shown to be ripe for destruction. In it we have perhaps the most striking example of that baseless, vortex-like movement, upon which we have already commented, and which is here imparted to a whole society. Dostoevsky was the best possible critic of that society, because he was born in it, and because he possessed in a degree only possible to a great artist the explosive elements that were tearing it apart. In this social order, there sprang up a baseless revolution, dedicated solely to destruction, and finally melting into the insubstantial. When questioned upon the aim of his conspiracy, Pyotr Stepanovich replied that it had acted

> ". . . with the idea of systematically undermining the foundations, and destroying society and all principles: with the idea of nonplussing everyone and making hay out of everything, and then, when society was tottering, sick and out of joint, cynical and sceptical, though filled with an intense eagerness for self-preservation and for some guiding idea, suddenly to seize it in their hands, raising the standard of revolt and relying on a complete net-work of quintets, which were actively, meanwhile, gathering recruits and seeking out the weak spots which could be attacked."

Out of this sterile society, directed to negation and destruction, came Stavrogin, Dostoevsky's most complete development of the romantic, "Byronic," egoist. The sensual basis of his egoism is made clear: he returns to his own town from a career of vice in Petersburg, a common tale of brutality arising out of the general break-up of moral standards. At least, so it seems at first: but the full truth is far more complex. As the book proceeds, Stavrogin is moved to an effort to outstrip all human limitations and to seek an absolute self-sufficiency. He desires, for example, to rise above all the restrictions of society and to expose its worthlessness; so when Gaganov repeats his self-satisfied "No, you can't lead me by the nose," Stavrogin is moved to take him at his word and perform the feat literally. And society (quite rightly) detected the nihilist in him: "They insisted on seeing an insolent design and deliberate intention to insult our whole society at once." Inevitably exiled, Stavrogin, like all the egoists of Dostoevsky, is driven in upon himself. He begins a career of negation and self-humiliation, which accounts for his "confession" of his marriage to the mad cripple and of his supposed connivance in her ultimate murder. But the satirical spirit of his relations with his society is also expressed in his own story of negation, for his career is inevitably a career of death. As an egoist he is bound to act. But his action cannot be directed to evil, as in Pyotr Stepanovich, for, as he writes in his last letter: "I don't like vice, and I don't want it." Nor can he even act "greatly" like Kirilov, whose epileptic mysticism recalls *The Idiot*, though on a clearer level of frustration:

"Kirilov, in the greatness of his soul, could not compromise with an idea, and shot himself: but I see, of course, that he was great-souled because he had lost his reason. I can never lose my reason, and I can never believe in an idea to such a degree as he did."

Kirilov and Pyotr Stepanovich represent the two inevitable resolutions of the self's lust for egoistic fulfilment. The one drives himself into a "mysticism" that cracks the frontiers of the sensible and causes the breakdown of human personality; the other embarks upon a career of vice and destruction, and ends, in Fedka's words: "for all the world like a filthy human louse." Stavrogin stands between them, recognizing the futility of both, but seeing no trace of a third possibility. And so—"from me nothing has come but negation, with no greatness of soul, no force. Even negation has not come from me." So, like Svidrigailov, he hanged himself as the last act of his vanity.

I think that Stavrogin is really the last step in Dostoevsky's "metaphysical" progress. There remains *Karamazov*. As a novel, in the usual acceptance of the term, it is magnificent. The relations of the tragic family, and in particular the story of Mitya and his father, are wonderfully drawn; the account of the murder is superb. But that does not affect our enquiry. We are concerned here with the "spiritual message," the resolution of his former dilemmas, that Dostoevsky tried to insert into the structure of his novel; everything else was at least implicit in the earlier work. Our interest, in this case, must be primarily in Alyosha. Now the most striking point about Alyosha seems to be the complete discontinuity between his virtue and the general characteristics of the *Karamazov* world. It is, in fact, pasted on to the main body of the work. I do not see how a sensitive reader can avoid being conscious of this definite artistic flaw; it is implied even by Berdyaev, who confesses that he is incompletely drawn. We are, in fact, back in the atmosphere of sentimental regeneration with which Dostoevsky sought to avoid the crucial antithesis of *Crime and Punishment*. Note, too, that the supposedly "Christian" teaching of Alyosha hardly contains a word of the Incarnation, after Alyosha's rather half-hearted suggestion in reply to Ivan. It is a purely personal mysticism, often using Christian terminology, but rather sentimental and pantheistic in its force. It lays stress upon "watering the earth with your tears," but the reader is troubled by lack of feeling for the real earth of creation; Dostoevsky's earth is merely there to be wept upon. His lack of sympathy for the sensible and the tangible lands him finally in sentimental weakness.

This is not to say that Alyosha's "spirituality" is not affected by the thought and feeling of the later works, but the effect is not altogether wholesome. It is seen best in what he learned from Father Zosima, and all the beauty of Dostoevsky's prose cannot conceal the effect of Rakitin's comment: "His elder stinks." Zosima's teaching covers, rather than takes

account of, the corruption of the flesh, and it is suggested more than
once that its source is pride. "How can you presume to do such deeds?"
the monk asked him, in connection with the healing of Lise (and, of
course, Dostoevsky gives no real suggestion of a miracle), and it is purposely left doubtful whether the question tells most against Zosima or
his questioner. There is something repellent, too, about the story of the
murderer who was led by Zosima to confess his crime. When he comes
back at the last moment to murder his friend, we feel that he is driven
on by that typical egoism which may issue either in the destruction of
another human life or in that strange self-centred craving for humiliation which the sensation of an open confession would satisfy so well.
And Zosima, let us remember, was Dostoevsky's answer to the Grand
Inquisitor.

But if one cannot accept Dostoevsky as a spiritual guide for modern
man, he is unrivalled in his exploration of certain aspects of modern
disorder. His very "metaphysical" keenness enables him to express most
clearly the way in which humanity is being cut off from a full and integrated experience. For example, Berdyaev writes as follows on
Dostoevsky:

> Nothing is gained by love; it is simply a tornado that bears men to
> shipwreck. Why? Because it is a manifestation of self-will and as such
> breaks up the human person and cleaves it in twain. . . . For him, sexual
> love signifies the loss of the integrity of human nature.

It is interesting to see how this observation connects Dostoevsky with a
theme essential to English literature, especially in the metaphysical tradition. Shakespeare and Donne were also occupied with the contradiction
essential to human passion—the contradiction between the desire for
absolute unity which prompts it, and the final independence of the
separate personality upon which that desire breaks. But in the great
English poets the contradiction is resolved by the intensity of emotion.
The element of separation by "devouring" time is seen as necessary to
a greater intensity of living, as the condition of a new life of "sensation"
(using the word to imply a completeness of human experience, bodily,
mental, and spiritual), whose value is absolute. Dostoevsky's "metaphysical" impatience made such a conception impossible for him. As
Berdyaev says: "for the Russians, culture is an obstacle in the way of
their impetuous rush towards a consummation." We have seen in Dostoevsky, as nowhere else, where such impetuous rushes must inevitably
lead us. In fact, "culture" and "love" are more closely connected than
might appear, and the bringing of these two passages is amply justified.
For in these two activities the human being (not merely his body or
mind, or even his "soul" which is, in fact, inseparable from these) comes
into its closest contact with reality. A man who disregards "love"—and

love considered in part as a sexual act—disregards the finest of all contacts by which human life may be enriched; if he is a Christian, he also despises something to which the Church has given the dignity of a sacrament. And a man who neglects "culture" turns away from the sum of experience and the quintessence of man's essential contacts. Dostoevsky, placed in a world which had reached this stage of denial, explored its consequences to the full, and his findings are written in his novels. In them a man is revealed with quite extraordinary discriminations of feeling, but with these directed to an impossible end. The result is a dreadful retaliation of the flesh, an amazing sensitivity to what I can only describe as "metaphysical" pain. Consider, for example, how Lise, having "lacerated" Alyosha, shuts her finger in the crack of the door in an agony of self-detestation. Here, as in many instances, we touch upon the provinces of pathology and psychology; but it is one of the purposes of this essay to insist that the evaluation of this experience must be a critical one. The finding of criticism, I suggest, is that Dostoevsky was the master of all explorers of physical and spiritual disorder, and that his findings expose an erring adventure in human experience— the experiment, ultimately, of replacing the true balance of living by the despotic activity of the independent mind.

# Chronology of Important Dates

N.B. Dates of events in Russia are given according to the Julian calendar (or Old Style) which, during the nineteenth century, was *13* days *behind* the Gregorian calendar used in the West.

| | |
|---|---|
| 1821 | October 30. Fyodor Mikhailovich Dostoevsky born in Moscow, in hospital for the poor where his father was resident physician. |
| 1837 | Death of mother, Marya Fyodorovna née Nechaev. |
| 1838 | Enters military engineering school in Petersburg. |
| 1839 | Father killed by peasants on his estate Darovoe (Government Tula). |
| 1843 | Leaves engineering school as lieutenant and joins engineering department of War Ministry. |
| 1844 | Resigns from Army. Publishes translation of Balzac's *Eugénie Grandet* in periodical (*Repertuar i Panteon*). |
| 1845 | Finishes his first novel, *Poor People* (*Bednye lyudi*) and is hailed by Belinsky as a great writer. |
| 1846 | January 15: *Poor People* published in *Petersburg Miscellany* (*Peterbursky sbornik*). The second novel *The Double* (*Dvojnik*) appeared two weeks later in *Notes from the Fatherland* (*Otechestvennye zapiski*). |
| 1847 | "The Landlady" ("Khozayka") in *Notes from the Fatherland*. |
| 1848 | "The Faint Heart" ("Slaboe serdtse"), "An Honest Thief" ("Chestnyi Vor"), "White Nights" ("Belye Nochi") in *Notes*. |
| 1849 | April 23: Arrested for part in Petrashevsky conspiracy. *Netochka Nezvanova,* an unfinished novel, in *Notes.*<br>December 22: Led to execution, but pardoned.<br>December 24: Put into irons and taken to Siberia by sled. |
| 1850 | January 23: Arrives at Omsk in Labor camp. |
| 1854 | February: Released from penal servitude and sent to Semipalatinsk (near Mongolian border) as common soldier. |
| 1856 | Promoted to Ensign. |
| 1857 | "The Little Hero" ("Malenkyi geroy"), composed in prison in 1849, published in *Notes* anonymously.<br>February 2: Marries Marya Dmitrevna Isaeva, née Constant, a widow, at Kuznetsk. Given back rank of nobleman. |
| 1859 | Allowed to resign from Army and return to Russia. Arrived at Tver in August. On December 16, returns to Petersburg. |

"Uncle's Dream" ("Dyadushkin Son") in *The Russian Word* (*Russkoe slovo*). "The Friend of the Family" ("Selo Stepanchikovo i ego obitateli") in *Notes from the Fatherland.*

1860 The Introduction and the first chapter of *The House of the Dead* (*Zapiski iz mertvogo doma*) published in *The Russian World* (*Russkyi mir*). A two-volume collection of Dostoevsky's writings published.

1861 His brother Mikhail's monthly *Time* (*Vremya*), starts publication. *The Insulted and the Injured* (*Unizhennye i oskorblennye*) published there in installments. In book-form in the same year. The whole of *The House of the Dead* reprinted in *Time.*

1862 *The House of the Dead* in book-form. June-August: first trip abroad, to Paris, London, and Geneva. "An Unpleasant Predicament" ("Skverny anekdot") in *Time.*

1863 "Winter Notes on Summer Impressions" ("Zimnyia zametky o letnikh vpechatlenyakh") in *Time. Time* suppressed in May. Second trip abroad, August-October. Paris, then with Appolinaria Suslova to Italy, by ship from Naples to Livorno. Back after gambling at Homburg.

1864 Becomes editor of *Epokha* (*The Age*). There "Notes from the Underground" ("Zapiski iz podpolya"). April 15: Death of his wife in Moscow. July 10: Death of brother Mikhail.

1865 *Epokha* ceases publication. Third trip abroad July-October. Meets Appolinaria Suslova in Wiesbaden and returns via Copenhagen. A new two-volume collection of his writings.

1866 *Crime and Punishment* (*Prestuplenie i nakazanie*) appears serially in *The Russian Herald* (*Russkyi vestnik*). October: Dictates "The Gambler" ("Igrok") to stenographer Anna Grigorevna Snitkim. "The Gambler" published in third volume of collected works.

1867 February 15: Marriage to Anna Grigorevna—*Crime and Punishment* in book-form—April 14: The newly-weds leave Russia for Dresden. July 10: The encounter with Turgenev in Baden-Baden. August: Arrives in Geneva.

1868 *The Idiot* (*Idiot*) appears serially in *The Russian Herald*. March 5: A daughter Sofya born who died May 24. Moves to Vevey, Milan, and in November to Florence.

1869 Travels via Vienna and Prague to Dresden. There (September 26) birth of daughter Lyubov.

1870 "The Eternal Husband" ("Vechnyi muzh") in *Dawn* (*Zarya*).

1871 Returns to Petersburg (July 8). A son Fyodor born July 16. *The Possessed* (*Besy*) serially in *The Russian Herald.*

1872 The Third Part of *The Possessed* in *The Russian Herald.*

1873-4 Editor of *The Citizen* (*Grazhdanin*).

1873 *The Possessed* in book-form.

1874      *The Idiot* in book-form. March 26: Arrested and confined for violation of censorship rules. June-August: Trip to Ems and Geneva.

1875      *A Raw Youth (Podrostok)* serially in *Notes from the Fatherland*. May-July: Trip to Berlin and Ems. August 10: Birth of son Alexey.

1876      *A Raw Youth* in book-form. July: Again in Ems. *The Diary of a Writer (Dnevnik pisatelya)* started—eleven numbers: "A Gentle Spirit" ("Krotkaya") in November number.

1877      Nine new numbers of *The Diary*: in April number "The Dream of a Ridiculous Man" ("Son smeshnogo cheloveka").

1878      May 16: Death of son Alexey (Alyosha). June: Visit to Monastery Optina with Vladimir Solovyov.

1879      *The Brothers Karamazov (Bratrya Karamazovy)* serially in *The Russian Herald* up to Book IX of Part III. July-September: In Ems.

1880      The rest of the *Brothers* in *Russian Herald*. Published in book-form in December. June 8: Speech at the Pushkin Jubilee in Moscow. The speech printed in Moscow paper and in August in a single number of *The Diary of a Writer*.

1881      Dies January 28 in Petersburg two days after hemorrhage of lungs. February 1: Burial in cemetery of Alexander Nevsky Monastery.

# Notes on the Editor and Authors

RENÉ WELLEK (born 1903) the editor of this volume, is Sterling Professor of Comparative Literature at Yale University. He is the author of *Kant in England* (1931), *The Rise of English Literary History* (1941), *Theory of Literature* (with Austin Warren, 1949), and *A History of Modern Criticism, 1750-1950*, in four volumes, of which two were published in 1955. He has received honorary Lit.D.'s from Oxford, Harvard, and Rome.

DMITRI CHIZHEVSKY (spelled also Čiževśkyj or Tschiževskij) (born 1894) is a Ukrainian scholar who is now Professor at Heidelberg. His books in Russian and German include studies of *Hegel in Russia, A History of Old Russian Literature*, etc. Professor Chizhevsky spent seven years at Harvard (1947-54).

IRVING HOWE (born 1920) is Professor of English at Stanford University. His books, besides *Politics and the Novel* (1957) include studies of *Sherwood Anderson* and *William Faulkner*.

SIGMUND FREUD (1856-1939) needs no identification.

MURRAY KRIEGER (born 1923) is Professor of English at the University of Illinois. Besides *The Tragic Vision* (1960) he has written *The New Apologists for Poetry* (1956).

D. H. LAWRENCE (1885-1930). His criticism has found many admirers recently.

GEORG (or György) LUKÁCS (born 1885), a Hungarian living in Budapest, is the most eminent Marxist critic. His books in German, besides *Der russische Roman in der Weltliteratur* (1949) include *Goethe und seine Zeit* (1947), *Der historische Roman* (1955), etc. Lukács was for a short time Minister of Education of the Nagy Government during the 1956 revolution.

PHILIP RAHV (born 1908) is editor of *Partisan Review* and teaches at Brandeis University. *Image and Idea* (1949) is a collection of his essays.

DEREK TRAVERSI (born 1912) is a Welshman who is now with the British Council in Madrid. He has written for *Scrutiny* and *The Criterion* and published three books on Shakespeare.

ELISEO VIVAS (born 1901) came from Colombia as a boy. He is now Professor of Philosophy at Northwestern University. His books include *Creation and Discovery* (1955) and *D. H. Lawrence* (1960).

V. V. ZENKOVSKY (born 1881) is a retired Professor of the Russian Theological Institute in Paris. His writings, in Russian, include *A History of Russian Philosophy* (2 vols., 1948) and, in German, *Aus der Geschichte der ästhetischen Ideen in Russland* (The Hague, 1958).

# Bibliographical Note

All of Dostoevsky's more important writings are listed in the Chronology. The Introduction refers to practically every book and many articles on Dostoevsky in Russian, German, French, and English. I list here items useful for the study of the history of Dostoevsky criticism and influence in Western languages.

## GENERAL

Anon. "Dostoevsky and the Novel," in *Times Literary Supplement, XXIX* (June 5, 1930), 665-6.
Romein, Jan Marius. *Dostojewskij in de westersche Kritik.* Harlem, 1924. In Dutch. Bibliography.

## ON RUSSIAN CRITICISM

Fiske, John C. "Dostoevsky and the Soviet Critics, 1947-8," in *American Slavic and East European Review,* IX (1950), 42-56.
Jackson, Robert L. *Dostojevskij's Underground Man in Russian Literature.* The Hague, 1958.
Komarovič, V. "Die Weltanschauung Dostojevskij's in der russischen Forschung 1914-1924," in *Zeitschrift für slavische Philologie, III* (1926), 217-228.
———, "Neue Probleme der Dostojevskij-Forschung 1925-1930," *Ibid.* X (1933), 402-28; and *XI* (1934), 193-236.
Seduro, Vladimir, *Dostoyevski in Russian Literary Criticism 1846-1956.* New York, 1957. Ample bibliography. See, however, my review in *The American Slavic and East European Review, XVII* (1958), 376-8.

## ON GERMAN CRITICISM

Kampmann, Theoderich, *Dostojewski in Deutschland. München,* 1934. Universitäts-Archiv, vol. 50.
Setschkareff, Vsevolod, "Dostojewskij in Deutschland," in *Zeitschrift für slavische Philologie, XXII* (1954), 12-39.

## ON FRENCH CRITICISM

Hemmings, F. W. J., *The Russian Novel in France 1884-1914.* Oxford, 1950.
Minnse, Hanns Friedrich, *Die französische Kritik und Dostojewski.* Hamburg, 1932.

## ON BRITISH AND AMERICAN CRITICISM

Beebe, Maurice, and Newton, Christopher, "Dostoevsky in English: A Selected
    Checklist of Criticism and Translations," in *Modern Fiction Studies, IV*
    (1958), 271-91.
Brewster, Dorothy, *East-West Passage,* London: Allen and Unwin, Ltd., 1954.
Muchnic, Helen, *Dostoevsky's English Reputation (1881-1936). Smith College
    Studies in Modern Languages,* Vol. XX (1939), Northampton, Mass.
Neuschäffer, Walter, *Dostojewskijs Einfluss auf den englischen Roman.* Heidel-
    berg, 1935.
Phelps, Gilbert, *The Russian Novel in English Fiction.* London: Hutchinson
    & Co., Ltd., 1956.
Wasiolek, Edward (ed.) *Crime and Punishment and the Critics.* San Francisco:
    Wadsworth Publishing Co., 1961.

# TWENTIETH CENTURY VIEWS SERIES *

* Also available in limited clothbound edition.